WHY SOME THINGS SHOULD NOT BE FOR SALE

OXFORD POLITICAL PHILOSOPHY

General Editor: Samuel Freeman
University of Pennsylvania

Oxford Political Philosophy publishes books on theoretical and applied
political philosophy within the Anglo-American tradition. The series
welcomes submissions on social, political, and global justice, individual
rights, democracy, liberalism, socialism, and constitutionalism.

Imposing Values: An Essay on Liberalism and Regulation
N. Scott Arnold

Liberalism and Prostitution
Peter de Marneffe

Why Some Things Should Not Be for Sale: The Moral Limits of Markets
Debra Satz

WHY SOME THINGS SHOULD NOT BE FOR SALE

The Moral Limits of Markets

DEBRA SATZ

UNIVERSITY PRESS

2010

OXFORD
UNIVERSITY PRESS

Oxford University Press, Inc., publishes works that further
Oxford University's objective of excellence
in research, scholarship, and education.

Oxford New York
Auckland Cape Town Dar es Salaam Hong Kong Karachi
Kuala Lumpur Madrid Melbourne Mexico City Nairobi
New Delhi Shanghai Taipei Toronto

With offices in
Argentina Austria Brazil Chile Czech Republic France Greece
Guatemala Hungary Italy Japan Poland Portugal Singapore
South Korea Switzerland Thailand Turkey Ukraine Vietnam

Published by Oxford University Press, Inc.
198 Madison Avenue, New York, NY 10016

www.oup.com

Oxford is a registered trademark of Oxford University Press

Library of Congress Cataloging-in-Publication Data
Satz, Debra.
Why some things should not be for sale : the moral limits of markets / Debra Satz.
p. cm. — (Oxford political philosophy)
ISBN 978-0-19-531159-4
1. Free enterprise—Moral and ethical aspects.
2. Capitalism—Moral and ethical aspects. I. Title.
HB95.S33 2010
174′.4—dc22
2009035769

3 5 7 9 8 6 4 2

Printed in the United States of America
on acid-free paper

To Richard C. Friedman

Contents

Acknowledgments   ix

Introduction   3

PART I

1.   What Do Markets Do?   15

PART II

2.   The Changing Visions of Economics   39
3.   The Market's Place and Scope in Contemporary Egalitarian
Political Theory   63
4.   Noxious Markets   91

PART III

5.   Markets in Women's Reproductive Labor   115
6.   Markets in Women's Sexual Labor   135
7.   Child Labor: A Normative Perspective   155
8.   Voluntary Slavery and the Limits of the Market   171
9.   Ethical Issues in the Supply and Demand of Human Kidneys   189
10.   Conclusion   207

Notes   211
Bibliography   237
Index   249

Acknowledgments

I have been thinking and writing about this topic for a long time and along the way I have accumulated a lot of debts. If anyone ever demanded that those debts be cashed out in monetary terms, I would be broke. Luckily I have benefited from our social norms of reciprocity and kindness, and I hope to repay these debts in that currency.

Some people helped by leading me to have a sense of possibility, a reason to hope that the world was not a fixed place to be merely accepted or tolerated. These people led me out of not only the external poverty in which I grew up, but also the poverty of having leveled aspirations. Here I must thank my father, who filled our house with books, and Richard Friedman, who set me on the road I have taken and kept a strong wind at my back.

Many people generously helped with advice and information, reading parts of the book and in some cases the entire manuscript. I would like to thank the following people and to ask forgiveness of anyone else whose name I unintentionally omit. Rob Reich, Josh Cohen, John Ferejohn, Elizabeth Hansot, Andrew Levine, Elizabeth Anderson, Susan Okin, Barbara Fried, Zosia Stemploskawa, Adam Rosenblatt, Allen Wood, Tom Nagel, Lewis Kornhauser, Seana Shiffrin, Jonathan Wolf, Yossi Dahan, Ben Hippen, Anabelle Lever, Liam Murphy, and Paul Gowder each provided me with helpful comments. Everything here is better as a result of their efforts.

I have presented parts of this work on various occasions and received excellent suggestions. I thank the following organizations and the audiences: the Philosophy Department at the University of Michigan and Marshall Weinberg for endowing the chair that enabled me to spend three months in Ann Arbor; the Colloquium in Legal, Political, and Social Philosophy at New York University Law School; the Law, Economics, and Politics Colloquium at New York University Law School; the Aristotelian Society; the University of Manchester; the

MIT Philosophy Department; the Ramat Gan Law School; the University of Victoria; the Princeton Center for Human Values; the University of Toronto Law School; the University of Texas at Austin Law School; the Stanford University Workshop on Global Justice, and the University of Melbourne.

I have also benefited from the work of a number of gifted Stanford undergraduate research assistants, including Eric Pai, Joseph Shapiro, Jose Campos, Caleb Perl, and Alexander Berger. One of the great pleasures of teaching at Stanford is the chance to interact with so many talented and passionate students. I have also relied on the amazing staff support in the Philosophy Department and at the Bowen H. McCoy Family Center for Ethics in Society. I could not have finished this without unloading some of my administrative work on Joan Berry in particular. Thanks to all of you.

I have had financial support during the time of the writing of this book, including fellowships from the Stanford Humanities Center and the Princeton Center on Human Values, a research grant from the vice provost for undergraduate education at Stanford, and funding as a Marta Sutton Weeks Faculty Scholar, also at Stanford. I am grateful for all of this support, which provided me invaluable time to work. I must also mention the Neon Rose Guest Cabin in Point Reyes Station that allowed me a room of my own (with a view of the bay!) to finish this book.

Some of these chapters appeared in earlier incarnations, and I am grateful to the editors of the following journals for permission to reprint updated versions of these early arguments: *Philosophy and Public Affairs* (chapter 5), *Ethics* (chapter 6), *The World Bank Economic Review* (chapter 7), *Social Philosophy and Policy* (chapter 8), and the *Aristotelian Society* (chapter 9). A very distant relative of chapter 4 appeared in *Globalization, Culture and the Limits of the Market*, edited by Stephen Cullenberg and Prasanta Pattanaik (New Delhi: Oxford University Press, 2004). A closer cousin of chapter 2 will be appearing in *Nineteenth Century Philosophy*, edited by Allen Wood (Cambridge: Cambridge University Press, 2010).

My friends have undoubtedly heard a lot more about this book and the trials of writing it than they would have liked. I have been very fortunate to have a wonderful community of friends ranging from Palo Alto to the Bronx. Their friendship and companionship sustained me through the ups and downs. I am especially grateful to Kathryn Pryor for helping me to maintain my focus.

Thanks are also due to my editor at Oxford University Press, Peter Ohlin, and the generous comments of the editor of the series in which this book is appearing, Samuel Freeman. Judith Hoover's copyediting helped get the manuscript into final shape.

I have been blessed with a good that no amount of money could ever buy: a happy family. I am grateful for the love and support of my husband, Don Barr, and our son, Isaac Barr Satz. Don read much of the book, talked with me about it, offered editorial suggestions, and supported me in all of my efforts. Isaac has brought his knowledge of the rival theories of distributive justice to bear on his Little League games, bringing great joy to his mother.

WHY SOME THINGS SHOULD
NOT BE FOR SALE

Introduction

Markets are important forms of social and economic organization. They allow vast numbers of people who are otherwise completely unknown to one another to cooperate together in a system of voluntary exchange. Through markets, people are able to signal to one another what they want, disseminate information, and reward innovation. Markets enable people to mutually adjust their activities without the need for a central planning authority. Furthermore markets are widely recognized as the most efficient way we have to organize production and distribution in a complex economy.

It is not surprising, therefore, that with the collapse of communism, markets and the political theories that advocate expanding the market have been enjoying a considerable resurgence. Markets are not only spreading across the globe, but they are also extending to new domains, such as environmental pollution.[1] For many people market institutions are assuming the role of an all-purpose remedy for the defects of the cumbersome government bureaucracies of the Western world, the poverty of the Southern world, and the coercive state control of the planned economies. This remains true despite the recent economic downturn.

At the same time as markets have expanded their reach, new controversies have arisen concerning the morality of markets in human organs, reproductive services, diamonds that fuel bloody civil wars, sex, weapons, life-saving medicines, addictive drugs—and now credit derivatives. Markets in these goods are seen as fundamentally different from, and elicit very different reactions than, markets in automobiles or soybeans. Such markets, we might say, strike many people as noxious, toxic to important human values. These markets evoke widespread discomfort and, in the extreme, revulsion.

Consider child labor, a case I take up in chapter 7. Child labor is common in many developing societies and indeed was once prevalent in what is now the developed world. Some economists and policy advisors have argued that banning child labor is a mistake because some families rely for their survival on the labor of their children. At the same time many believe that protecting young children from working is a moral requirement for any decent society.

Consider a second example: human kidneys. Selling a kidney is currently illegal in every developed society, even though in such societies there is a chronic shortage of donor organs. From an economist's perspective, the ban on selling is inefficient because it is likely that monetary incentives would increase supply and thereby save lives. But some people would not accept the sale of organs under any circumstances. I discuss this case in chapter 9.

What considerations ought to guide the debates about such markets? Are there some things that should not be bought and sold? More generally, what is it about the nature of particular exchanges that strike us as noxious? How should our social policies respond to these noxious markets? I have been thinking and writing about these questions for more than a decade, and this book presents and defends my answers.

My answers have been shaped, to a significant degree, in response to the dominant perspectives on markets and their limits found in contemporary economics and political philosophy. Although these perspectives contain important insights, I have found the theoretical categories they employ of only limited use in answering these questions. This is because both groups of scholars generally assume that markets are a homogeneous institution, raising similar issues across distinct domains. But this assumption is mistaken. Markets not only allocate resources among different uses and distribute income among different people, but particular markets also shape our politics and culture, even our identities. Some markets thwart desirable human capacities; some shape our preferences in problematic ways; and some support objectionably hierarchical relationships between people. Efficiency is clearly not the only value relevant to assessing markets: we have to think about the effects of markets on social justice, and on who we are, how we relate to each other, and what kind of society we can have. For example, even if markets in goods such as child labor were efficient, we would still have reasons to object to such markets if they had harmful consequences for children or threatened democratic governance.[2] In this book I challenge the one-dimensional view of markets found in many economics textbooks and seek to address markets as institutions that raise political and moral questions as much as economic ones.

I also reject the flattened-out view of markets still found in much contemporary liberal philosophy. Most liberal egalitarian theorists analyze problematic markets through the lens of distribution and not (or not only) the economist's lens of efficiency. From the egalitarian's angle of vision, what underlies noxious markets—markets in sex, organs, child labor, kidneys, or bondage—is a prior and unjust distribution of resources, particularly of income and wealth. The problem with child labor, on this view, is the whip of poverty and hunger that compels parents to put their children to work, not the market in child labor itself.

This is a powerful view. Like these egalitarians, I also think that the fairness of the underlying distribution of wealth and income is extremely relevant to our assessment of markets, including those involving child labor. Certainly some of the markets that strike us as noxious do so because of their *origins* in destitution and desperation. But in this book I argue that we have reasons to block certain markets, to limit the domain of things that money can buy, even when such limits cannot be justified by considerations of economic desperation or by a prior unjust distribution of income and wealth. The kind of equality I advocate has noneconomic dimensions and depends on access to *specific* goods, such as education, health care, and employment.

In addition to criticizing the dominant contemporary approaches to the limits of the market, I also seek to revive earlier traditions of political economy and egalitarian political philosophy. These earlier traditions recognized the distinct nature of different kinds of markets. Early theorists of the market such as Adam Smith and David Ricardo were especially attuned to the ways that particular markets could promote, but also could undermine, relations of freedom and equality between members of a society. The classical political economists noted, for example, that labor markets could function in ways that shaped their participants as submissive inferiors and dominating superiors bent on exercising their arbitrary power. These thinkers also noted the ways certain markets were inherently characterized by asymmetric information and enforcement problems that allowed some market exchangers to exploit others. At the same time they believed that when properly structured and limited, markets had a very significant role to play in undermining the hierarchical organization of feudal society and advancing egalitarian social relationships.

Nineteenth-century social liberals such as T. H. Marshall argued that some specific goods, such as education, access to employment, health care, and votes, are necessary if citizens are to be equals and so should be guaranteed as a right. Rights are things that lie outside the domain of the market, at least to a certain extent. For example, to view health care as a right is to argue that there is some entitlement to health care that is independent of the cash nexus. The same holds true for the right to freedom of speech: even though access to very large audiences can be expensive, to view speech as a right entails that no one has to give a monetary payment to purchase the freedom to speak itself. As Marshall wrote, "Social rights in their modern form imply an invasion of contract by status, the subordination of market price to social justice, the replacement of the free bargain by the declaration of rights."[3]

Although I disagree in many details with thinkers like Smith and Marshall, my book revives in broad strokes these earlier arguments— that some markets shape individuals and society in problematic ways and that some specific goods need to be shielded from the operation of the market. The animating vision of this book, and of its central argument, is that of a society of equals: a society where there is "no more bowing and scraping, fawning and toadying; no more fearful trembling; no more high and mightiness; no more masters, no more slaves."[4] As we shall see, markets make an important contribution to the possibility of such a society, but to do so they need limits, and some goods need to be guaranteed to all.

THE PLAN OF THE BOOK

This book proceeds from and builds on some of my earlier essays, integrating them into a more general theory for assessing markets. The development of that theory proceeds in three parts. The first part of the book introduces the idea of the market as an economic and social mechanism for setting prices, coordinating behavior, and promoting choices. The approaches of welfare economics and neoclassical economics offer powerful arguments in favor of the market mechanism. In particular the market is often (but not always) better in a technical sense than alternatives: it is more efficient as an outcome for everyone involved. I explain and defend (in part) the insights from these two economic approaches to the market. Nevertheless a few examples can serve to highlight the limitations of these modes of economic reasoning. I argue that neither of these approaches can adequately explain our negative responses to certain kinds of markets (sex, weapons, pollution), nor can they explain why bans on particular markets (for votes, mercenaries, or salvation) might nevertheless be justified, even in cases where those bans generate inefficiencies.

The second part of the book builds the case for my own theory. I begin, in chapter 2, by setting out the view of markets found in classical political economy. For the classical economists the term *market* actually referred to a heterogeneous collection of economic relations. Adam Smith and his followers offered distinct theories of the functioning not only of consumer goods markets, but also of markets in land, labor, and credit. Their theories took account of the particular objects that different markets exchange: Smith pointed out the risky motivations of the borrowers of money; Ricardo and Malthus focused on the natural limits to the supply of land; and Marx singled out the distinctive nature of human labor power as a commodity whose purchase gives some people power and authority over others.[5]

Two features of the classical treatment of markets are important for the view that I develop. First, the classical political economists focused on the ways that certain exchanges can influence the people we become. In particular they saw that the labor market could shape the parties to the exchange in a way that a typical commodity market—a market in cars, for example—does not. These theorists noted that what a person can do and be, what he wants and what he can hope for, are importantly influenced by the structure and character of the labor market.

Second, these theorists noted that the structure of certain markets, the differing ability of the parties to exit the market and find alternatives, gives rise to relations of dominance and subordination between the parties. For example, they recognized that there are contexts in which some people have an urgent need for goods that other people control. In such circumstances the position of the weaker party is not only vulnerable to abuse and exploitation, but is utterly dependent on the will of another.[6]

In chapter 3 I explore the place of the market in contemporary egalitarian political philosophy. This is the most intramural of the chapters, providing details of recent philosophical arguments that have been made about the role of the market in a just society. Historically markets have provoked clashing opinions among egalitarians, but today most egalitarians acknowledge a substantial role for the market. At the same time some contemporary egalitarians have gone further; for example, the philosopher and legal theorist Ronald Dworkin has argued that the market is essential to our very understanding of what equality is. He concludes this because he thinks that equality requires that people have equal resources and that markets allow people with different preferences to acquire the goods that matter to them without violating the resource equality requirement. We need the market to show that the bundles of different goods that egalitarian theory says each of us has an initial claim on are in fact of equal value. One goal of this chapter is to argue that it is a mistake to think that markets can play this a priori role with respect to determining the shape of distributional equality. Markets are important institutions with a role to play in advancing social equality, but egalitarians have good reasons to reject some of the results that even perfect markets would throw our way.

Even egalitarians who treat markets as a merely instrumental mechanism for producing wealth tend to think that a focus on specific markets, markets in particular goods such as labor or kidneys, is a mistake. Most contemporary egalitarians are what the economist James Tobin once referred to as "general egalitarians."[7] General egalitarians recognize that targeted interventions in specific markets—rationing the sale of gasoline, for example—tend to be more inefficient than the generic redistribution of income. Some political philosophers also embrace general egalitarianism because they reject blocks on specific markets as paternalistic intrusions on personal liberty. They think that, unless others are harmed, restricting what people can do with their own income fails to treat them with respect. On the general egalitarian view, rather than looking at the workings of any particular market we should focus on the underlying distribution of resources. Once the underlying distribution of resources is fair, we should let markets do their work. If there are market imperfections, or if we think the market simply generates too much inequality, then we can correct these problems by a tax-and-transfer system.

I argue that tax-and-transfer egalitarianism has been too inattentive to the political and relational consequences of certain markets, the ways that certain markets shape us, our relationships with others, and our society. A just society requires restrictions on some of the market choices its citizens might make; an obvious example is a market in votes, but I hope to show that there are other, less obvious, cases as well.

The fourth chapter is the heart of the book, elaborating my theory of what makes particular markets noxious. The theory is complex. I identify four parameters that are relevant to the assessment of individual markets. These parameters are *vulnerability, weak agency, extremely harmful outcomes for individuals,* and *extremely harmful outcomes for society.*[8]

The first two parameters, vulnerability and weak agency, are characteristics of the *sources* of a market: they characterize what people bring to a market transaction.[9] Markets can arise in circumstances in which some people are so poor or so desperate that they accept any terms of exchange that are offered. Let us say that people in such markets suffer from *vulnerability*. Other markets arise in circumstances in which some parties have poor information about the goods they are exchanging, or in which some parties are not direct participants in the exchange but depend on others' decisions. Let us say that that people in such markets have *weak agency*.[10]

The second two parameters are characteristics of the *outcomes* of a market. Some markets may operate in ways that leave some of the participants in extremely bad circumstances, for example, circumstances in which they become destitute or in which their most basic interests are undermined. Let us say that such markets produce *extremely harmful outcomes for individuals*. Some markets produce *extremely harmful outcomes* not only for individuals but also *for society*: they undermine the framework needed for a society of equals, supporting relations of humiliating subordination or unaccountable power.

In chapter 4 I explain in detail the meaning of these four parameters and argue that scoring high along even one parameter (e.g., extremely harmful outcomes for children in child labor markets) can push a market into the "noxious" category. Yet although in principle any market can become noxious, I also argue that particular markets are *much more likely* to produce extremely harmful outcomes, manifest weak agency, exploit underlying vulnerabilities, or support extremely harmful and inegalitarian social relationships than other markets. For example, markets in health care, education, labor, and political influence all have, unlike apple markets, significant consequences for the structure of relationships between people in contemporary American society. These markets also have important effects on who we are, what we care about, what we can do and the kind of society that we can achieve. In the end, I try to show how many—if not all—noxious markets threaten democracy.

The argument of this chapter provides a framework for thinking about markets as well as criteria against which potential interventions in a market will need to be checked. It is not obvious that the best response to the existence of a noxious market is to ban it. In some cases banning a particular market may in fact intensify the problems that led us to condemn that market in the first place.[11] Legal or tolerated child labor, for example, is likely to be preferable to child prostitution in a black market. Where there are good reasons to refrain from blocking a particular market we may want to adopt measures that directly target the specific problems with that market, perhaps by changing background property rights or by income redistribution. Still, I intend to show that some particular markets need to be blocked altogether; there is sufficient reason to draw some bottom lines.

The third part of the book uses the theory I have developed to analyze current controversies about the scope of the market. Chapters 5 through 9 discuss markets in women's reproduction, prostitution, child labor, bonded labor, and human organs. In each case I call attention to dimensions of moral concern raised by such markets that are difficult to fully capture from the perspectives of economics and tax-and-transfer egalitarianism. In each case I look beyond considerations of efficiency and distributive equality to the broad cultural and political effects of these markets.

I should emphasize that this book is a work of political philosophy, not economics. It challenges *normative* aspects of the neoclassical and welfare economist's approaches to markets, not their *explanatory* power. The main categories of those approaches do not allow us to ask the full range of questions that I believe are relevant to the assessment of markets. Indeed these approaches were not designed to ask such questions. This book is also critical of the role that contemporary egalitarian theory has given to the market. When we think of markets only in terms of the distribution of goods and not in terms of the relationships of the people who produce and exchange those goods, crucial evaluative questions are also excluded from our decision frame. To evaluate markets we need to consider not only the production and distribution of goods, but also the social and political relationships that various markets sustain and support, including their effects on rich and poor, women and men, and the more or less powerful. We need to examine the effects of various markets on the social norms that underwrite our relationships with one another.

I have two aims in this book. The first is theoretical and is primarily addressed to contemporary political philosophers and philosophically minded economists; the second is practical and addresses current policy controversies. First, I hope to contribute to current discussions of equality. Among the questions that I consider are the following: In what ways do markets advance social equality? Are restrictions on the market transactions of consenting adults necessarily paternalist? What is the relationship between markets and equal citizenship in a democracy? My second more practical aim is to sketch an approach to markets that can be of use in guiding debates not only about the cases specifically discussed in this book but also in other cases, including controversies over the appropriate role of markets in the production and distribution of life-saving drugs, private prisons, education, the buying and selling of subprime mortgages, the regulation of carbon, and political influence. Of course each of these cases raises complex empirical matters that bear directly on what we should do in each case. The perspective I develop here is not intended as a blueprint.

Indeed, as will be apparent, my approach is importantly open-ended: I do not rank the various parameters for assessing markets against one another, nor do I offer mathematically precise definitions; there is no formula ascertaining how high a score along one of the parameters has to be before a market should be seen as noxious. Instead my argument will have been successful insofar as I have convinced my readers of the need for a fine-grained view of markets and their complex relationship to social equality.

PART I

1

What Do Markets Do?

Economists have written surprisingly little about the nature of a market, assuming perhaps that it is a simple concept with a clear or obvious referent. There is, for example, no definition of a market in many of the most widely used economic textbooks.[1] Yet in reality a market is a complex institution. As we will see in subsequent chapters, my view of markets is that they are even more complex than the basic account I give here suggests.

To begin, markets are institutions in which exchanges take place between parties who voluntarily undertake them.[2] Because all human action takes place within limits—I can't use my arms to fly simply by wishing it so—"voluntary" cannot mean the same thing as "unconstrained." All human action is constrained, by external and internal factors. There is a rich and subtle philosophical literature on the nature of voluntary actions, attempting to distinguish them from actions that are *unjustly* constrained.[3] For present purposes I will simply assume that in market exchanges both buyer and seller are entitled to the resources with which they transact, have the freedom to accept or refuse an offer of exchange, and can attempt to make another offer or strike a better deal with someone else.[4]

Additionally a market is not a single exchange between two individuals; indeed an exchange can be noxious without there being a noxious market.[5] Markets coordinate behavior through price signals, and to do this there have to be enough exchanges so that people are able to adjust their behavior in response to the actions and anticipated actions of others. If there are only two goods in the world, then you and I might exchange those goods with each other, but unless there is the possibility of coordination on future exchanges we don't really have a market, at least as I am using the term here.

The New Shorter Oxford English Dictionary defines a market as "a meeting or gathering place of people for the purchase and sale of provisions or livestock" and as "the action or business or buying and selling."[6] But markets are not merely meeting places or a series of individual transactions: they are social institutions that must be built up and maintained.[7] Initially markets may be thrown up spontaneously, but in the end they are socially sustained; *all* markets depend for their operation on background property rules and a complex of social, cultural, and legal institutions. For exchanges to constitute the structure of a market many elements have to be in place: property rights need to be defined and protected, rules for making contracts and agreements need to be specified and enforced, information needs to flow smoothly, people need to be induced through internal and external mechanisms to behave in a trustworthy manner, and monopolies need to be curtailed. In all developed market economies governments play a large role in securing these elements.

For this reason it is mistaken to consider *state* and *market* to be opposite terms; the state necessarily shapes and supports the process of market transacting. In Lewis Kornhauser and Robert Mnookin's memorable phrase, all (market) bargaining occurs in the shadow of the law.[8] Transacting individuals depend on the state for their basic security when they walk to the corner store to purchase food for their meals; they expect the state to enforce health and safety requirements concerning food production and handling; and they expect the shop owner to be sanctioned if he fails to keep up his end of the transaction. The fact that laws and institutions underwrite market transactions also means that such transactions are, at least in principle, not *private* capitalist acts between consenting adults, as the libertarian philosopher Robert Nozick famously claimed, but instead a *public* concern of all citizens whether or not they directly participate in them.

In addition to specific markets, such as markets in land, labor, or luxury goods like a yacht, there is what is sometimes referred to as "the market system" or the market economy. This further abstraction is usually taken to refer to a "society wide coordination of human activities" through mutual transactions.[9] Some people also use the term to refer to the integration of markets with "private property in the means of production."[10] But markets can coordinate behavior under very different property rules. I will use the term *market* in the context of discussing specific types of exchange transactions and *market system* as the abstraction that is supposed to link the set of all such markets. One important argument of this book is that in order to understand and fully appreciate the diverse moral dimensions of markets, we need to focus on the specific nature of particular markets and not on the market system.

MARKET VIRTUES

It is difficult to understand how a market system or any particular market works. Like ants in a colony, individuals cooperating in a market "have no dictators, no generals, no evil masterminds. In fact, there are no leaders at all."[11] The participants in a market are not obligated to follow another's orders with respect to what they buy and sell. Through markets individuals coordinate and mutually adjust their behaviors without relying on a conscious organizer to bring about the coordination. Somehow a market order arises out of millions of independent individual decisions, although such decisions are supported, as I stressed earlier, by an array of government and nongovernment institutions. Nevertheless the fact that coordination occurs largely through individual decisions and not through a central command and control structure explains and supports two particular virtues associated with markets, at least when they are working well: their link to efficiency and their link to liberty. Let us consider each of these virtues in turn.

EFFICIENCY

Market transactions link multiple chains of trades and involve cooperative behaviors spanning the globe. To give an example, workers in India whom I will never meet assembled my cell phone using materials imported from Africa and ordered on the Internet from suppliers, and the phone was transported to me by the employees of a transnational shipping company. Through the use of prices, markets signal what millions of goods are worth to sellers and buyers and intermediaries who will never meet each other. In doing so they function to mete out resources efficiently, indicating to sellers what and how much to produce, to consumers what price to pay, and to investors where to lay down their capital. Because rational individuals will exchange with one another only when they have something to gain, markets will (ideally) purge the economy of less desirable goods and move the trading parties to their most preferred positions, given their resources. The continual adjustment of supply and demand, registered in changing prices, allows markets to "clear" what has been produced. When inventory is cleared, there is no excess demand or excess supply: supply equals demand at some price.

A set of remarkable theorems formalizes the link between markets and efficiency. The first is the so-called fundamental theorem of welfare economics, according to which the result of any market equilibrium under perfect competition is Pareto optimal.[12] A social state is described as Pareto optimal if and only if no one's position (measured in terms of their preference satisfaction) can be improved without reducing the position of someone else. The intuitive idea behind the theorem is that people will engage in mutually beneficial exchanges and continue doing so until they cannot improve their positions by exchanging further. When all exchanges cease it is because an optimal allocation has been reached. Once that point is reached any deviation will make at least one person worse off.

A second formal result proves the converse proposition, that every Pareto optimal social state is a perfectly competitive equilibrium for some initial distribution of resources. It is worth keeping in mind that there is typically more than one Pareto optimum for any economy; in addition, given different starting distributions market competition will yield different results. This theorem allows that radical change from the status quo can still be efficient; it suggests that we can always find some initial distribution of resources that, along with the use of a market, will support a given Pareto optimal (efficient) social state.

These two results have intuitive ethical appeal. With respect to the first theorem, it seems obvious that it is better to make people better off and that if one of two prospects is better for someone than the other, and at least as good for everyone else, then it is better.[13] Yet although these efficiency results may be powerful in certain respects, they are actually of limited significance from a normative (ethical) point of view. Paretian efficiency does not give us overriding reasons for using markets or overriding reasons against interfering in them. As Amartya Sen notes, "A state can be Pareto optimal with some people in extreme misery and others rolling in luxury, so long as the miserable cannot be made better off without cutting into the luxury of the rich."[14]

We have good reasons to care about more than Paretian efficiency in our assessment of markets. For example, we have reasons to care that the initial distribution of resources in society is *fair*. Indeed if you think that individuals are *entitled* to certain property rights—by considerations of justice—then the fact that a certain social state is efficient relative to a *different* distribution of property rights has no normative force for you whatsoever. This is why objections to slavery are not undermined if it turns out that a slave system is Pareto efficient (insofar as any change in distributive allocations would make the slave owners worse off).

The second theorem might seem to help here since it allows for the incorporation of the distributive justice objection. If a critic doesn't like a particular Pareto equilibrium she can always redistribute initial resources the way she wants—abolish slave ownership, for example—and then allow competitive markets to produce another Pareto optimal result. Of course arranging for the redistribution is another matter.

In practice it is very difficult to find policy interventions that do not make at least one person worse off. Consider policies to promote the building of roads, hospitals, bridges, or schools. *Somebody* almost always prefers that these tasks not be undertaken; for example, a new highway benefits some businesses but hurts others located along the route of the older road. Nonetheless there may be good reasons to build the road. For this reason many economists prefer to think about efficiency in ways that allow the costs to some to be compensated by the extra gains to others. We can define a social state R as a *potential* Pareto improvement over a social state S if the winners in R could compensate the losers in R and still retain something over and above what they would have had in S. This idea of efficiency is sometimes referred to as Kaldor-Hicks efficiency, and it is effectively a form of cost-benefit analysis. Cost-benefit analysis tells us to adopt the policy (e.g., to build or not build the new road) that has the largest net benefit, other things being equal. However, we should bear in mind that a policy with the greatest net benefit may in reality fail to distribute some of that benefit to the losers, and thus this form of efficiency (unlike Pareto efficiency) can wind up endorsing policies that actually make some people worse off!

Although Kaldor-Hicks efficiency is a more useful concept than Pareto efficiency to use in evaluating economic policies, given that so many exchanges produce both winners and losers both concepts are still normatively narrow ways of assessing economic achievements. Both employ criteria that omit consideration of such issues as what is a *fair* distributive outcome. Indeed the development of these concepts of efficiency was partly motivated by the desire to separate the study of what economists saw as uncontroversial economic improvements from the more controversial questions of ethics and distributive justice.

I believe that such a complete separation is in fact impossible. For example, the acceptance of the Pareto criterion as the measure of economic improvement depends on a key normative assumption: that improvement is to be measured in the space of individual preferences. That is, on this view of efficiency, people are considered better off the more that their own (consistent) preferences are satisfied. Additionally this criterion was formulated to bypass interpersonal comparisons with respect to different individuals' preference satisfaction since such comparisons are considered meaningless because there are "no means whereby such comparisons can be accomplished."[15]

But surely not all preferences are equally worthy of satisfaction. First, some preferences are really urgent needs, whereas others are altogether frivolous. It is surely more important to satisfy the needs of those in extreme misery in Sen's example than to add more to the coffers of those already rolling in luxury. The fact that income transfers to the poor would make the wealthy worse off does not settle the case against such transfers. Second, some preferences, such as the preference for hurting others, would be accorded no weight at all from a moral point of view. Is it really an improvement if, all things being equal, the slaveholder's preference for more slaves is satisfied or the sadist's preference for inflicting pain?

For these reasons most political and moral philosophers (indeed most people) use criteria for assessing social policies that go beyond Paretian and even Kaldor-Hicks efficiency. They appeal to fairness as well as to conceptions of human well-being that allow us to compare the benefits and costs of different policies to different individuals. In comparing people's well-being we might be led to decrease the preference satisfaction of the millionaire to satisfy the urgent needs of the desperately poor. Indeed we might be led to reject preference satisfaction as the right metric for making and assessing interpersonal comparisons and for evaluating economic states of affairs. (Later in this book I discuss in more detail the limitations of focusing on preference satisfaction as a standard for assessing markets).

Nevertheless the efficiency theorems do give us some insight into the individualistic basis for the mutually advantageous nature of trade.

Individual decisions function, in the context of markets and prices, as signals for coordinating action to satisfy maximally agents' wants under given sets of constraints. In a market's best-case scenario, where information flows, there are no third-party effects of exchanges, no monopoly power, and the parties are completely trustworthy, the network of individual trade serves to generate improvements in getting people what they want. It thus produces efficiency relative to those wants; it limits waste and uses human and nonhuman resources efficiently. However, in real-world scenarios we cannot automatically conclude that the market is more efficient than alternatives. In almost all actual market contexts there are problems with information and enforcement that mean that intervention can improve on efficiency, a point to which I will shortly return.

FREEDOM

From a normative point of view, one of the key attractions of markets is their relationship to individual choice and decision. Markets:

- Present agents with the opportunity to choose between a set of alternatives (partly by providing individuals with incentives to create the material wealth which is a precondition of having an extensive array of choices)
- Provide incentives for agents to anticipate the results of their choices and thus foster a kind of instrumental (means-ends) rationality
- Decentralize decision making, giving an agent alone the power to buy and sell things without requiring him or her to ask any one else's permission or take anyone else's values into account
- Place limits on the viability of coercive social relationships by providing (at least formally) avenues for exit
- Decentralize information, thereby making abuses of power by authorities less likely
- Allow people to experiment, to try new commodities, to develop new tastes, to opt out of traditional ways of life
- Contribute to the undermining of racial, ethnic, and religious discrimination by appealing to the reciprocal self-interest of individuals in exchanging goods with one another and by fostering anonymous exchange

Liberal theories that assign substantial weight to individual freedom thus tend to allot a central role for market allocation, pointing to the market realm as a place where the capacities for individual choice, indeed where the liberal individual herself is developed. Markets call up our powers as individual decision makers who can veto as well as sign on to exchanges, and they give scope for the exercise of these powers. In this sense markets can be *instruments* for promoting freedom: they develop our capacities to choose. Additionally markets can be *components* of freedom. As Amartya Sen has noted, the freedom to engage in transactions with others, to decide on where to work, what to produce, and what to consume, are important parts of a person's overall freedom.[16] Choosing often has an intrinsic value; many of our actions have a special meaning for us precisely because we chose them. Think about buying a birthday gift for a devoted friend. Even if I could hire someone to make the choice and purchase for me, I may want to do it myself as a way of expressing and communicating my own feelings. Even if a well-designed computer program allotted people into careers that matched their talents, this would be quite different from allowing people to choose (perhaps with less happy outcomes) their own occupations. Many of us want our own values and judgments to be reflected in what work we do, what we consume, and which of (what Max Weber termed) the warring gods we serve in how we live.

Many political and social theorists have valued markets precisely because they believed that markets assist in the development and exercise of our capacities as individual decision makers. For even if, as Locke and Rousseau thought, we are *born to* a state of freedom, it is widely recognized that to develop and realize various freedoms requires education, planning, practice, and cooperation with others. The development of the free individual is in fact a tremendous *social* achievement. Markets have had an important role to play in facilitating freedom's achievement by stimulating the capacities we need to choose and providing these capacities with a wide arena for their employment.

Reliance on markets for the distribution of goods and services can also be an important way of respecting individual and divergent values. Two people do not have to agree on the importance of a good, or its place in a worthwhile life, in order to exchange that good on a market. Think of the buyer and the seller of a religious text such as the Bible. Buyer and seller may disagree radically as to the Bible's importance as well as about the appropriate attitude a person should take to the Bible, but they can still agree on its price. In a market system there is no preordained pattern of value to which individuals must conform; markets allow people to make their own judgments about what they want to buy or sell, how hard they want to work, how much they want to save, what they value and how they value it, and what they wish to consume. Indeed the market system institutionalizes the idea that, potentially, *anything* might be traded for anything and *anyone* might enter into the great trading game.

In a justly famous passage in *The Communist Manifesto* Karl Marx celebrated this cosmopolitan and liberating character of a market system:

> All fixed, fast frozen relations, with their train of ancient and venerable prejudices and opinions are swept away, all new-formed ones become antiquated before they can ossify. All that is solid melts into air, all that is holy is profaned, and man is at last compelled to face with sober senses, his real conditions of life and his relations with his kind. . . . In place of the old wants, satisfied by the production of the country, we find new wants, requiring for their satisfaction the old products of distant lands and climes. In place of the old and national seclusion and self-sufficiency, we have intercourse in every direction, universal interdependence of nations.[17]

True, Marx was ambivalent about the liberating effects of the market system—he thought that under capitalism too many of those who work were under the subjection of their employers and limited by their own poverty—but as this passage makes clear, he also saw the potential for markets to link people together in a fundamentally new way, in opposition to the "venerable prejudices" that had previously bound people in traditional "fixed and frozen" roles. The idea that markets place people in new social relationships with one another—relationships that are horizontal, egalitarian, and anonymous—is a theme sounded by the market's earliest defenders as well as by its detractors.

Sometimes it is thought that the type of freedom that markets support is essentially negative freedom, freedom from interference by others. In the marketplace the consumer is held to be her own "sovereign," not subject to anyone else's authority. (As I noted, this is literally false: markets always depend on property rules, enforced through public coercion, that interfere with some individual liberties. If you own the car, then I am not simply free to use it. Ownership of real estate and land, likewise, puts enormous restraint on people's freedom of movement. But markets also can support a more positive kind of freedom, the freedom to be in control of one's own life, by reducing servile dependency and undermining hierarchical social relationships. Adam Smith singled out this feature of markets as their "most important" effect, along with "good government":

> Commerce and manufactures gradually introduced order and good government, and with them, the liberty and security of individuals, among the inhabitants of the country, who had before lived almost in a continual state of war with their neighbours and of servile dependency upon their superiors. This, though it has been the least observed, *is by far the most important of all their effects.*[18]

Under feudalism wealthy landlords employed hundreds of retainers, servants, and peasant farmers, all of whom depended on them for both their subsistence and protection.[19] By contrast, Smith points out, commerce and manufacturing liberate individuals from such degrading servility because in a well-functioning labor market, no one is dependent on any one particular master. Any worker can, at least theoretically, move to another employer in the event of humiliating or arbitrary treatment.[20] And in a competitive market no single person has the power to set prices: prices depend on the choices of all.

Of course, it is important not to overstate this contrast between market freedom and feudal dependence; many laborers did and still do have to obey an arbitrary master on the factory floor. Bosses wield power over their employees that these same employees do not wield over employers.[21] But two features of competitive labor markets work to temper the degree of humiliating servitude that workers face on the job.

The first mitigating feature is that market relationships are impersonal relationships based on mutual self-interest. As Smith reminds us, "It is not from the benevolence of the butcher, the brewer or the baker that we get our dinner, but from their regard to their own interest."[22] The motivation of self-interest that fuels a market differs from those motivations involved in the exercise of an arrogant and personal power. In Albert Hirschman's words, in a market society "passion" tends to be tamed by "interest.[23] Under the pressure of competition the motivation for abusing and lording it over inferiors and the temptation of unleashing volatile emotions such as vengeance, honor, and envy have to be disciplined by the need for productive efficiency.[24] Moreover markets link anonymous strangers, people who have no personal relationships with one another, and therefore no personal axe to grind.

The second mitigating feature of competitive labor markets is that they allow, to varying degrees, for the possibility of exit. The need actually to *enlist* loyalty, commitment, and accountability on the part of their employees gives employers a reason to mitigate the power that they might otherwise wield. *Exit* is a powerful influence on the shape of human relationships and interactions. In many circumstances the mere threat by a person to exit a relationship may lead others to consider her interests more carefully and to treat her better.

Employees also exit from their employers when they leave their job, in contrast with feudalism; they go home to a realm in which their employer is not assumed to have authority. Feudalism gave the owners of land (the lords) the rights they needed to exercise direct control over the people who lived on their land (the peasants), including the right to punish them and to give them orders to go to war with neighboring landowners. Although there have been "company towns," capitalist managers do not ordinarily give orders to their employees outside of their working hours and have little direct control over non-work-related aspects of an employee's life. In developed capitalist economies residence is largely separated from work, although as we shall see later in this book, in some parts of the developing world such exit can be foreclosed by the shape of the labor market itself.[25]

Of course, much of the curtailment of employers' arbitrary and abusive power was achieved not only through the employers' own prudent decisions about the requirements of maximizing productivity, but also, and perhaps especially, through the advent of labor unions. A critical function of unions on the factory floor has been to protect the freedom and equality of workers by providing a counterweight to employer power.

And even though markets can be seen to promote independence and individual freedom we should not lose sight of the fact that they can also coexist with political regimes that deny or curtail basic political freedoms. Finally, those who fare very badly in the market system—who hold down personally unrewarding jobs for little pay, have no viable alternatives with which to support themselves, lack information, and so on—might reasonably claim that they have only a minimal and degenerate form of freedom.

Nor are markets the only route to personal freedom and independence. A person can experience important freedoms within a nonmarket context, such as when she participates in a collective political endeavor or shares in a project with her friends and family. Many of our important collective and individual freedoms do not rely directly or even indirectly on a market. Indeed some of these freedoms, such as the freedom to participate in a tight-knit homogeneous community or to be able to escape competitive interactions with others, may be effectively undermined by the existence of a market.[26] Nor is there any guarantee that all of the freedoms that markets enable will be meaningful freedoms; freedom from servitude and abuse is crucially important, but having the opportunity to choose between dozens of toothpaste brands does not significantly advance a person's freedom.

THE BACKGROUND CONDITIONS FOR THE MARKET'S LINK TO EFFICIENCY AND FREEDOM

Markets do not automatically or spontaneously realize the virtues of efficiency or freedom. For markets to promote these values, there has to be a suitable platform in place. Theorists from Adam Smith to David Hume have recognized that economic activity presupposes property, rules of exchange, and contract and enforcement. Moreover different platforms will have dramatically different effects on the compatibility between markets and the values of freedom and efficiency. In other words, a positive relationship between particular markets and the values of freedom and efficiency is contingent: it depends, at least in large part, on the platform on which markets are erected. I describe in generic terms the most important elements of this platform below.[27]

Property Rights

Markets work efficiently only where there are established and protected property rights. This requires the existence of legal and regulatory frameworks to ensure that contracts are enforced and the given property rights are respected. But functioning markets require that the state do more than simply intervene to prevent theft and fraud. There also need to be mechanisms for resolving commercial disputes; there has to be a sound banking system that provides businesses with access to credit;

and there needs to be a system of taxation to pursue necessary collective goals such as education, building and maintaining infrastructure, and the administration of justice.

Property rights are also relevant for the real freedoms a person can achieve. For example, a market in which some people can be owned limits the freedom of those who may become the property of others. A market that leaves people with few social entitlements may undermine the ability of the poor to achieve important substantive freedoms. Even if, to paraphrase Anatole France, in a market system the poor and the rich are equally free to dine at the most expensive restaurant in New York City, this freedom is not worth very much to the poor. Before a person can be said to have the effective opportunity—the real freedom—to be and do many things, she must have access to a number of goods that markets may or may not provide. A person may be unable to participate in collective decision making, achieve a kind of personal independence, or even function as a market agent if she is hungry or illiterate or cannot escape premature morbidity.

More generally all property rights enable certain freedoms and place limits on other freedoms. Some private property rights endow individual owners with exclusive authority over their property and thus simultaneously exclude all others.[28] In addition all property rights are the products of laws and conventions that back them up and enforce them.[29] My ownership of a good means little if I am powerless to prevent others from seizing it. An important implication of this observation is that the free market is necessarily based on the coercive power of property rules, government regulations, and social conventions. True laissez-faire is not even logically possible.

Free Information

Unless buyers know what commodities are selling for, they may overpay for them. If a seller controls price and product information, then buyers can be misled into buying a shabby product, and there is no incentive for the seller to cut his prices. In the presence of reliable information, an exchange that looked to be in the buyer's benefit might turn out to have been a mistake. Efficiency requires that decisions be made with adequate information on benefits and costs.

Information does not always flow freely in a market. It is costly to come by, it takes time and effort to learn what goods are available and what their prices are, and it is even more costly to determine their quality. And both buyers and sellers have an incentive for holding on to information to increase their own market power. To ensure the flow of information requires many institutions, conventions, regulations, and norms. Services such as the Yellow Pages, Google, and company trademarks lower the costs of finding information for consumers. Wholesalers and trading companies lower costs of information to businesses. Government regulations attempt to assure quality control and accurate information about products.[30] Nevertheless in some exchanges large asymmetries of information are likely to remain between buyers and sellers; examples include health care markets and the market for used cars.[31] In these cases it is hard for buyers to ascertain the quality of the goods that are for sale. As we shall see, child labor markets are also often closely tied to poor information.

Even when information on products is available people are notoriously bad at processing it; they regularly distort the probabilities of risks associated with different products, and they are easily overloaded by too much information. For example, even reasonably informed people may choose to downplay the risk of cancer due to smoking because, although knowing the statistics, they do not see cancer as something that can happen *to them*. Recent work on biases in decision making has demonstrated that people routinely overestimate the importance of nominal losses, overestimate their probability of success, and respond to "framing effects" in the ways that decisions are posed.[32] In such cases biases mean that it may be possible to improve on market outcomes through some kind of intervention (educational campaigns, changing default starting points, marketing). There is no invisible market hand automatically producing efficient outcomes; as Joseph Stiglitz has remarked, Adam Smith's "invisible hand" is invisible because it is not there.

Trust

Markets function well only when the participants are trustworthy. Because in many transactions there is a time lag between purchase and sale, buyer and seller depend on each other to honor their agreements. Because obtaining information and monitoring are costly, markets are more efficient when the parties do not aim to deceive one another. This means that although it is often said that markets are fueled by a maximizing self-interest, they must also be underwritten by social sentiments and norms. *Homo economicus* may be out only for himself, but he must not generally steal, lie, cheat, or murder in order to maximize his gains if markets are to work.[33] Theft involves an exchange of goods, but clearly it is not a market exchange.

Interestingly markets have different and opposing effects on the possibilities for trust and trustworthiness in a society. On the one hand, to the extent that a trustworthy reputation is important to market success, markets encourage intelligent pursuit of *interest* over reckless passion.[34] When one party behaves in an untrustworthy manner, other parties may refuse to trade with him in the future. Knowing this, it is not in his self-interest to default on his contractual agreements. In this way self-interest can serve as a basis for mutually beneficial behavior. On the other hand, however, the possibilities for trust depend on several factors that are themselves affected by markets. People seem to be more likely to trust those with whom they repeatedly interact, with whom they share beliefs and values, and with whom they are able to engage in direct communication. Markets negatively affect all of these factors by increasing the number and heterogeneity of trading partners.[35] The anonymous nature of market exchanges tends to favor short-lived exchanges and a pairing of individuals that is more random than in a small community of friends. As the number and heterogeneity of trading partners increase, the monitoring and enforcement costs also increase, and self-interest becomes a less reliable basis for producing socially good results. Although markets enable participants to economize on virtue, those exchanging cannot economize too much.

Anti-Monopoly

An efficient market needs to keep the tendency to monopoly in check; in particular, competition is necessary for the two theorems of welfare economics to hold. In perfect competition no one has any power over anyone else, all are assumed to act independently of one another, and no one can determine prices. Competition thus disciplines companies; they must produce high enough quality products at low enough prices to stay ahead of their competitors. Monopolists face no such incentives; they can persist in offering shoddy products at inflated prices, and they can impose arbitrary prices because there are no alternatives. To forestall the formation of monopolies societies must sometimes rely on antitrust legislation, laws against price fixing, and regulations regarding mergers and takeovers.

Even with such measures many markets are not perfectly competitive. Economies of scale convey advantages in production that lead large producers to corner the market. Some industries are natural monopolies in which it makes little sense to have multiple suppliers. For example, there would be greater social costs to have two water systems running in parallel than having just one, given the costs of digging pathways that go to the same place.

Important freedoms are also undermined by the absence of alternatives. Under monopoly buyers cannot get what they want from many sellers, and in cases of needed goods they are completely dependent on one supplier. Consider the power of the person who owns all the water in a desert. Monopoly is a particular form of compulsion, re-creating a feudal relationship of dependency right in the heart of a liberal market society.

In sum, well-functioning markets require supports. Such supports are not all or nothing, but plainly admit of degrees. The great majority of actual markets lie somewhere in between the textbook extremes of perfect competition and pure monopoly. Individuals come to the market with very differing assets and differing knowledge about alternatives, which can make some parties far more dependent on the transaction than others.

State regulations, redistribution, and widespread acceptance and use of norms such as sympathy and honesty can bring markets closer to their ideal conditions. For example, the state can enforce property laws, curtail monopolies, regulate communications systems, and underwrite compulsory education. Yet even if these four props are in place—even if there are established property rights, free information, trust, and competition—markets can still fail to be efficient or realize liberal freedoms. And even if they do support efficiency and liberal freedoms we may still find markets in some goods unsettling. I will postpone detailed discussion of how markets can fail to link to freedom until a later chapter, when I discuss how labor markets can be compatible with extreme servitude and dependency.³⁶ And I will postpone discussion of how even efficient and freedom-enhancing markets can nevertheless be problematic until chapter 4, when I discuss markets in specific goods like safety and education. I conclude this chapter by focusing on the main contemporary economic concern with markets: their efficiency. Why does the link between markets and efficiency sometimes fail, even when good supports for the market are in place?

MARKET FAILURE

It is well recognized in economics that market transactions can sometimes impose costs on uninvolved third parties. These costs are usually referred to as "externalities," and they form the core of the economist's theory of market failure. As an example, consider that the effects of pollution cannot be restricted only to the parties whose exchanges produce it. Many of the world's greatest environmental problems today are due to the external unpriced effects of increasing industrial production and fuel consumption. Likewise the sales of international weapons can spill over to have effects on people who are far removed from the parties to the transaction. Other bases of market failure include non-zero transaction costs and technologies that give rise to economies of scale, making only monopolistic or oligopolistic firms viable, as well as the existence of natural monopolies.

When markets fail because of externalities it is because there are some costs that have been introduced that individuals acting in the market have not accounted for. Some of these costs may actually be beneficial—public goods and not public bads—but the ones that concern us are usually not. The production of public bads as a byproduct of market exchanges forms the basis for the economic case for their regulation.

At one time economists proceeded as if externalities were unusual, and the rule was that most transactions had little effect on the individuals who were not direct parties to the exchange.³⁷ But a little reflection will show that this assumption is mistaken. Almost any exchange in a dense, interdependent, and complex society is likely to impose a cost on third parties. Building high-rise apartment towers block the sunlight for neighboring houses. Cars bring congestion. Cigarette smoke circulates. In fact whenever I have preferences over your actions or their effects we also have an externality. If I disapprove of a particular religious text because I despise that religion, then your buying or selling this text generates an externality for me, a negative cost that I must now absorb.[38]

In practice economists tend to be quite opportunistic as to where and when they invoke the concept of externality.[39] Indeed they usually appeal to externalities as a basis of regulation in ways that track the traditional "harm principle" of liberal theory, according to which the bare fact that I do not like a certain outcome does not constitute *harm*, that is, a genuine *cost* to me that calls for redress.[40] But nothing in economic analysis generates or supports this particular interpretation of costs or harm; the economic argument for identifying inefficiencies in the case of only certain externalities—pollution but not intolerance of religious diversity—feeds off moral theory done elsewhere.[41] That's not necessarily a problem, as long as we attend to the moral theory and make it explicit in our understanding of inefficiency.

Markets can also fail to provide needed public goods, where these are understood to include goods (such as national defense) that provide positive externalities, are nonexcludable, and are costly to produce. In such cases, although it is to everyone's benefit that the good be provided, it is in no one's individual benefit to provide it. If national defense is provided it will benefit all those who live in a country, even those who do not pay their share of the costs of maintaining it. Many goods are purely or partially public in nature. (And sometimes we face decisions about whether to consider a good a public or a private good. Although education is often treated as a public good, it *could* be treated as a private good.) Of course even if markets generate inefficiencies due to externalities, the alternatives might be worse. Perhaps some market inefficiency is preferable to a lot of government regulation, with its slow, clumsy, and lumbering bureaucracy. That is why market failure generates only a prima facie case for intervention, not an-all-things considered case.

The logic of the economic approach to markets leads us to view market failure as an indicator not that the market's system of allocation is defective, but as a sign that the market system is not complete.[42] If the scope of the market could be enlarged to include the external third party effects—if sunlight, congestion, pollution, secondhand cigarette smoke, and religious distaste could be priced and sold—then the externalities could be reabsorbed. A complete market, universal in scope and across all future temporal states of the world, promises *in theory* to eliminate all externalities. Indeed much economic reasoning is at least theoretically imperialistic about the range of the market. In the standard Arrow-Debreu general equilibrium models, for example, there is assumed to be a market for every conceivable good, present and future, and every conceivable circumstance.[43]

Economists' response to the inefficiencies of actual markets suggests that they have some independent normative commitments and beliefs—a belief, for example, that the market's inefficiency costs will turn out to be less burdensome than the intrusions of state regulation, and the assumption that third-party cost is defined by only certain kinds of losses. It is open to any of us to endorse a different and more complex view of the concept of market failure.

LOOKING AHEAD

To this point I have stressed the idea of markets as economic and social mechanisms for setting prices, coordinating behavior, and promoting individual choices. As we have seen, contemporary economics offers some powerful arguments in favor of the market mechanism. Markets are often (but not always) better in a technical sense than alternatives, superior as an outcome (in terms of individual preferences) for everyone involved. Markets help develop and give range to individual choice and decision. This chapter explains and defends (in part) these arguments. But it also cautions us to not treat these arguments as a priori. Markets are not *necessarily* better at promoting these values than alternatives, including, in many instances, in-kind redistribution by the state. To evaluate markets and their alternatives we need to examine messy empirical cases.

The economic arguments in favor of markets proceed without attaching any independent moral value to the commodities being produced and exchanged. It doesn't matter whether the goods on the market are bibles, guns, butter, human organs, "blood diamonds" that fuel bloody civil wars, or sex. Nor is the quality of the goods relevant. It all looks the same in the economist's equations. As Lionel Robbins explained in 1932, economics deals with the ubiquitous elements of scarcity, means, and ends, and the means and ends can be filled in with any content whatsoever.[44] All markets are explained in the same terms.

Moreover market failure is understood in the same terms in all of these different cases. Rather than address questions of ethics, most economists purport to employ a division of labor whereby they explain only the economic consequences of the use of particular markets for efficiency while others worry about ethics. But, as I have argued, such a division of labor is impossible: what counts as an inefficiency or an economic improvement involves prior ethical judgments. For if the only resource we have for thinking about efficiency is subjective preference, then we will have to count dissatisfactions based on envy at another's success as economic costs. But this seems ludicrous. It follows that any plausible measure of the costs of various activities presupposes a substantive conception of what is important to human welfare, of which subjectively felt harms count as costs. Efficiency turns out to have a moral dimension after all.

In this book I will argue that neither standard efficiency analysis nor the generic concept of market failure can tell us when we should use markets to allocate particular goods and when other mechanisms are more appropriate. Let me anticipate my discussion in the coming chapters with a few simple examples.

Consider the vote. As James Tobin notes, "Any good second year graduate student could write a short examination paper proving that voluntary transactions in votes would increase the welfare of the sellers as well as the buyers."[45] But no one seriously proposes that we distribute a society's votes through a market; the legitimacy of the political process rests on the prohibition of such transactions.

Consider the labor market. Should employers be allowed to demand sexual favors in compensation for a higher wage?[46] Should individuals be allowed to sign slavery contracts with one another? Both quid pro quo sexual favors and slave contracts are widely held to be reprehensible. The interesting question is why this is so and whether efficiency or the standard analysis of market failure is in any way at issue.

Military service is often viewed as a civic duty and something to be praised when undertaken. At the same time, the hiring of mercenaries is widely condemned. Why do people condemn an act when done for pay that they would praise if done for duty?[47]

A central thesis of this book is that we must expand our evaluation of markets, along with the concept of market failure, to include the effects of such markets on the structure of our relationships with one another, on our democracy, and on human motivation. Even if markets in sexual favors or votes or mercenaries turned out to be efficient, and even if they arose from voluntary agreements, such markets might still be objectionable—*would* be objectionable, I shall argue—insofar as they arise from weak agency, exploit the underlying vulnerabilities of the most vulnerable, or have extremely harmful consequences for individuals or their societies.

In the next two chapters I explore alternative frameworks for thinking about markets. In chapter 2 I present the neglected and rich approach of the classical political economists. Whereas contemporary economics has tended to think of markets in very abstract terms, the classical economists saw markets as heterogeneous, and they sharply distinguished between markets in land, labor, and capital. Their assessment of different markets explicitly called attention to the structure of power and to the effects of markets on human motivation, human capacities, and social relationships. This tradition has been neglected in economics, and I argue that we have much to learn from it. Chapter 3 examines some contemporary egalitarian frameworks for considering the role of the market and its moral limits, including those of Ronald Dworkin and Michael Walzer. In chapter 4 I present and defend my own view of these limits.

PART II

2

The Changing Visions of Economics

The view of the market as a homogeneous mechanism operating across different types of exchanges is distinctly modern. The classical political economists, especially Adam Smith, David Ricardo, and Karl Marx, held a very different view of markets and of their place in society. Our modern understanding of markets in terms of their formal properties and our ability to build tractable models far surpasses those of the classical political economists. But something important has been lost. This chapter focuses on these earlier thinkers' larger overall vision and its contrast with that laid out in chapter 1. This alternative vision had far-reaching implications for their views of the nature and limits of markets and the justice (or injustice) of many market transactions.[1] Aspects of this earlier vision are present in some later post-Jevons economists, such as Marshall, Pigou, and Pareto, but I will end my discussion with the marginalist revolution that occurred in economics during the 1870s. I want to bring into the sharpest focus the contrast between the classical political economist's understanding of the market as a system of heterogeneous relationships between social classes with competing interests and the later approaches founded on an image of the economy as a set of exchange relations between independent individuals.

In this chapter I discuss the particular answers that the classical economists gave to the question of the nature and limits of markets. There are two features shared by their answers that I wish to highlight. First, they emphasized the *social embeddedness* of markets. They saw that markets could not become the sole institution or sole organizing principle of a liberal society without destroying that society. More specifically they recognized that markets require limits if a liberal society, based on the equality and freedom of its members, is to be maintained. This is an idea that was revived in the twentieth century by Karl Polanyi, who argued that a society based on self-regulating markets alone could not work.[2] A

society held together only by markets would not be able to stably reproduce itself over time. Most economists today recognize the truth of
Polanyi's stability argument about a self-regulating market society, but
they ignore one of his central conclusions, which is that labor markets
have features that distinguish them from other types of markets.

Second, and relatedly, the classical political economists recognized
that markets were heterogeneous and that some markets shape society
as well as individuals. For example, thinkers as diverse as Smith and
Marx believed that the way human labor power is produced and sold
has not only profound effects on the workers whose labor it is, but also
external effects on society as a whole. Because I think that these are key
insights—the embeddedness of markets and the effects of particular
markets on individual preferences and capacities—I want to explore
them at some length in this chapter.

However, it is important to begin with some caveats. First, I am
focusing on only a handful of thinkers. At the time these economists
were writing, there were quite different traditions; the French physio-
crats (especially Quesnay), Montesquieu with his *doux-commerce* thesis
(that is, the thesis that commerce makes for gentle manners),[3] and John
Stuart Mill serve as prominent contemporaries that I exclude. Although
these thinkers share some ideas with the views I explore here, their overall theories do not serve to illuminate the line of thought I am pursuing.
Second, as I alluded earlier, I am restricting myself to a specific time
period. The decline of feudalism gave impetus to new ways of thinking
about human nature and about economic order. Feudalism looms large
in the background of the arguments that I consider here. Thus although
there are late nineteenth- and twentieth-century economists, including
Amartya Sen, whose ideas overlap with the classical political economists,
I want to keep my focus on thinkers who highlight the ways that markets
can support and threaten a liberal social order.

THE SMITHEAN VIEW OF MARKETS

The rich man in his castle,
The poor man at his gate,
God made them, high or lowly,
And order'd their estate.[4]

Under feudalism a person's status was assigned by birth, and the world was divided into inferiors and superiors. The second half of the eighteenth century saw a social order based on hierarchical and fixed status differentials between social groups under pressure from a new way of thinking about social and political relations, based on individual freedom and consent. But how could individual freedom and consent be made compatible with social *order*? Wouldn't reliance on everyone's separate and self-interested choices produce conflict? In *Leviathan* Thomas Hobbes argued that only an absolute sovereign with unlimited power could secure a stable social order among independent free individuals.[5] Adam Smith provides the world with a different answer. A central claim of his *Inquiry into the Nature and Causes of the Wealth of Nations* (1776; the last revised edition appeared in 1784) is that, in the context of market relations, independent individuals would not only produce increased wealth but would also make a liberal social order.

Smith's striking innovation was to see the market as a form of *social* organization. His arguments concerning the economic efficiency effects of markets (and the division of labor) are well known, but his important arguments about the market system's *social* effects have been largely ignored or misunderstood.

Smith celebrated the freedom to buy and sell not only as an impetus to economic growth and the wealth of nations, but also as a form of emancipation from a particular kind of political oppression. As I noted in chapter 1, Smith argued that markets undermined social relationships built on servility:

> Commerce and manufactures gradually introduced order and good government, and with them, the liberty and security of individuals, among the inhabitants of the country, who had before lived almost in a continual state of war with their neighbors and of servile dependency upon their superiors. This, although it has been the least observed, is by far the most important of their effects.[6]

To understand Smith's argument, consider the contrast between the organization of feudal society and the freedom of the new industrial order based on market exchange. Under feudalism peasants and laborers were dependent on the feudal landowners for their subsistence and for protection from violence by others. This extreme dependency supported relations of servility between the lord and his subjects, the peasant's bowing and scraping before his superior. Peasants had a duty to obey the lord's commands, no matter how arbitrary or humiliating or costly such commands were. An important point about this servile relationship between serf and lord is that it was generally *voluntary*: the serf was tied to his master by apparently voluntary acts of loyalty. Although in theory the peasant might have been free to leave and find an alternative master,[7] mobility was difficult, and the bundled package of work and home often made it impossible for him to change one without changing all his social ties. Given his economic, political, and social circumstances, subservience to the lord was frequently the peasant's best option.

How did markets change this relation between inferior and superior into a relation between equals? Smith argued that markets liberate individuals from their abject dependence on one powerful person by allowing them to sustain themselves through exchanges with thousands of anonymous and indifferent customers: "Each tradesman or artificer derives his subsistence from the employment, not of one, but of a hundred or a thousand different customers. Though in some measure obliged to them all, therefore, he is not absolutely dependent on any one of them."[8]

Freedom of commerce creates the possibility of multiple and optional webs of relationship with anonymous others, thus undermining the relations of personal and direct subjection and servility that characterized feudalism. This end of abject servility to masters (along with good government) was "by far the most important" effect of markets.

The extension of the market system creates a society of horizontal relationships based on free interaction, equality, and reciprocal self-interest. Because market exchanges are based on each participant's mutual agreement, such exchanges implicitly recognize the participants as persons who have standing and are able to make claims on their own behalf. Buyer and seller meet as free persons. Because market exchanges are governed by the idea that goods are exchanged for their equivalents, they are realms of equality. Because market exchanges do not presuppose that the interests of the participants are identical (all that matters is that each has something to gain), they are also compatible with social coordination among independent individuals with diverse values and preferences. Rather than appealing to norms based on natural hierarchy, in a market each looks only to his own advantage. In a quite different context even Marx noted that market exchange is a realm of "freedom, equality, property and Bentham."[9] The development and spread of labor markets and consumer product markets thus enabled large numbers of people to enjoy a kind of personal independence, or at least an end to absolute dependence, that had simply not been possible before.[10]

Yet Smith also recognized that the ability of laborers to escape from servility to a master through markets is dependent on a number of conditions, including how competitive the labor market actually is and the skill levels of the laborers. If the labor market is not competitive and if workers are deskilled and superfluous, they will voluntarily agree to terms that leave them utterly dependent on and subordinate to their employers. Under such conditions employers have a power of control analogous to the feudal lords. As Rodbertus pointedly observed, hunger can serve as a whip as readily as a piece of leather.[11]

Smith was also extremely aware of the tendency of the merchants to attempt to bring the state in as an ally in controlling their workers a tendency that he argues must be resisted. By contrast, he was tolerant of governmental regulation of wages on behalf of laborers: "Whenever the regulation . . . is in favor of the workmen, it is always just and equitable; but it is sometimes otherwise when in favor of the masters."[12]

As this passage testifies, Smith was no simple critic of government intervention in markets; he never viewed markets as freestanding institutions. Moreover his rationale for intervention in the case of labor markets was not efficiency, but "justice and equity." He was worried about the coercive nature of labor contracts, about the ability of the employers to "force the other into a compliance with their terms."[13] He also accepts government intervention when the aim is to reduce poverty. Another example of this is his support for progressive taxation on carriages in proportion to their price, so that "the indolence and vanity of the rich is made to contribute in an easy manner to the relief of the poor."[14]

Why, then, is Smith so often viewed as a simple proponent of free trade and free markets and an antagonist of the visible hand of government?[15] I think that although some writers have viewed Smith as opposed to government intervention per se, it is helpful to recall that Smith's arguments against government intervention in markets are focused on a specific social order: feudalism. Many of the regulations that he vociferously condemned were vestiges of a precapitalist and undemocratic social order: the narrow interests of monopolistic merchants seeking to protect their inflated profits and the rules of the powerful guilds that restricted the free entry of individuals into professions and trades. Of the feudal guilds, for example, he writes that "a thousand spinners and weavers" may be dependent on "half a dozen wool combers," who by refusing to take on apprentices can "reduce the whole manufacture into *a sort of slavery to themselves.*"[16]

Rather than propounding a doctrine of a spontaneous and self-correcting market order, Smith actually stressed that markets function as vehicles of freedom, equality, and efficiency only under very definite institutional arrangements. It requires a "separate independent state" to promote the well-being and freedom of the poor, a state that has cut itself loose from the power of the rich merchants, the guilds, religious groups, and prejudicial social norms. Indeed Smith worried that the system of law would never be completely secure against such interests and would need to be counteracted by a universal system of education, as well as regulation of labor markets to protect the freedom of the worker.

Smith's perspective on the comparative benefits of capitalist labor markets over feudal labor-tying arrangements differs from those that would be revealed by the framework of much contemporary economics. He explicitly recognizes that the introduction of capitalist markets depended on restrictions on property rights that, at least initially, were neither voluntary nor Pareto-improving. To anticipate later chapters and to reiterate my argument in chapter 1, a *free labor market* is the product of state regulation. It requires policies that restrict the remedies that the law makes available to employers, for example, banning the use of imprisonment for nonperformance of a labor contract and curtailing feudal ownership rights over the products of the serf's labor.[17] But in the context of feudalism these restrictions were certainly not Pareto improvements; they made the lords worse off.

HETEROGENEOUS MARKETS

Smith and his classical political economy followers offer distinct theories of the functioning of not only consumer goods markets, but also land, credit, and labor markets. Consider labor markets. Unlike a car market,

Smith argues, a labor market shapes the capacities of the human beings whose labor power is purchased. As he puts it in *Wealth of Nations*:

> The employment of the great body of the people comes to be confined to a few operations; frequently to one or two. But the understandings . . . of men are necessarily formed by their ordinary employments. The man whose whole life is spent performing a few simple operations of which the effects too are perhaps always the same . . . has no occasion to exert his understanding or to exercise his invention in finding out expedients for removing difficulties which never occur. He naturally loses, therefore, the habit of such exertion and generally becomes as stupid and ignorant as it is possible for a human creature to become. . . . [He is incapable] of forming any just judgment concerning many even of the ordinary duties of private life. Of the great and extensive interests of his country, he is altogether incapable of judging.[18]

In this passage reflecting on the division of labor in a pin-making factory, Smith claims that a worker's *preferences and capabilities* are shaped by the organization of work. He observed that as markets push forward the development of the division of labor, not only is economic growth produced, but also workers who are incapable of taking part in social decision making. The growth of the division of labor in industry deprives these workers of their "intellectual, social and martial virtues."[19] Whereas contemporary economic theory tends to view a person's preferences and capacities as *given* inputs into an economy, Smith believed that the parties to certain kinds of exchanges are themselves partially constituted in the market.

Interestingly, in this passage Smith makes a causal claim: workers' preferences and capacities change *because of* the structure of the labor market, shaped by the increasing division of labor which itself is fueled by the quest for efficiency. These preferences and capacities, then, are not taken as givens. Moreover these preferences and capacities are relevant to our assessment of markets: labor markets can have troubling social, cultural, and political effects precisely by shaping preferences and capacities. To put the point a bit tendentiously, in the labor market workers make not only pins and widgets, but they also make aspects of themselves. And how they make themselves affects not only the price of their labor but also the kind of society that is possible. In the pin factory, according to Smith, workers lose their power of independent thinking and become ill equipped to judge or deliberate about the policies of their country.

The growth of the division of labor and the creation of distinct spheres of laboring activity—fueled by labor markets—are also central to Smith's understanding of social inequality. According to Smith, the division of labor, whose extent is limited by the extent of the market, shapes our *differing* and thus unequal preferences, interests, and capacities:

> The difference of natural talents in different men is, in reality, much less than we are aware of; and the very different genius which appears to distinguish men of different professions, when grown to maturity, is not upon many occasions so much the cause, as the effect of division of labour. The difference between the most dissimilar characters, between a philosopher and a common street porter, for example, seems to arise not so much from nature, as from habit, custom and education. When they came into the world, and for the first six or eight years of their existence, they were, perhaps, very much alike, and neither their parents nor play-fellows could perceive any remarkable difference.[20]

It would perhaps take a detailed psychological and sociological argument to fully substantiate this claim, although later in this book I'll look at some evidence concerning the effects of different kinds of labor relations on worker's self-conceptions. But the basic point to consider for present purposes is that if work and the preparation for work significantly influence who we are, then labor markets cannot be judged by their efficiency alone.

Labor is special for Smith in yet another way. Because labor power is embodied in human beings, whose own effort and compliance affect their productivity, the buyers of labor power have an interest in motivating their workers to work hard. But workers have opposing interests. Because the amount and quality of work cannot be completely specified in a contract, some system for controlling work must be devised. But the system of control itself will have important effects on the laborer, his productivity, his capacities and his relationship to his employer.

Smith's assessment of labor markets thus gives us a wider set of criteria for their evaluation than efficiency. Extending his framework, we might say that a labor market would fail, even if it were efficient and even if it were voluntary, if it placed workers in relations of servile dependence with manufacturers or deskilled them to function as mere tools. It would fail if it eroded workers' sense of justice and public spirit, the qualities "most useful" to society and their fellows.[21] We can describe some of these effects as "externalities," but some of the effects fall only on the parties to the contracts. Additionally, as I have argued, the concept of an externality is too blunt to tell us why and when we should be concerned with particular markets.

In what can only be an embarrassing anomaly for those who view him as an advocate of laissez-faire, Smith also argued in favor of regulating credit markets. Although he objected to the legal banning of interest on money, he gave a qualified approval of the existing usury laws in Great Britain that limited the rate of interest that could be charged on a loan to 5 percent:

> In countries where interest is permitted, the law, in order to prevent the extortion of usury, generally fixes the highest rate which can be taken without incurring a penalty. . . . The legal rate, it is to be observed, though it ought to be somewhat above, ought not to be much above the lowest market rate. If the legal rate of interest in Great Britain, for example, was fixed so high as eight or ten percent, the greater part of the money which was to be lent, would be lent to prodigals and projectors, who alone would be willing to give this high interest. Sober people, who will give for the use of money no more than a part of what they are likely to make by the use of it, would not venture into the competition. A greater part of the capital of the country would thus be kept out of the hands which were most likely to make a profitable and advantageous use of it, and thrown into those which were most likely to waste and destroy it.[22]

Why did Smith oppose usury? Access to credit is important for production, so why block potential exchanges between willing borrowers and willing lenders? The explicit reason he gives in this passage from *The Wealth of Nations* is that the pursuit of private gain (by prodigals and projectors) can sometimes lead to social loss: if reckless speculators possess too much capital and invest it on useless projects, this is bad for the wealth of the country.[23] Moreover lenders have only inadequate knowledge of the motivations and future actions of their borrowers; they cannot ensure that their borrowers will behave in ways that allow them to repay their debts. Therefore the market in capital must be regulated; we cannot depend on markets alone to appropriately distribute capital and risk. Smith's analysis of credit markets has relevance for our contemporary economic crisis and the role of financial instruments such as credit derivatives and subprime mortgages within it.

Because the parties to an exchange come to the market with different vulnerabilities to each other and with different information and different capacities for exit from their relationships, because certain market exchanges shape the parties, and because there are important social goods that a market is unlikely to supply, Smith rejected laissez-faire. Although favorably inclined to the logic of the market mechanism, he believed that intervention in and oversight of the market was frequently justified.

Perhaps the most important case Smith sees for governmental intervention in the economy—for setting limits to the operation of markets—is education. He believes that the "corruption and degeneracy of the great body of people" is inevitable without some attention from the government.[24] Many of his arguments for education can be translated into an economic framework as resting on the fact that education generates positive externalities; basic education (for example, literacy) provides a communal benefit that transcends the gains of the person being educated. Conversely failure to educate children produces public bads: less labor mobility, greater poverty, and less economic growth. Arguing along these lines Smith harshly criticizes the irrationality of failing to provide public expenditure for education: "For a very small expense the publick can facilitate, can encourage, and can even impose upon the whole body of the people, the necessity of acquiring those most essential parts of education."[25]

But Smith is also insistent that beyond its effects on productivity education is important to the development of human sensibilities and capacities. He writes that the lack of education for the children of the poor is "one of their great misfortunes." A child laborer who has been denied an education finds that "when he is grown up he has no ideas with which he can amuse himself."[26] To be uneducated is not simply to be missing out on potential earnings for oneself or for one's society; education is also important for things we cannot buy: the ability to value and to know, to make informed choices about ourselves and our path in life, to experience the world in a different way than an uneducated person. To quote the twentieth-century writer James Baldwin: "The purpose of education, finally, is to create in a person the ability to look at the world for himself, to make his own decisions, to say to himself this is black or this is white, to decide whether there is a god in heaven or not. To ask questions of the universe, and then to live with those questions, is the way he achieves his identity."[27]

And if democratic rule is to work, the mass of people need to be educated to be capable of participating in public discussion.[28] There is no reason to think that markets will supply the appropriate level of education for all.

SMITH AND PARETIANISM

The uncoordinated actions of individuals in a market were taken by Smith to be sometimes (but not always) better at producing good results (e.g., liberty, security, equality, and wealth) than the visible hand of conscious state policies, especially since the latter was likely to be disproportionately attentive to the interests of the wealthy. Smith's fundamental insight—that the market choices made by rational individuals can (under certain conditions) coordinate social production among diverse individuals and generate efficient social order—was formalized in the twentieth century by Pareto and Walras. As mentioned in the previous chapter, the so-called fundamental theorem of welfare economics states that in a free market world in which everyone can trade everything, the allocation of resources will be Pareto optimal.

Adam Smith, of course, knew nothing about the "fundamental theorem" of welfare economics, which he greatly antedated. And I have argued that Smith's defense of markets did not rest primarily on their purported allocative efficiency, but rather on their connection to social relations based on freedom and equality. But it is worth highlighting three further differences between Smith's approach and the standard Paretian justification of competitive markets.

First, Paretians justify markets because markets allow individuals to optimally satisfy their preferences under constraints. But Smith recognized the central role that both markets and social institutions play in *shaping* individual preferences. If markets themselves importantly shape a person's preferences, if our preferences are "endogenous" to markets, -that is, originating from within markets, then it is circular to appeal to a market's ability to satisfy those preferences as its central justification. Market outcomes cannot be ranked unambiguously by preference rankings if the preference rankings themselves depend on markets.[29]

Second, Smith was interested in the role of markets in enabling substantive freedoms, including freedom from extreme dependency on others, and not only in their role in satisfying preferences. In contemporary economics this perspective has been rather marginal, although Amartya Sen has picked up and developed Smith's perspective. Rather than evaluating a market solely in terms of its ability to satisfy a person's subjective preferences, Sen asks us to examine its effects on a person's actual capabilities, that is, the person's ability to do and achieve. Important capabilities, for Sen, include the capability to be nourished, to be literate, and, borrowing from Smith, to "appear in public without shame." To see how markets affect these capabilities, we have to focus not only on the moment of an individual's particular market choices, but also on the way market institutions can enhance or restrict a person's *range* of choices, that is, the real options that are open to her.[30] From this perspective, closing off some market choices might be justified if it enables other, better choices that would not have been available otherwise. For example, as I discuss in chapter 7, closing off the option of child labor in a society might lead to higher adult wages than would otherwise be the case, as well as leading to better education for children. Placing limits on labor hours and regulating working conditions might lead to improved worker health, enhanced cooperation, and a fairer distribution. More choice is not necessarily better choice, especially if judged from the perspective of the specific capabilities that different choice sets make possible.

Third, and related, Smith made an important contribution to economic thought with his observation that specific types of exchanges have constitutive effects on their participants. For this reason I doubt that Smith would accept "the market" as the essence of those practices we conventionally label "the labor market" or endorse the view that employment regulations should be driven entirely by efficiency criteria. Indeed his perspective—that labor markets shape workers' capacities and preferences—can be expanded to embrace a vision of the role that work plays in our lives that links work to some level of material well-being (a minimum wage), democratic organization (union organizations, worker's rights on and off the job, the workplace as a site for furthering democratic capacities, perhaps by lessening the sharp divide between manual and mental labor), and for some balance among our different life activities (hours regulation). At the very least Smith himself clearly recognized that the functioning of labor markets inevitably raises questions relevant to the structure of public life, in a way that the functioning of a market in cars or apples does not.[31]

Smith saw the marketplace as a political and cultural as well as an economic institution, where differing interests wielded power and where some types of exchanges shaped the participants. If markets in such domains are political and cultural institutions, then market failure takes on a different meaning than is supplied by the Pareto criterion. If labor markets are organized in ways that produce servility or passivity or undermine the collective decision-making skills on which a democratic society depends, then we might judge such markets a failure even if they are efficient. Ultimately Smith's insights and economic perspective cannot easily be summed up by a single principle of free exchange between consenting adults. Smith saw the market as a complex heterogeneous institution, bringing people into different kinds of relations with each other for different purposes. From this broader perspective, not only efficiency but also the effects of a particular market on the structure of political power and on human development are relevant to its assessment.

A (BRIEF) EXCURSION ON MARKET PRICE AND VALUE

A central concern of *The Wealth of Nations*, and of the classical political economists, was the distribution of the social product among the three great social classes—capitalists, landlords, and workers—in the form of profits, rents, and wages. The relationships between these classes and their behavior in the market are central to Smith's theory of economic growth. Yet *The Wealth of Nations* suggests two different theories of the contribution of these different classes to the production of wealth, related in turn to two ideas Smith propounds about the value of commodities: a cost of production theory (developed by Ricardo and Marx) and a subjective welfare theory (developed by Bentham, Walras, and Jevons).

According to Smith's cost of production theory, the ultimate factor determining the relative prices of goods is the amount of labor the good "commands." In an economy in which there is no capital accumulation and no privately appropriated land, this would be equal to the labor embodied in the goods.[32] Under those conditions the whole product of labor would belong to the laborer. But once production is no longer wholly owned and controlled by the workers, the price of commodities must include profit and rent as well as wages. The price of the commodity will then be determined by the sum of the wages and profit and rent paid to produce it. To express this in terms of cost of production, we must think of profits and rents as residues: because labor commanded is seen as the source of value, profits and rents are not determined independently. In this theory the price of a good can be specified independently of individual choices and psychological factors. For each commodity, its price is governed by its normal costs of production (except for goods produced under monopoly conditions).

The Wealth of Nations also contains suggestions of an "additive" way of thinking about a good's value, in which the price of a commodity is determined by the incomes—in the form of wages, profits, and rents—paid to produce it. According to this theory, prices are determined by the supply and demand of the three different "factors" of production. This additive theory provides the foundations for a theory in which individual buyers and sellers of goods decide on the quantity to demand or to supply on the basis of a given price. This theory requires individualist foundations, and those who adopted this theory stressed Smith's comments about the "toil and trouble" of labor and the pains people took to avoid it. The additive theory thus ultimately gave rise to a theory of subjective individual utility or welfare as the basis of price. Later economists seized on and amplified the idea that an "invisible hand" of the market connected each individual's goal of maximizing his preference satisfaction with a production system that produced the goods preferred with maximum efficiency at the lowest possible prices.

Both theories of value are strands of Adam Smith's thought, and they issue in two very different directions: in one direction the concepts of costs of production and the role of the various social classes are fundamental in determining prices, and in the other direction the ideas of the individual economic actor and competitive equilibrium are fundamental. During the nineteenth century this second direction of Smith's thought about exchange value would eclipse the first and be seen as fundamental to his economics, and indeed to economics as a whole. As we will see, this shift in the understanding of value has consequences for views of markets.

DIMINISHING RETURNS AND THE
THEORY OF LAND RENTS

The classical political economists also viewed markets in land as distinct from other markets because the good under consideration (land) was in fixed supply. Here we come to the theory of diminishing returns and the theory of ground rent. Robert Malthus developed these ideas more or less simultaneously with David Ricardo, Sir Edward West, and Robert Torrens in 1815.[33]

According to the principle of diminishing returns in agriculture, the improvement of cultivation becomes progressively more expensive in that equal inputs of labor and capital applied to land yields diminishing outputs. This decline in the rate of return was taken by Malthus and the others to hold whether the labor and capital are "intensively" applied to lands already under cultivation or "extensively" applied to new (and often inferior) lands. These diminishing outputs on the basis of capital and labor are then reflected in the rising costs of agricultural products such as grain and corn.

The four theorists inferred from this principle that the price of land is regulated by the least favorable circumstance under which production is carried on. When increased demand leads producers to cultivate inferior land or to intensify production on given land, the price of agricultural goods will rise, because the costs of labor and capital employed in producing the marginal unit of these goods will rise. But the price of these goods will be the same, whether obtained on more fertile land (and thus with less labor and capital inputs) or less fertile land. Malthus and the others argued that, given the assumption that capital and labor both obtain their marginal product—that is, that they are paid proportionately to their added productive contribution—there is a surplus that will fall to the landlord holding the superior land, paid in the form of rent.

Ricardo used this argument to condemn the British Corn Laws, protectionist barriers against the import of agricultural goods passed in 1816, which forced national agriculture to increase productivity by intensifying the investment in agriculture and leading landowners to develop less fertile lands. The Corn Laws allowed for the maintenance of high land rents to the detriment of the profits of manufacturers, the suppliers of financial capital. Drawing on the principle of decreasing returns, Ricardo argued that there would eventually be catastrophic results from the decreasing returns to agriculture.

Here's the basic Ricardian argument: Most of the money to finance investment comes from the profits of manufacturers, not from the rents obtained from ownership of land. Landowners, who can earn very high incomes simply from the possession of land, do not need to save and reinvest. If rent is high, those manufacturers who would invest their capital in the service of outperforming their competition will be unable to do so because they must pay rent; thus national growth will stall. Indeed Ricardian economics aimed to demonstrate that the interests of the landlords are antithetical to industrial progress and the wealth of the nation: "The interest of the landlord is always opposed to the interest of every other class in the community."[34]

One consequence of Ricardo's theory is that rent is not a cost of production—it does not enter into price—and is not payment for using up natural or social resources.[35] In Ricardo's words, "Corn is not high because a rent is paid, but rent is paid because corn is high."[36] Rent bore no relationship to the landlord's actual costs of production. Nor did it help produce additional wealth or stimulate productivity. Rather rent grew simply because over time fertile land became progressively scarcer, driving up the marginal price of agricultural production.

It is a small step from these observations to the practical conclusion that the returns from private ownership of land were completely unearned, and that land's confiscation by the state would make no difference to production.[37] Unlike workers and capitalists, landlords neither improved the situation of others by their appropriation, nor did they expend any effort or labor of their own. Ricardo did not himself draw the full and radical political implications of his diagnosis, but others recognized the significant upshot of Ricardian theory: the landlord's private ownership and control of land threatened to derail economic growth and progress.[38] Because of their fixed quantity and uneven quality, land markets give rise to quite distinct regulatory considerations. The ownership of land can be nationalized without loss to productivity.

MARX'S VIEW OF LABOR MARKETS

As we saw, Smith believed that markets importantly advance liberal freedom and equality. But the extent of their contribution depended on features such as the competitiveness of particular markets, the existence of alternatives, and the presence of nonmarket supports such as education and redistributive taxation for the poor. Karl Marx followed Smith in thinking that capitalist labor markets made possible a significant improvement over social relationships founded on servility or outright slavery. For example, in *Capital* he celebrates the American Civil War as "the one great event of contemporary history,"[39] not because of the efficiency it produced, but because of the freedoms its way of organization of production—free labor, not slave labor—enabled.

At the same time, however, Marx believed that capitalist labor markets were founded on property rights that necessarily limited the freedom of workers. Even if workers were well paid, he argued, they would still remain dependent on their employers and vulnerable to their power. Why? True, workers depend on employers, but don't employers also depend on workers? Why should there be unequal dependence and vulnerability? It is worth exploring Marx's arguments for this claim in more detail.

In the first place, Marx argued that capitalist labor markets depend on differential ownership: workers own only their ability to labor, and capitalists own most other productive assets. That is, a worker typically lacks independent access to the means of production (machines, physical plant) and so relies on a capitalist to employ him. Without this difference in underlying ownership relationships, without workers who own nothing but their ability to work, Marx argued that capitalism wouldn't have emerged as a stable social system. Marx's story of "unhappy Mr. Peel" nicely illustrates this point:

> A Mr. Peel . . . took with him from England to the Swan River district of Western Australia means of subsistence and of production to the amount of $50,000. This Mr. Peel even had the foresight to bring besides 3,000 persons of the working class, men, women and children. Once he arrived at his destination, Mr. Peel was left without a servant to make his bed or fetch him water from the river. Unhappy Mr. Peel, who provided for everything except the export of English relations of production to Swan River.[40]

In other words, capitalism comes into existence only when workers have no other option but to sell their labor power. If given the choice, as in Western Australia, workers are more likely to want to acquire their own land rather than work for the capitalists in a factory. Marx's parable of Mr. Peel serves to reveal what Marx takes to be the central (and historically created) feature of a capitalist society: the widespread existence of formally (legally) free, but only *formally* free, labor. Whereas Smith viewed capitalist labor markets as an important sphere of human liberty, Marx believed that in such markets most workers were not substantively free agents, because in a capitalist society they are dependent on employment (by the capitalists) to survive. Workers' dependence on the decision and will of the capitalists generates uncertainty and pressure to defer to the latter's demands. As Marx quips in *Capital*, once we pierce the veneer of free and equal exchange between workers and owners, the "exclusive realm of Freedom, Equality, Property and Bentham," we find dependency and subordination.[41] In most contexts a worker urgently needs the job that the capitalist supplies; a capitalist, by contrast, can readily substitute one worker's labor power for another's. Besides which, there are many more workers than capitalists, making it more difficult for workers to organize and coordinate their behavior to increase their bargaining power.

In the second place, Marx famously thought that workers were destined to immiseration and poverty. Under competition continued investment in technology works to keep labor in a state of excess supply, generating unemployment and subsistence. Not only are workers in capitalist societies insecure and dependent, but they are also very poor. This poverty makes it hard for them to hold out for better terms of employment.

In the third place, Marx, like Smith, saw labor as shaping human preferences and capabilities. On Marx's view, human beings transform nature through their labor and, in so doing, simultaneously transform themselves. Yet capitalist production, with its developed (and deskilled) division of labor, as exemplified in Adam Smith's pin-making factory, gives workers little opportunity for developing a range of capacities or for finding meaning in their jobs. Instead many workers are treated as, and serve as, "appendages to machines," performing mindless and repetitive tasks throughout their working lives. Not only do workers gain no satisfaction from working on such tasks, but they are working as animals and machines would work, not as human beings.[42] Indeed Marx's normative condemnation of capitalism focuses on its degradation of human beings to animals and things, and *not* on its distribution of wages and profits.[43]

It might be argued that not all of these problems are necessary features of capitalist labor markets—that many workers (at least in the developed world) are not deskilled automatons, enjoy more than subsistence wages, and identify with their jobs. But it takes regulation of labor markets and a system of entitlements and rights to blunt this possibility.

THE MARGINAL REVOLUTION AND THE RISE
OF NEOCLASSICAL POLITICAL ECONOMY

If the classical economists sharply differentiated between markets in labor, land, credit, and other commodities and worried about the shaping effects of labor markets, contemporary economists, at least until very recently, have not.[44] In the 1870s a dramatic shift in economics took place, which led to the virtual abandonment of the cost of production theory of the classical economists, the displacement of class relationships from the center of economic analysis, and the unification of different types of markets.

Three figures were central to the marginal revolution in economics: William Stanley Jevons (1835–82), Carl Menger (1840–1921), and Leon Walras (1834–1910). Although these thinkers had many important differences, together they initiated a new line of thinking in economics. At the center of this new approach to economics stands the problem of the allocation of *given* scarce resources among alternative uses. Indeed analysis of that problem becomes the defining feature of economics. As Jevons put it, "The problem of economics may be stated thus: *Given a certain population, with various goods and other sources of materials: required, the mode of employing their labour which will maximize the utility of the produce.*"[45] Economics is now to be conceived as an inquiry into the optimal allocation of given resources under conditions of scarcity.

The basic idea behind marginalism is itself rather simple; indeed we have already encountered an example of it in the analysis by Ricardo and Malthus of ground rent. Assume that individuals seek to deploy their resources to maximally satisfy their wants. At the optimal position marginal prices will then be equalized, that is, the gains to be derived from deploying a resource for one use will exactly equal the losses involved in withdrawing it from another, alternative use. Wherever diminishing returns are obtainable from putting a given unit of a resource to a particular use, the optimum result is obtained when values are equalized at the margin; rent is just a special case of a more general theory. Marginalism thus allowed economists to explain all prices in common terms, something that the earlier cost of production theory had failed to achieve.[46]

The marginalists were able to provide a mathematically elegant explanation of the determination of prices. More important, they were able to show that a system of perfect market competition would lead to an equimarginal distribution of resources. Formalizing and extending Smith's more inchoate metaphor of the invisible hand, the marginalists demonstrated that under certain assumptions rational individuals would behave in a market so that the optimal allocation of given resources among alternative uses was achieved. This idea—that a market order produces maximal benefits *for all* as an unintended consequence of its operations—has been of the greatest importance for twentieth-century political thought and practice. It is also, as we have seen, both a development of and a distortion of the more modest claims that Adam Smith had made concerning the market mechanism. It overlooks his earlier insistence that the market itself is a cultural and political institution permeated by power relations, and, needless to say, it disregards his cost of production theory.

Many contemporary economists believe that the marginalists delivered a decisive blow to the cost of production theory of the classical economists, and to the theory of exploitation that the Ricardian socialists and Marx erected upon it.[47] Perhaps this is so. Certainly the new models were more tractable. But it could also be claimed, with at least as much plausibility, that the marginalists did not so much refute the classical economists as change the subject.

The marginalists' approach to economics has several distinctive features that, taken together, transformed economic theory. First, marginalism enabled economists to unify their approach across distinct kinds of markets: consumer markets, labor markets, capital markets, and markets in land—markets that, as we have seen, the classical economists had treated independently. The effect of marginalism was to generalize Ricardian rent theory to all factors of production: land, labor, and capital. The marginalists linked all markets in a single system of equations, culminating in Walras's construction of a general equilibrium for the entire market economy.

Second, by abstracting away from the features of particular kinds of markets, the marginalists also abstracted away from the social relations in which markets are situated. The analysis of the social relations between the three great social classes—a focus that had preoccupied the classical political economists—became viewed as exogenous to economics. Markets are now viewed as complete and self-enforcing; in the marginalist framework there is little room for ideas of social class or market power. Economics no longer contemplates the capitalist and his control over his employees, the landlord's lack of contribution to productive growth, or the dynamic tendencies of differing markets.

Third, the marginalists were able to reformulate the puzzle of how labor inputs related to price that had so puzzled the classical economists. Abandoning the cost of production theory, the marginalists simply defined price in terms of marginal utility. In dividing resources among competing uses, efficient allocation will equalize returns at the margins. Whereas the classical economists treated the three different components of production as fundamentally distinct, the new economics treated all factors the same. Factors were rewarded because they were scarce relative to consumers wants for the products that factors could produce. The marginalists thus derived not only prices from their principle, but also allocation: both factor and product prices were to be explained by marginal utility. But this principle unified different domains at the cost of narrowing its focus: it can explain distribution and price only at a fixed point in time, on the basis of given factors.[48] This approach contrasts sharply with the classical economists' concern with the *dynamic* aspects of an economy. The classical economists investigated the possibilities for economic growth or stagnation under the assumptions of changing population, expanding human wants, differing human motivations, and the changing quantity and quality of resources. The marginalist approach, with only a few exceptions (e.g., Pigou and Schumpeter), simply ignored or assumed away the questions posed by such long-term analyses. Indeed with the elimination of social relations and social change, economics took on the character of applied mathematics.

Fourth, the early marginalists took from the philosophical utilitarians the idea that a rational individual seeks to maximize his utility, where utility is understood in terms of subjective preference satisfaction. On this interpretation of utility, it is up to the individual alone—so long as he is properly informed and rational—to calculate and rank-order the value of the different aims for which his resources may be

deployed. An immediate consequence of this is that values and preferences are now shifted outside the province of economics to private
individual choice and decision. Economics is hereafter silent about individual subjective market choices. Classes with their distinct social aims
have disappeared, displaced by individually rational maximizers of
utility. Here too the contrast with the classical political economists—
Smith's worries about prodigals and projectors, Ricardo's criticism of
the landlords for forgoing investment, Marx's concerns with the narrow
human capacities of industrial workers—could not be greater.

Left aside, or simply assumed, were the social, psychological, cultural
and institutional factors that shaped exchange value.[49] These included
the ways that preferences and capacities were formed, the influence of
ownership and property on the economy and on individual freedoms,
and all phenomena relating to long-term growth. Instead the marginalists left us with the dubious equation of a market system with the greatest aggregate happiness, understood in terms of the maximal satisfaction of preferences under constraints.[50] This claim is, of course,
philosophically and empirically controversial, and would also have been
rejected, at least as a sweeping generalization, by all of the classical
political economists.[51]

CONCLUSION

There is one striking theme in the story of the changing nature of political economy. The fundamental divide that tears through the eighteenth
and nineteenth century is not primarily a divide of technical knowledge
or rigor (although it is that) or even political orientation. It is fundamentally a question of vision. The classical political economists viewed
the economy not so much as a series of homogeneous relations between
individuals and the things they wanted, but as a system of heterogeneous relationships between social classes. For Adam Smith, Ricardo,
and Marx the central question to be addressed was the distribution of
the social product among the three great social classes. As Ricardo put it,
"To determine the laws which regulate *this* distribution is the principle
problem in political economy."[52] Moreover this was a question that
raised both explanatory (positive) and normative issues. The condition

of the working poor, for example, had been a central focus of concern for the political economists. Smith, John Stuart Mill, the Ricardian socialists, and Marx bequeathed a rich tradition of critical social thought, including arguments about the coerciveness of labor contracts as well as awareness about the asymmetric power of agents bargaining over the distribution of the social surplus. Moreover, for the classical political economists these issues were tied to their respective visions of a good society. How to achieve that good society, and whether or not it could be maintained once achieved or would fall into a stationary state and decline, were principal questions that preoccupied these thinkers.

By the end of the nineteenth century, by contrast, the question of how to optimize consumer preferences had become the central question for economics. The neoclassical paradigm ushered in by the marginalist revolution takes the preferences of households, factor endowments, and forms of property as given inputs and on that basis generates a theory of prices. The economy is now viewed as an autonomous sphere of activity, independent of law, convention, or power. The marginalist's celebration of the market assumes away, for example, the presence of massive political power that would undermine the market's optimizing effects. Furthermore human wants and resources are taken as given; people are simply assumed to have certain "preferences" and "endowments" whose justice or nature is not relevant to the economic assessment of markets. The new economics enabled its practitioners to build tractable and unified models (which have admittedly generated some very important insights into the workings of an economy). Yet almost everything that the classical economists considered of interest in economic life—in particular their crucial insights into the social effects of different markets on human capacities and social relationships and the ways that different markets are socially embedded—has been omitted. The next chapters attempt to recapture these insights and put them to use in thinking about particular markets.

3

The Market's Place and Scope in Contemporary Egalitarian Political Theory

When a poor man goes to the market, often he comes home only with tears.

—African Proverb

In this chapter I examine two prominent but divergent contemporary views about the relationship between markets and equality. On the first view, although markets have an important role to play in society, egalitarians should seek to rectify the distributional inequalities that markets create by using a tax-and-transfer system. For example, if there is market-generated inequality that is judged to be objectionable, such as an inequality in access to health care between the rich and the poor, the appropriate egalitarian response is the redistribution of income to those less favored so that they can choose to provide for their health needs (or not) by themselves. If egalitarians do not like the unequal distribution of health care, then they should look to the distribution of income and wealth. If they do not find the underlying distribution of income and wealth acceptable, then that is what they should change, using a tax-and-transfer system. I call this view, borrowing the term from the economist James Tobin, *general egalitarianism.*[1] General egalitarians believe that the goal of efficiency entails that any desired redistribution take place through progressive taxation and transfer, not through a limit on the scope of the market. The reason for their preference for the former over the latter is that "specific interventions, whether in the name of equality or not, introduce inefficiencies, and the more specific the intervention the more serious the inefficiency."[2] Most egalitarian economists accordingly tend to be general egalitarians.

Not only is government intervention in a specific market alleged to entail undesirable inefficiencies, but it is sometimes argued that such intervention is an unjustified restriction on individual freedom. It is objectionably paternalistic, the argument proceeds, to provide individuals with specific goods such as health care or food. Instead freedom is best served by giving individuals income and letting them decide which of their preferences they themselves wish to satisfy. The government fails to treat its citizens with respect when it seeks to determine which of their individual goals, health care or music lessons, is most worthy of pursuit, regardless of the goals that these citizens themselves prefer. Many liberal political philosophers also tend to be general egalitarians in Tobin's sense. Some think markets serve both liberty and efficiency, whereas others would reject government restrictions on specific markets on the grounds of liberty alone.

Different theories will, of course, differ as to how much tax and transfer a society should undertake, and different theories will attach different weights to efficiency and liberty as opposed to equality.[3] But the basic point I want to stress is this: General egalitarians think that, with a few exceptions I will discuss, a tax-and-transfer system is the best way to harness the market's virtues of efficiency and/or liberty to egalitarian goals.

On the second contrasting view, egalitarianism requires that particular goods not be distributed using a market at all, even when blocking exchanges in these goods is inefficient. I call this view, again drawing on Tobin's terminology, *specific egalitarianism*. Specific egalitarians believe that there are some scarce goods that should be distributed (in kind) equally to all.[4] They are often egalitarians only with respect to specific goods, not in general. Candidates for such goods include health care, basic necessities, and goods related to citizenship such as education and military service. Many of the people who support social policies such as universal health insurance hold this type of view; they favor universal access to medical care even though they are not in favor of a general egalitarian redistribution of income.

In examining the merits of each perspective I consider how each respectively deals with a range of cases that I call "*Titanic* cases."[5] These are examples about which many people seem to have specific egalitarian intuitions. Recall that when the *Titanic* sank there were enough lifeboats for first-class passengers, but those in steerage were expected to go down with the ship. Most of us, I believe, find this objectionable. General egalitarians might try to accommodate this conviction by pointing out there was an initial unfair distribution of purchasing power that determined who sailed first class and who was relegated to steerage. Nevertheless I suspect that many of us would continue to find the example objectionable even if purchasing power had been fairly distributed and the inequality arose simply because some individuals cared more about, and were willing to pay more for, securing a lifeboat than others. Specific egalitarianism is a more promising approach for accommodating this conviction, but I will argue that the specific egalitarian theories that I consider are not adequate.

My discussion of *Titanic* cases will pave the way for my own theory about the limits of markets, which I develop and defend in the next chapter. On my theory there is a strong case for regulating or curtailing particular markets to the extent that their operation undermines or blocks the capacity of the parties to *interact as equals*, even if such markets arise through voluntary individual consent and on the basis of an initial equality of conditions. The ideas of interacting as equals, and of the social and political preconditions for interacting as equals, are complex ideas, related to but not identical to other conceptions of equality, and I leave their discussion to the next chapter. I mention them here because they shape my discussion of the alternative views I consider below.

Both the general and the specific egalitarian theories treat markets as *mechanisms* to be assessed by the extent to which they achieve or undermine important values. But some people think that the great strength of a market system is *moral:* the way that it holds people responsible for their own lives and choices. On the moral view, the market holds each of us responsible for our market choices, while at the same time ensuring that the benefits we obtain from these choices depend on the costs and benefits of those choices to others. According to this view's proponents, the market establishes a kind of equality between individuals, where differences between the resources that they have reflect only differences in their preferences for work, leisure, risk, and so forth.

I begin this chapter by exploring the possibility of a deeper connection between markets and equality than is found in alternative theories, including my own. I will argue that the case for a conceptual link between markets and equality fails. Markets have important roles to play in society, but they cannot be used as the *fundamental* standard by which we determine what resources people are entitled to.

THE MORAL VIEW OF THE MARKET AS CONCEPTUALLY LINKED TO EGALITARIANISM

Some ground clearing: Given that human beings are different in myriad ways (e.g., individuals differ in strength, sex, age, values and preferences, health status, and levels of talent), any ideal of human equality inevitably must be abstract. Furthermore policies that attain equality in one dimension often create inequality in another. For example, equality in income can entail unequal reward for effort. We cannot be each other's equals in every way, so we must decide which dimensions of our differences matter. Every egalitarian theory needs to do this.[6]

One suggestion, advanced by Ronald Dworkin, is that our equality is best understood in terms of the idea that individuals should be treated *as equals*; in particular he argues that the state is obligated to treat all of its members with equal concern and respect.[7] Dworkin goes so far as to claim that all liberal political philosophies are committed in a fundamental way to this abstract idea of equality, although they offer very different understandings of its implications.[8] For example, some philosophers argue that treating people with equal concern and respect means giving them equal prospects for achieving good lives, whereas others argue that it means giving people equal rights over their property and labor.

Dworkin calls his own interpretation of the distributive implications of treating people as equals *equality of resources*. Its basic idea is that two people are treated with equal concern and respect when they are (initially) provided with an equal share of the society's total resources.[9] It seems obvious, for example, that a state would not be treating its citizens with equal concern and respect if it gave its white citizens twice as many resources as its black citizens. Dworkin's theory extends and deepens this intuitive idea.

We might imagine that the principle of equality of resources could be implemented by a planning agency that kept track of the amount of a society's available resources and the size of its population. Yet Dworkin claims that we cannot achieve an equal division of assets, which is what equal respect and concern demands, without reliance on a market: "The idea of an economic market, as a device for setting prices for a vast variety of goods and services, must be at the center of any attractive theoretical development of equality of resources."[10] Why? If the implication of treating individuals as equals is that they have equal resources, why not simply give to each person an equal amount of all of the resources that are available for redistribution?[11]

The problem with the proposal to divide up society's resources equally is not merely that many goods are not likely to be uniform in quality; some pieces of land, for example, are bound to be better than others.[12] The core problem with this proposal is that, even given an equal initial division, different people will have different preferences for goods and services. If people have different preferences over resources, then they will not be equally satisfied with the resources that they are given. Some will want to cede a portion of their resources to obtain other resources. To decide what the different resources are worth, and to preserve equal value, we need a metric of comparison. According to Dworkin, the market gives us the metric; it sets the value of any particular resource in terms of how important that resource is for others.[13]

Dworkin asks us to imagine a society in which all the available resources are up for sale in an auction.[14] Everyone starts with an equal amount of purchasing power—clamshells, in his hypothetical example—with which they can bid on these resources. People exchange their clamshells for resources, and exchange with one another, until a set of market-clearing prices is arrived at. (When the markets clear, supply of the goods is equal to the demand for the goods at some price.)[15] In this model the differences between each individual's resources are simply the result of the choices that each has made. The auction parallels the ideal market of Walrasian microeconomic theory: the interaction of the preferences of everyone in the community over all the society's goods and services gives us the equilibrium prices for any one individual's goods and services.[16]

Given the background of an initial equal division of resources, the auction is meant to guarantee that people wind up with different but, for them, equally valuable resources. After the auction the division of these resources is "envy free"—everyone prefers his own bundle of resources to those of others—or is at least indifferent. (If anyonedid prefer a different bundle, she could have bid for it rather than the resources that she did bid for in the auction.) Differences in people's resource bundles now reflect only their different preferences, attitudes toward risk, and life ambitions. If one person prefers more expensive food and luxuries than another, this may affect his relative well-being, but he is wholly responsible if he chooses to buy French burgundy instead of beer and so has fewer resources left to buy books.[17] This combination of markets and initial equality thus enables Dworkin to answer what he takes to be a central question for distributive justice: How can we ensure that individuals face equal circumstances while also having and exercising a special responsibility to make a success of their own lives?

Dworkin's answer to this question is not fully supplied by the auction; equality in external resources (i.e., clamshells) is not enough to ensure that individuals really face equal circumstances when making their (market) choices. This is because individuals will differ in their internal personal resources, such as their level of inborn talent potential and physical powers. Although the state cannot redistribute all the differences in internal resources between people, Dworkin argues that it can mitigate their effects by offering compensation to those whose internal resources are less valuable on the market than those of others. To determine the extent of compensation that a person is owed, we must again rely on a market, in this case a hypothetical insurance market. The hypothetical market in insurance supplements the auction in external resources.

Dworkin's argument is complex, but the basic idea is this: Imagine that no one knows whether they have or will acquire a given physical or mental impairment, although each knows the consequences of having this impairment and its statistical probability in the general population. Through a hypothetical insurance market, individuals can, using some of their original clamshells, purchase insurance to protect themselves against the probability of having these impairments or being otherwise disadvantaged in the distribution of internal resources.

In this situation chosen levels of insurance would likely differ. Given your other goals and preferences, you might be willing to spend a significant percentage of your original share of resources as insurance against being so disadvantaged; I might want to spend less. But Dworkin argues that in the case of "general handicaps . . . that affect a wide spectrum of different sorts of lives," we should assume that most people would take out roughly similar insurance policies.[18] A society can then tax people as if they have taken out insurance policies against these forms of disability and provide cash benefits for actual people with disabilities at the level at which the average person would have insured. Once the hypothetical market has determined the value of insurance premiums for disadvantages in internal resources and the payouts to be distributed, and once the external resources have been divided up using the auction, then equality of resources has been achieved. Everyone has been treated with equal concern and respect—everyone has been provided by the state with equally valuable resources—and no one has any basis for complaint on the grounds that they have been treated unfairly.

Or do they? However compelling Dworkin's view of equality is on its own terms, I believe that he is mistaken to suppose that the market is *intrinsically* connected to the distributive implications of treating people with equal concern and respect. Markets may be especially useful instruments for achieving many important social and personal aims, but they cannot tell us, even under Dworkin's demanding initial conditions, what resources people are entitled to or what distributive outcomes are fair. To know what resources people are entitled to and what distributive outcomes are fair we have to look elsewhere than to the equilibrium prices established (under the assumption of initial equal resources) by their subjective preferences and their voluntary choices expressed through their market behaviors.

Why? To begin with, Dworkin's model assumes that the preferences for goods and services that people bring to the market are authentic, well supported, and exogenously given.[19] But many of our preferences are not like that. They are sometimes formed by whim, confusion, tradition, peer pressure, and social context.[20] Our preferences, even our life's ambitions, do not come from nowhere. Indeed I have already argued that markets themselves can help shape our preferences. If our preferences are formed in any of the ways I just mentioned, then they may not reflect what is really important for us: a way of life that we are genuinely committed to.

If my envy of your bundle of goods is based on preferences formed by misinformation or advertising or whim, then this seems a poor basis for recalibrating the distribution of our resources. Some people want to keep up with the lifestyle of anyone who has things that they themselves do not have.[21] Others do not feel satisfied with their lives unless they have the latest gadget, and are continually chasing after new goods (whose capabilities differ little from their predecessors but are well-marketed). Many people reverse their preference orderings given small changes in their environment, and few people possess a set of predefined preferences for every contingency. In many experiments context and the procedures involved in making choices powerfully influence the preferences that are implied by the elicited choices. Some people choose things simply because of social norms in their community. Given this, why should we assume that all of the preferences that people express in markets matter for ethical purposes?

Although Dworkin's model depends on individuals having resources that are equally valuable to them for the pursuit of their own projects, some people may choose resources that have no real value for these aims. So, as Dworkin acknowledges, we will need to bring in a principle that secures the conditions for authenticity of the parties' preferences before the auction proceeds.[22] This is a step in the right direction, but it is a tall order.

Elsewhere in his work Dworkin defends a "challenge" model according to which a life goes well insofar as it is "an appropriate response to the distinct circumstances in which it is lived."[23] Perhaps filling out that model would enable us to think about the preferences that are not only authentic, but also worthy of satisfaction. At the same time Dworkin stresses that his account of distributive justice (i.e., equality of resources) does not depend on his challenge model. Instead, following contemporary economic theory, his account largely treats our preferences as *given* (perhaps they are subject to consistency demands; perhaps they could be subject to certain informational demands). This may make sense for explanatory purposes, but this assumption does not seem well motivated when we are dealing with ethical questions. Why should a society's obligations to its citizens—that is, the distributional implications of treating its citizens with equal concern and respect—track mistaken, fleeting, confused, maladaptive, conformist, or inauthentic preferences?[24] And if preferences change on the basis of distributions that themselves depend on initial property rules about what can be owned, we have the circularity problem I noted in chapter 1.

Even if our preferences were authentic, consistent, and stable, even if we could somehow clean up our motivational psychology, satisfying individual preferences through Dworkin's hypothetical ideal markets is compatible with a failure by the state to treat its members as equals. To appreciate this point I want to consider three examples: individuals with disabilities, female caregivers, and those who make imprudent and risky choices.

At first glance Dworkin's framework appears well designed to handle the advantages and disadvantages that attach to the internal resources different individuals have.[25] Although individuals must bear the costs of their own decisions, his proposed framework compensates people for the differences in their internal resources for which they are not responsible. People who are less lucky in what John Rawls calls the "natural lottery" would accordingly be compensated, presumably via a tax-and-transfer system.[26] A person who turns out to suffer from innate deficiencies in mental and physical assets will receive additional external resources determined by the hypothetical insurance market (i.e., cash) that he can use to make up for these deficiencies and thus achieve equality of resources.

As promising as this approach is, the problem is that the disadvantages that disabled people face in society are not solely, or even mainly a function of the private resources they have at their disposal.[27] Disabled people have been marginalized and excluded from public spaces, discriminated against in employment, and subjected to demeaning stereotypes. Even a large amount of extra money will not help disabled people achieve inclusion in society as equals, unless society also alters its physical structures and its social norms and expectations. Indeed recognizing this, disability rights activists have long pressed for regulatory measures aimed at social inclusion—for the refiguring of public spaces so that they are accessible to all, for accommodations in technology and work organization that diminish the consequences of impairments—and they have challenged the stigmatizing view of disabled people as defective and less than others. Few, if any, disabled people would be satisfied with resource compensation if it left their inferior and marginalized social status intact.[28]

Dworkin's auction is focused on the distribution of *individually* held resources; the nature of the *social world* in which individuals make their transactions and relate to one another is not central to his egalitarian theory. Although he acknowledges that the social world matters—all auctions must proceed on the basis of property rules, individual and collective liberties, norms, and the like—he puts these issues to the side in his discussion of equality of resources. Yet often it is precisely the social world, the social, political, and cultural background of our market choices and actions, that is the appropriate target of egalitarian criticism. Inclusion of the disabled in society's institutions generally requires making changes to the social, political, cultural, and material organization of society. Equalizing individually held resources can go only so far in advancing this central egalitarian goal, and disabled people may nevertheless have a legitimate complaint that they are not being treated with equal respect.[29] At the very least, then, Dworkin's scheme will need to be amended so that it includes ex ante policies of social integration to facilitate the participation of disabled people in society. A market cannot guarantee that such policies will be enacted or accessible spaces built, as that will depend on factors such as the percentage of disabled people in the population and the distribution of preferences.

Consider, as a second example, the gendered division of labor, in which women assume disproportionate responsibility for domestic chores and raising children.[30] This division of labor in the family disadvantages women in the workplace, given that most workplaces do not accommodate workers' caretaking responsibilities, and women disproportionately shoulder these responsibilities. Women who assume primary responsibilities for parenting and the household cannot generally pursue the most highly paid careers and some of the most rewarding ones. These careers reward investment in human capital, not raising children, and are structured on the assumption that the worker has a spouse at home who can devote herself to the household. At the same time the implicit discrimination and stereotyping that help lead to women's lower pay for work equivalent to men's reinforce the allocation of domestic work in the family to women. It makes good economic sense to withdraw women and not men from the workforce to assume parenting duties if women's pay prospects are lower than men's.

Dworkin's market scheme offers no guidance as to what is problematic about current job structures or the gendered division of labor.[31] At best his view simply puts this issue to the side, perhaps for the political system to decide. However, from an *egalitarian* standpoint the gendered division of labor in the family and at work is objectionable. It perpetuates and reinforces the social subordination of women to men by hindering women from pursuing the most rewarding jobs and opportunities; it socializes women to have lower expectations than men; and it reinforces women's lower pay and dependence on a (male) primary wage earner for support.

How would Dworkin's theory respond to women who forgo paid work in order to care for their children or elderly parents? His theory would seem to imply that compensation to such caregivers is unnecessary because the inequality in income reflects a lifestyle choice, a difference in ambitions and aspirations between men and women that leads women to value caring over additional income that would be available in the market economy.

To be fair, Dworkin does argue that his theory can accommodate criticisms of inequality between the genders. He claims that "whatever differences now exist between the genders in their desires to combine a career with child care [are] very likely, at least in considerable part, the upshot of social expectations that are themselves the consequences of long-standing and unjust patterns of discrimination and stereotyping."[32] The question is how Dworkin's response to the problems posed by the gendered shaping of ambitions and choices fits in his own theory of choice-sensitive resource equality. Although it can be argued that women form their ambitions in response to the preferences of others and within existing social constraints, this is true of human ambitions generally. And Dworkin's view places great weight on an individual's responsibility for her own choices. So on what basis can he object to the choices that women make with respect to their careers?

Of course, it may be possible to use Dworkin's own writings on affirmative action, which stress the relevance of the history of unequal treatment, to craft some criteria for identifying those preferences that should not be given weight in the assignment of benefits and costs and those that should. This, however, involves a difficult extrapolation, because the perpetuation of gender inequality has proceeded in a very different way than the perpetuation of racial inequality; in particular, at least for most of the twentieth century, gender inequality has been supported by preferences internalized by women themselves rather than by legal discrimination, along with an inflexible job structure that makes those preferences seem rational.[33]

Even if we could identify certain preferences as somehow illegitimate, we still need to confront the question of remedy. Would the gendered family and workplace become acceptable if women were simply paid to stay in the home? This is a complicated question. Although paying women for the labor of child care might arguably be an improvement over the status quo, women would have better opportunities and more freedoms if work schedules and expectations were restructured to accommodate the need for dependent care on the parts of both women and men. Women and men would interact on terms of greater equality if, for example, parental leave were available to all on terms that did not compromise the careers of those who made use of such leave. But once again the need for this restructuring, though perhaps compatible with Dworkin's market-based theory of equality, remains invisible from within it. It thus offers us little guidance about how to identify the institutions that would under-write men's and women's equality. But surely this is a critical issue for egalitarians concerned with treating all with equal concern and respect.

Consider a third case, the case of an individual who makes a bad gamble.[34] Even if background institutions were restructured to include women and the disabled as equals, some bad gambles would remain a fact of life. On Dworkin's theory, a person cannot complain about a consequence if she has chosen it, or chosen the risk of it. Individuals must bear the costs of their risky choices, for, as we have seen, *a person's claim to an equal share is limited by her responsibility for her choices.* Nothing in Dworkin's theory would prevent a person, if she were impru-dent, from winding up in extremely bad circumstances, in which she is now subject to gross exploitation by others. Yet why not think that treating and respecting people as equals demands protecting them from exploitation, extremely unfair exchanges, and demands placing limits on the amount of power one person can exercise over another?[35]

Dworkin might respond to this example by pointing out that not only are we responsible for our own choices, but that it is important to make us internalize the costs of the burdens that we impose on others. We do not want to give people incentives to make poor and socially costly choices. This is a fair point. Any society needs to concern itself with the problems of "moral hazard" that can arise when an individual does not bear the full consequences of his actions and therefore has a tendency to act less carefully than he otherwise would do. But protect-ing people from exploitation and destitution does not require unlimited transfers to those who have made risky choices. Nor does it preclude attaching some conditions to the receipt of aid.[36]

I think that we should acknowledge the desirability of minimizing the incentives for people to engage in extremely risky gambles; nonethe-less people do sometimes make choices that turn out to have very bad consequences.[37] This is part of the reason why egalitarian social movements have fought for unconditional social insurance programs such as worker's compensation, disability insurance, and universal health coverage. These programs place ceilings on the levels of risk that people are vulnerable to, irrespective of whether or not they are responsible for having assumed these risks.

To be sure, Dworkin's fully developed theory ends up qualifying his core idea of equality-tracking individual responsibility in important ways. For example, he does grant that we can have special reasons, "based on a theory of political equality," for forbidding someone to gamble with his freedom or his religious or political rights.[38] In cases where there are externalities, he also suggests that mandatory regulation of markets may be necessary, whatever particular individuals prefer. And as we have seen in Dworkin's use of the hypothetical insurance market, he argues that we can make "rough and general judgments" about what average people of normal prudence would have chosen with respect to health insurance, and perhaps also with respect to welfare provisions and unemployment insurance.[39]

Thus reasons of ensuring equal political rights and paternalism may lead us to accept mandatory minimum provisions that will restrict market outcomes. But his theory *in principle* places no limit on the extent of inequality in the divisible resources held by different individuals given their choices. In a passage in his book *Sovereign Virtue* he writes:

> In principle . . . individuals should be relieved of consequential responsibility for those unfortunate features of their situation that are brute bad luck, but not from those that should be seen as flowing from their own choices. If someone has been born blind or without talents others have, that is his bad luck, and, so far as this can be managed, a just society would compensate him for that bad luck. But if he has fewer resources than other people now because he spent more on luxuries earlier, or because he chose not to work, or to work at less remunerative jobs than others chose, then his situation is the result of choice not luck, and he is not entitled to any compensation.[40]

However, if having adequate material resources is a standing condition of the ability of people to interact in society as equals, and if interacting as equals is a central egalitarian commitment, then, contrary to Dworkin, redistribution cannot be fully conditional on a person's own degree of *responsibility* for his plight.

Although there is reason to allow markets to influence distributional outcomes—because of their coordinating and incentive roles and because of the wide berth they give to freedom of choice—it does not follow that egalitarians must accept *all* of the results that even idealized markets would produce. I have so far argued that this is so for two main reasons.

In the first place, not all preferences that are expressed on the market matter for moral purposes. We have reason to concern ourselves with the stigmatizing norms that help determine the value of different kinds of labor, exclude some people from full membership in society, and fail to reward the labor of parenting. When we look back at the way some preferences were formed or at the kind of preferences they are, we may find reason to discount their importance.[41] We may reject, for example, a market role for preferences when they are based on or express contempt for others.[42]

In the second place, when we look forward at the effects of individual market preferences we have reasons to maintain the background conditions that prevent one person from becoming utterly dependent on the whims and power of others. Regardless of a person's responsibility for his bad market choice, society's interest in maintaining relations of equality extends far beyond the consequences of a single act of choosing. Focusing on what distributions markets throw up will not tell us under which conditions people can interact as equals.[43]

GENERAL EGALITARIANISM

The view that I have referred to as general egalitarianism recognizes that markets may produce an unacceptable amount of social inequality even when they arise on the basis of individual choice. This market-generated inequality might reflect background inequality of conditions, differences in individual abilities, bad judgments, or distortions on the operations of the market due to externalities, non-zero transaction costs, monopolies, or incomplete or asymmetric information.[44] Or it might reflect a skewed or otherwise problematic distribution of preferences in society: consider a society that pays child care workers less than it pays zookeepers.

When the market generates an outcome that is judged to be objectionable, the general egalitarian prefers to transfer money rather than to reallocate goods in kind. Once the distribution of purchasing power is made acceptable, she believes that we should allow competitive markets to do their work because competitive markets produce optimal economic results. Interfering with the market in specific goods simply leads to greater inefficiencies than might otherwise be the case.[45]

Thomas Schelling gives an illustrative example: Suppose that faced with a shortage of gasoline and resulting high prices, policymakers restrict a market in gasoline and give every family a nontransferable coupon that they can use to purchase it.[46] Some poor people will undoubtedly make use of the coupons, but others (say, those without cars) will prefer to have money. Some rich people will undoubtedly want to buy more gasoline than their coupon entitles them to. A poor person might not be interested in purchasing gas but very interested in buying additional food for his children. A rich person might not be especially interested in buying more groceries but might want to buy more gas. In this example, restricting the operation of the market by making the coupons inalienable serves to make the poor worse off than they would have been if the restriction on transfer had been lifted. If the restriction on selling coupons were lifted, poor people who needed gas could use their coupons and those who needed groceries could sell their coupons to others for cash. Rich people who wanted more gas could buy the coupons from the poor. Lifting the restriction is a Pareto improvement, as defined in chapter 1. However, once you see the rationale for allowing the coupons to be traded, notice that we could have obtained the same result by allowing the price of gas to rise in an unrestricted market, taxing the price increase, and transferring the tax revenues to supplement the incomes of the poor. In that case, everyone would be better off in terms of what they want.

Some liberal philosophers are also drawn to general egalitarianism because they are suspicious of the ability of governments, or third parties, to be better decision makers than the first parties whose interests are directly involved. They believe that an individual will achieve greater preference satisfaction if he is making his own decisions about what to buy and sell rather than relying on a third party to decide for him. Indeed there is a large literature in economics concerning what is referred to as the "principal-agent problem," in which a person who needs to get something done (known as the principal) must motivate her agent to act as closely in accord with her wishes as possible. This is less easy than one might think. Not only can it be costly to transmit information, but the principal can have opposing interests to the agent.

Of course some principals cannot make decisions for themselves; they must rely on others. It is generally recognized that young children and adults with severe cognitive impairments require paternalistic interventions. But by the same token many people reject as insulting the idea that competent adults cannot be trusted to make the decisions about their own lives. When welfare state programs that seek to aid the poor deliver their aid in the form of nontradable vouchers for food and housing, they thereby replace poor people's own judgments about what is good for them by the program's own discretion. To some this replacement supports the objection that welfare states treat the poor like children.[47] From a general egalitarian perspective, there is little to be said in favor of such paternalistic interventions.[48] Neither the value of efficiency nor the value of freedom of choice is likely to be served by such interventions. Instead it is held to be better on grounds of both freedom and efficiency that if there is to be some redistribution, it should take the form of money with which the poor can make their own choices about what they wish to consume, how they want to spend their time, and what risks they are willing to assume.

These concerns about efficiency and paternalism certainly have some merit, but they do not establish that egalitarians should refrain from seeking to limit the scope of the market. First, as I discussed chapter 1, every market depends on background rules. In turn, these default rules rule out some choices (e.g., robbery) and make some choices more likely than others.[49] For example, some societies have adopted an "opt out" system of organ donation, in which the presumption is that a person's organs are available for transplant after his death unless he explicitly opts out. Other societies, such as the United States, have "opt in" systems in which the opposite presumption is in place. These different default arrangements affect the number of available cadaver organs. More generally psychologists have found substantial framing effects, in which the legal and organizational rules have powerful influence on the choices of those affected. We do not make choices from nowhere and we need to determine the default rules. It is hard to see why paternalist considerations should not influence society's choice of these rules.

Second, from the standpoint of our obligations to one another and the state's obligations to its own citizens, not all goods mean the same thing as money. The general egalitarian view assumes that resources are fungible; that is, other resources can substitute for them. (Money substitutes for gas in Schelling's example.) This assumption is also a feature of

Dworkin's theory, where to equalize resources between people, his theory requires a common currency (clamshells in his model). But not all goods play the same role as money in our political and moral theories. In particular I can think that there are goods that people have a claim to—life, public health, and public safety—without thinking that these people have *the same claim* on the cash equivalent that might (or might not) be used to buy these goods.

T. M. Scanlon provides a powerful illustration of the difference between two related types of claims in his paper "Preference and Urgency." Suppose a person sees himself as under an obligation to redress an urgent need, such as an obligation to transfer some of his resources to prevent a person from starving. Scanlon asks us to now imagine that this starving person would happily choose to forgo a decent diet in order to build a monument to her god. It does not follow that the potential donor must see himself under an obligation to transfer resources to contribute to the cost of the monument. The basis for his obligation to the starving person arises from her (more or less) objective needs, and not the importance that she herself places on those needs within her own subjective conception of her life.

When we consider examples like Scanlon's monument builder in the context of the state's obligations to it's citizens, some form of in-kind provision looks superior to monetary distribution based on tax and transfer. In kind provision blocks the recipient from using resources in a way that undermines what is arguably the very basis of the state's obligations to its citizens, which is the latter's urgent needs.[50] Moreover the basis of this blockage is not paternalistic; it is focused on a view about the source of the donor's *obligation*, not on a view about what is in the recipient's best interest.

SPECIFIC EGALITARIANISM

A different egalitarian approach to the market takes the equal distribution of certain specific goods to be an implication of our equality. Or, at the very least, proponents of this approach recognize that certain scarce goods "should be distributed less unequally than the ability to pay for them."[51] People do tend to react quite differently to inequalities in access to medical care or to legal assistance than they do to inequalities in automobiles, clothes, and yachts. Even if income is distributed unequally, it does not follow that all goods should be distributed as unequally as income. But which specific goods are to be distributed equally? How should we decide?

In the contemporary philosophical literature the most influential discussion of that topic remains that given by Michael Walzer in his book *Spheres of Justice*.[52] Walzer argues that when we are considering how a good should be distributed we should ask whether its being so distributed would be consistent with the social meaning of that good. For example, he points out that it is in the nature of our concepts of honor, divine grace, and true love that these things have no market price. At the very least, using the market to distribute these goods would represent a change in the way people understand these goods; our current usages would be undermined. Someone who offers to buy my friendship does not really understand what it means (in our culture) to be or to have a friend. There are also some goods that people regard as simply irreplaceable, without any equivalent.[53] As Kant said about human beings, they have a dignity and not a price.[54]

In Walzer's approach markets are not merely neutral accounting devices for determining and tracking the value of goods. Markets can *change* and *degrade* the meaning of a good. Richard Titmuss's classic study, *The Gift Relationship*, provides a good case for thinking about how this might happen. Titmuss argued that allowing a market in blood changes the social understanding of blood donation from a "gift of life" to a mere cash equivalent. Moreover, by changing the meaning of blood, the use of markets leads to the procurement of blood of lower quality and also makes it less likely that blood will be freely and altruistically given. Titmuss argued that this change in meaning explained certain contrasts between the American and British systems of blood donation.[55] Walzer's theory extends Titmuss's argument about effect of markets on meaning to cover other goods such as membership, Nobel Prizes, basic education, health, and political equality. The very meaning of these goods, he claims, requires that we limit the role of the market in their distribution; otherwise the meaning of these goods will be corrupted.

Walzer argues that there are certain goods whose social meaning requires that they be distributed equally and not according to markets because markets distribute goods on the basis of people's ability and willingness to pay. In particular he claims that the meaning of health care requires that it be distributed on the basis of equal medical need. This is an interesting idea, but as Walzer's theory stands it is pretty much hopeless as a general political foundation for limiting markets. Many social meanings are contested. With respect to health care, for example, there are serious and long-standing controversies about its meaning.[56] Many Americans seem to believe that state intervention in health care should be limited to cases in which the market fails: to provide coverage for the old and the disabled, to those who cannot afford insurance, and to finance fundamental medical research, which is a public good. Beyond this there is considerable, if contested support for market provision. If we disagree with this position it does no good to cite the social meaning of health care as the reason for our disagreement, because it is precisely the social meaning (and its implications) that is here in dispute.

Others try to improve on Walzer's conventionalist foundation by arguing that we should base our attitudes toward market distributions on our *best understandings* of goods in the light of all of our values and evidence. Elizabeth Anderson argues that there are important differences in the appropriate attitudes we should take to different goods: whereas some goods are rightly viewed as tradable commodities, others are objects of respect or reverence or should be considered irreplaceable and without equivalent. By tracking differences in the ways we *appropriately* value specific goods, she argues, we can determine which goods are properly treated as market commodities.[57] Michael Sandel argues that we corrupt many moral and civic goods if they are bought for money. His examples include cases that I consider later in this book: commercial surrogacy, organ sales, and military service.[58] Margaret Jane Radin claims that markets in certain goods closely connected to our "personhood" undermine our flourishing as human beings and so should be blocked, or at least highly regulated.[59] On Radin's view, our best understanding of a flourishing human life sets the basis for limits on markets in specific goods.

Each of these strategies for limiting markets is interesting and often illuminating. However, they share two important weaknesses: there are rival views of the meaning of many particular goods (and of human flourishing), and, more importantly, there is only a tenuous connection in most cases between the meaning we give to a good and its distribution by a market.

First, consider that as a practical matter we may be unable to reach consensus on the best meaning of many specific goods. (This can be true even if the account given of a good's best meaning is in fact correct.)

Second, even where we accept a particular interpretation as providing the best meaning of a good, there is not necessarily any close connection between this understanding and the use of markets. Markets are typically instrumental mechanisms for achieving our ends; a market price is rarely the direct expression of our evaluative attitudes toward a good. As I pointed out in chapter 1, a religious person can buy a Bible without believing that its price expresses her views about its worth. A person who thinks health care is a right might still favor the use of a private market–based insurance system coupled with health care provision for the indigent. I can endorse food as a basic need that should be guaranteed, while also supporting some of its distribution by markets.

Additionally our evaluation about the acceptability of using a market to distribute a good is often conditioned by empirical factors, such as the elasticity in the supply of the good. When a scarce commodity is in fixed supply, arrangements for distributing it equally, or based on any other nonmarket criterion, can be made without worrying about efficiency. As an example, if the supply of kidneys available for transplantation is fixed, then we may think it most appropriate to distribute kidneys by nonmarket means. However, if allowing a market in kidneys also dramatically increases the supply, then the case for blocking that market will presumably look weaker. This is why we may be worried about the distribution of a specific good in some contexts but not others.

I see no reason to think that our evaluation of particular markets, even those markets that people intuitively view as deeply problematic, is usually tracking the meaning that the goods involved have for them or closely tracks goods connected to flourishing. People bring diverse understandings to markets; this is also true of the markets that provoke our discomfort. Two people may disagree about the meaning of a good or about what constitutes a flourishing life, but both find themselves uncomfortable with using a particular market to distribute that good.

One prominent example worth considering when evaluating these specific egalitarian approaches to the limits of markets is the public uproar occasioned by a memo from Lawrence Summers, then the chief economist of the World Bank, to his colleagues. The memo read in part:

Just between you and me, shouldn't the World Bank be encouraging more migration of the dirty industries to the LDCs [less developed countries]? I can think of three reasons:

1. The measurement of the costs of health-impairing pollution depends on the foregone earnings from increased morbidity and mortality. From this point of view a given amount of health-impairing pollution should be done in the country in the lowest cost, which will be the country with the lowest wages. I think the economic logic behind dumping a load of toxic waste in the lowest wage country is impeccable and we should face up to that.
2. The costs of pollution are likely to be non-linear as the initial increments of pollution probably have very low cost. . . . Only the lamentable facts that so much pollution is generated by non-tradable industries (transport, electrical generation) and that the unit transport costs of solid waste are so high prevent world-welfare enhancing trade in air pollution and waste.
3. The demand for a clean environment for aesthetic and health reasons is likely to have very high income elasticity. . . . Clearly trade in goods that embody aesthetic pollution concerns could be welfare enhancing. . . .

The problem with the arguments against all of these proposals for more pollution in LDCs (intrinsic rights to certain goods, moral reasons, social concerns, lack of adequate markets, etc.) could be turned around and used more or less effectively against every Bank proposal for liberalization.[60]

Summers is completely correct when he writes that the economic logic behind toxic dumping to LDCs (presumably in return for economic compensation) is "impeccable." If the parties to the trade are rational, then, given that the *economic* consequences of increased pollution are far lower in LDCs than in developed countries, people in the LDCs should be willing to sell pollution rights to people in developed countries for a price that the latter should be willing to pay. The *Economist*, to which the memo was leaked, found the language "crass" but noted, "On the economics his points are hard to answer."[61] So what explains the outcry that the publication of this memo occasioned? Why were so many people outraged by the idea of an international market in toxic waste?

There is a lot to consider here, but I do not think that Summers' critics need be committed to any particular view about pollution's *meaning*. For instance, someone who reacts negatively to Summers' memo can hold, with perfect consistency, that it is appropriate to allow corporations to buy and sell rights to pollute within the United States. And a person can value the environment aesthetically or spiritually without believing that those values are necessarily undermined by the use of a market, at least if the market is regulated in certain ways. Someone who criticizes Summers' proposal may not find the market commodification of pollution to be itself objectionable. Similarly two people might hold different views about the place of nature in a flourishing life but still find his memo troubling.

Although some goods do have a meaning that resists commodification—think of friendship, love, and Nobel Prizes—the overwhelming majority of goods do not. Our negative reactions to certain markets must depend in these latter cases on other considerations, considerations that I argue cut across differences in types of goods. For now, observe that if markets in a standard commodity produced extremely harmful consequences, perhaps because a sudden price drop in the good drove its producers to destitution, we would likely respond differently to markets in that good than we do now. I will discuss Summers' memo, and my own diagnosis of the problems with his proposal, in the next chapter.

TITANIC CASES

The specific egalitarians are right about something: there are inequalities in particular goods that strike most people as especially troubling. The interesting question is why this is so. As we have seen, general egalitarians and specific egalitarians offer different answers to this question. I now want to examine more closely how each of the views that I consider would deal with a puzzle arising from what I will call *Titanic* cases.

Consider this striking passage on the sinking of the *Titanic* from Thomas Schelling:

> There were enough lifeboats for first class; steerage was expected to go down with the ship. We do not tolerate that anymore. Those who want to risk their lives at sea and cannot afford a safe ship should perhaps not be denied the opportunity to entrust themselves to a cheaper ship without lifeboats; but if some people cannot afford the price of passage with lifeboats, and some people can, they should not travel on the same ship.[62]

Schelling does not explicitly endorse our policy of limiting inequality in safety aboard boats, but he does underscore that imposing such limits is a widely supported practice in our society.[63] Why do we now accept, as a matter of social policy, that the inequality in access to lifeboats aboard the *Titanic* was objectionable?

A general egalitarian would argue that what made the inequality in access to lifeboats objectionable is the unfair background distribution of income and wealth. According to the general egalitarian, if it is not fair that some people have so little money that they can only afford to travel in second or third class on the ship while others have so much that they can purchase luxury accommodations, then the outcome of that inequality is not fair as well. Our reaction to the *Titanic*, on this view, is best explained by our rejection of the starting economic positions of the poor and rich passengers.

As we have seen, something like this is Dworkin's view. And undoubtedly many of our reactions to unequal outcomes are best explained in this way, by our objections to the prior distribution of resources. Consider the very low proportion of students from poor families attending elite colleges and universities; roughly about 3 percent of such students come from the bottom quartile.[64] One factor that makes this proportion look especially objectionable is the highly unequal K–12 education that rich and poor children receive. Because of their poor preparation, many poor children never had a chance to fairly compete for an elite university education. We would probably react differently to such disparities in college attendance based on income if we found out that poor children were admitted to elite colleges at the same rate as their wealthier peers but chose not to attend because they were more interested in remaining at colleges in their home communities.

But does a concern with prior inequality adequately explain our discomfort with the *Titanic* case? To reflect on whether this is so, imagine that there was equality in purchasing power—assume everyone has an equal number of dollars with which to buy their tickets—and the inequality of access to lifeboats simply arose because some people cared more about ensuring their safety than others. After all, there are people who routinely engage in risky activities such as skydiving and mountain climbing. We do not prevent people from pursuing these activities. What is so objectionable, then, about allowing people to make their own consumption decisions about how much safety they want to buy? Why not allow people to buy the kind of safety they want?[65]

I believe that many people will continue to feel discomforted by the *Titanic* example, even if the unequal access to lifeboats arose by choice. If pressed to explain this lingering discomfort, a general egalitarian might try appealing to information problems: perhaps people buy second-class tickets only when they lack sufficient knowledge of the risks. On the actual *Titanic*, after all, the passengers *were* all deluded: they thought the boat was "unsinkable." Perhaps if the passengers had known of the risks they would not have assumed them. Indeed it seems reasonable to assume that people, on average, would not wish to run the downside risk that the *Titanic* example poses.

Recall that Dworkin makes an argument along these lines in his discussion of the purchase of disability insurance. Dworkin's view holds individuals responsible for the costs of the gambles they make. So if insurance against blindness is available, and two sighted people have an equal chance of suffering an accident that will blind them and know this to be the case, and one buys insurance and the other not, then Dworkin's theory does not argue for any redistribution if the latter person becomes blind. That person is held responsible for his failure to purchase the insurance.

However, because many blind people are blind at birth and most sighted people are sighted at birth and no one ever had the chance to buy insurance before the fact, Dworkin argues that we should suppose "most people would make roughly the same insurance decisions against general handicaps such as blindness," and that we should insure everyone at the level that the average person would choose. That is, even though those individuals born blind did not (and could not) purchase insurance against their blindness, we can assume that they *would have* purchased it if they had the chance and compensate them accordingly. So perhaps even though some passengers on the *Titanic* found themselves in seating classes that did not include the right of access to a lifeboat, we can assume that, on average, prudent individuals *would have* wanted it.

I agree that information is relevant to our evaluation of a person's choices, and in the next chapter I will discuss the role of such information in our judgments about the morality of specific markets. However, let's further revise the example of the original (and actual) *Titanic*. In this newly revised example, people not only have sufficient income to buy first-class tickets but also are assumed to know that there are risks to traveling without a lifeboat and are willing to take them, much as skydivers and mountain climbers are also so willing. This revised *Titanic* example is more like the case of sighted people who would fail to purchase insurance against becoming blind even when they knew the risks and have the choice to do so. Dworkin would hold these people responsible for their choices.

Of course, it is possible to invoke a paternalistic argument for not allowing people to forgo certain safety requirements; prudent individuals might wish to place themselves under certain restrictions in order to prevent themselves from doing things in moments of weakness or irrationality that would undermine their long-term interests. Gerald Dworkin makes an argument of this sort in his paper "Paternalism":

> I suggest that since we are all aware of our irrational propensities, deficiencies in cognitive and emotional capacities, and avoidable and unavoidable ignorance it is rational and prudent for us to in effect take out "social insurance policies." . . . I suggest we think of the imposition of paternalistic interferences in situations of this kind as being a kind of insurance policy which we take out against making decisions which are far reaching, potentially dangerous, and irreversible.[66]

I doubt that our reactions to the revised *Titanic* example depend on problems in anyone's cognitive or emotional capacities or on ignorance. After all, someone can, with full rationality, decide to take a risk to meet her goals. Every time I ride in my car, take an airplane, or just walk out the door I assume a small but potentially significant and irreversible risk of death. Are the risks in my revised example different from this? If not, then the case for paternalism based on imprudence does not seem very plausible.

Perhaps as important, even if we accept a paternalistic argument for requiring access to lifeboats, the argument doesn't explain what is problematic (if anything is) about the *inequality* in safety aboard the boat.[67] Interestingly Schelling contends that our discomfort with the *Titanic* example is primarily directed against the fact of *inequality* on the *same boat*. I think there is something to Schelling's suggestion. To see if you agree, ask yourself whether the case would be equally objectionable if in one society none had access to lifeboats on ships, and in another society everyone had access to them, and both societies had equal resources. Can a specific egalitarian offer reasons for objecting to the revised

Titanic example? She might try to argue that the social meaning of safety is such that it should be distributed equally to all. But that seems implausible as a general statement; after all, we allow people to buy cars that offer differential levels of safety in the event of an accident. Larger, heavier (and often more expensive) cars not only are safer for those that drive them, but are more dangerous to drivers of smaller, lighter cars in the event of a collision. Very few people have objected to the existence of some inequality in safety attaching to people driving in different cars. Of course, in the case of cars there are minimum safety requirements. But to address the importance of such baseline minimum requirements requires, I will argue, going beyond the specific egalitarianism views I have surveyed to bring in considerations that cut across different types of goods.

Both the general and the specific egalitarian views that I have outlined have difficulty in *explaining* our reactions to the revised *Titanic* case. Although they point to intuitively plausible factors for the assessment of allowing people to purchase tickets on ships with unequal access to lifeboats—the legitimacy of background starting positions, the adequacy of the parties' information, and the specific nature of certain goods—none of these factors seems relevant in the idealized *Titanic* case. Perhaps that case is, after all, unobjectionable.

I think, however, that there is a further aspect of both the real and the revised *Titanic* cases, an aspect that is so far missing from my discussion and from the other contemporary approaches that I have surveyed. The *Titanic* examples, both the initial example and my revised version, involve people standing in certain relationships with one another, people who interact in certain ways. First, think of what it would mean to find yourself on a sinking ship, which your society has built and sanctioned, where some of your fellow passengers have no claim on a seat in your lifeboat. Suppose these passengers struggle to board your lifeboat. The lack of sufficient safety places you in a particular relationship with these would-be invaders. You hold extreme power over them: Do you throw all of them out of the boat to their likely deaths? Do you offer to cram a few of them in for a price? Do you allocate a few seats to those who agree to be your personal slaves? Second, even beyond your face-to-face interactions with the people on the boat, *if the option of ship passage without lifeboats is available*, then some people in your society may face problematic choices, such as having to travel on risky ships or lose their jobs.

And as a citizen, you would be implicated in the enforcement of these arrangements.

Rather than resting the case for regulating *Titanic* cases on paternalism, I will argue that a better case can be made by appeal to the conditions under which cooperating members of a society can interact as equals. In refusing to allow some people to buy seats on a boat without access to lifeboats while others do, the state is in effect protecting the conditions for its citizens to interact as equals. The idea of what it means to interact as equals is, of course, a complex idea, which needs elaboration and defense. I turn to that task in the next chapter.

4

Noxious Markets

ABSTRACT MARKETS VERSUS
NOXIOUS MARKETS

What is wrong with markets in everything? What is it about the nature of particular exchanges that concerns us, to the point that markets in some goods appear to be clearly undesirable? How should our social policies respond to such markets? Where and for what reasons is it appropriate to regulate a market, and when should we seek to block it? These are the difficult but important questions that this chapter attempts to answer.

Several brief clarifications about my scope and aims here. First, as is evident from the discussion thus far, my project does not involve an overall assessment of "the market system."[1] Markets allow people to accomplish many important social and individual tasks under modern conditions of interdependence and diversity. The point of my inquiry is not to raise general questions about the market system or about markets in the abstract. Rather, I am concerned here with the differing characteristics of very particular market exchanges: in human body parts, child labor, toxic waste, sex, and life-saving medicines. Markets in these goods provoke reservations even among those who are otherwise great enthusiasts about the market system.

Second, I put aside questions concerning the rationing of essentials in cases of extreme scarcity, "tragic choices," as they are referred to in the legal literature.[2] These are cases in which no amount of money or effort will produce enough of urgently needed goods. Market allocations in tragic choice cases raise distinct considerations from the examples considered here, as such cases do for all the alternative systems of allocation, including those using lottery, age, or merit.

Let me recap the discussion so far. Chapter 1 focused on the dominant framework of contemporary economics that supports market interventions only where markets fail to be efficient.[3] Proponents of this approach can be divided between those who believe that perfectly efficient markets are "moral-free zones" to which morality simply does not apply,[4] and those who believe that it is simply not the place of economists to evaluate the morality of differing markets. But when particular markets fail, this approach does not tend to support the *elimination* of those markets. Indeed economic theory is inherently imperialistic about the scope of the market; as we have seen, the solution to market failure is often taken to consist in the *enlargement* of the scope of the market. (Consider the introduction of markets in pollution to incorporate pollution's costs to third parties.) There are no theoretically set limits for the scope of the market. In addition markets and the corresponding idea of market failures are everywhere conceived of in the same terms. This stands in sharp contrast to the approach of the classical political economists that I explored in chapter 2.

Chapter 3 examined important contemporary approaches to the limits of the market. Drawing on the work of Ronald Dworkin, I critically examined the view that markets have a necessary *moral* role to play in egalitarian theory because markets make each of us responsible for the allocation of effort and resources in our own lives, while at the same time ensuring that the benefits that we derive from our choices depend on how important our effort and resources are to others. As we saw, Dworkin's theory gives us no reason *in principle* to set limits to the scope of the market with respect to goods and services, except perhaps for paternalistic considerations.

I also explored the prevalent general egalitarian approach that, although critical of the economist's exclusive focus on market efficiency and market failure, accepts the legitimacy of relying on markets in most domains. Proponents would use markets to produce efficient outcomes and then support ex post transfers of income to achieve their desired egalitarian distribution.[5] Like contemporary economics, its proponents tend to treat most markets as the same: markets in soybeans are not fundamentally different from markets in body parts. The basic default strategy employed for dealing with market problems is to redistribute income and not to block particular markets or to redistribute specific goods in kind. Many proponents of this view also appeal to antipaternalistic considerations for preferring cash to in-kind transfers.

I also examined specific egalitarian approaches, which ground a distinction in markets—between those that are acceptable and those that are not—based on the meaning *of the goods being traded*. The idea here is that distribution should track our conventional or best understandings of the nature of the goods we seek to distribute. As we saw, these authors argue that markets corrupt the nature of certain goods, trading in things that money should not buy.

The theories considered in chapter 1 and chapter 3 have important insights on which I will draw: market failures (including externalities), distributional equality, and the importance of access to specific goods are important considerations in assessing markets.[6] Yet my underlying theory about the limits of markets also differs. I argue for a more nuanced view of the idea of market failure, one that takes into account how markets shape our relationships with others in ways that goes beyond the idea of unabsorbed economic costs. A market exchange based in desperation, humiliation, or begging or whose terms of remediation involve bondage or servitude is not an exchange between equals. On my view, lurking behind many, if not all, noxious markets are problems relating to the *standing* of the parties before, during, and after the process of exchange.

I will also argue in this chapter that some markets are noxious and need to be blocked or severely constrained if the parties are to be equals in a particular sense, as citizens in a democracy. In making this argument I draw on the writings of Adam Smith and the other classical political economists discussed in chapter 2. Recall that these thinkers recognized that markets require certain background conditions—specification of and enforcement of entitlements and property rights—in order to support relations of freedom and equality. The markets of the classical political economists were populated not by the abstract individuals with given wants that tend to characterize contemporary economic theory, but by landless peasants and wasteful landlords and by impoverished workers who stood in asymmetrical power relations with their employers. Moreover agents' preferences, capacities, and relationships were understood to be shaped by the structure and nature of particular markets. Like these theorists, the approach to markets I defend recognizes market heterogeneity and stresses the need to consider other values besides efficiency and distributional equality narrowly conceived. But, as I argued in chapter 3,

I think we should reject the main contemporary alternative arguments for limiting markets based on the social meaning of goods. As I see it, a major problem with noxious markets is not that they represent inferior ways of valuing goods (as those who link the limits of markets to social meanings claim) but that they undermine the conditions that people need if they are to relate as equals. At any rate, so I shall argue.

NOXIOUS MARKETS: THE BASIC PARAMETERS

I begin with a characterization of four parameters in terms of which we can differentiate the markets that people find especially objectionable from other types of markets. Several of these parameters are *internal* to the perspective of economics in that scoring high on them will often undermine efficiency. However, there are also political and moral rationales for limiting noxious markets. That is why the addition of more markets is not always the appropriate response to a noxious market. In some cases our goal should be to curtail a particular noxious market, not to make it work better.[7]

The first two parameters characterize the *consequences* of particular markets.

1. Some markets produce extremely *harmful outcomes*. That is, the operation of some markets leads to outcomes that are deleterious, either for the participants themselves or for third parties.[8] Consider market exchanges that lead to the depletion of the natural resource base of a country or to the fueling of a genocidal civil war. Or consider a stock market transaction that wipes out a person's resources.

Of course, many markets have harmful outcomes without eliciting our revulsion; we think that the ups and downs of prices come with the territory. But some market outcomes are so negative, so extremely harmful that they almost always evoke a strong reaction. How harmful is that? Following up on a suggestion by Ravi Kanbur, we might consider as a natural starting point for answering this question a market whose operation leaves a person destitute.[9] For example, a grain market whose operation leaves some people starving because they cannot afford the price at which grain is set through supply and demand is bound to make us feel uncomfortable.

Yet markets can also be extremely harmful to individuals in ways that go beyond destitution. Amartya Sen usefully distinguishes between two types of interests that people have: *welfare interests* concern a person's overall good, and *agency interests* concern a person's ability to participate in deciding matters that bear on that good.[10] These interests are interdependent, but they are distinct. (A benign dictator, for example, could meet all my basic welfare interests.) We can define a set of *basic* interests for people, interests in minimum levels of well-being and agency, and define extremely harmful market outcomes as outcomes that leave these basic interests unsatisfied. The idea of basic interests is meant to capture the idea that there are universal features of an adequate and minimally decent human life, a "line beneath which no one is to be allowed to sink."[11]

2. In addition to leading to extreme individual harms, certain markets can also be *extremely harmful for society*. The operation of these markets can undermine the social framework needed for people to interact *as equals*, as individuals with equal standing. There are, of course, running disagreements among philosophers concerning the meaning of "interact as equals," as well as the scope of this ideal. I take the content of this ideal to be given by the preconditions necessary for individuals to make claims on one another and interact without having to beg or to push others around. Markets help enable this ideal, as the basis of market claims is reciprocal self-interest of the parties.[12] But they can also undermine it. Consider markets that operate to undermine the capacities that a person needs to claim her rights or to participate in society; this is a problem with child labor markets and bonded labor, cases I discuss in the third part of this book. Or consider that particular markets may condition people to be docile or servile, shape them into passive accepters of a status quo. Whereas contemporary economics sees the capacities and preferences of agents in a market as givens, particular markets—think of media, education, and caregiving—shape us. Moreover they may shape us in ways that are in tension with a society of equals.

A special case is a market that is harmful for the standing of the parties as equal citizens in a democracy. This case ratchets up from the more minimal notion of equal standing: it has to do with the equality of individuals as co-deliberants and co-participants in making laws that apply to themselves. This kind of equality presupposes additional constraints on markets and their scope. Recall James Tobin: "Any good second year graduate student in economics could write a short examination paper proving that voluntary transactions in votes would increase the welfare of the sellers as well as the buyers."[13] Nevertheless the legitimacy of the democratic process depends on the prohibition of such transactions. I will discuss this case later in this chapter.

The next two parameters characterize the *sources* of particular markets, the underlying condition of the market agents:

3. Some markets are characterized by *very weak or highly asymmetric knowledge and agency* on the part of market participants. The Pareto efficiency results assume that agents are fully aware of the consequences of their actions and have complete information about the goods exchanged.[14] But, as is widely noted by economists and others, in most circumstances these assumptions do not hold. Agency failures can occur because some of the direct participants lack important knowledge or because the market has serious indirect effects on people who are not involved in the market transactions.[15] If one or both of the parties to a contract are mistaken about the material facts or about the future consequences of their contract, we cannot assume that the exchange is a Pareto improvement.

All real markets, of course, involve imperfect information. But in some cases this imperfect information is apt to produce extremely harmful consequences. This may be most likely in cases where is a significant time lag between the initiation and the completion of a transaction.[16] It is hard to predict one's future preferences. Consider the case of a woman selling her ability to have a child. In this case we might suspect that a woman who has never been pregnant cannot really know the consequences of selling the right to the child she bears.

Of course the fact that a contract has potential risks for an agent does not mean that the contract should not bind the agent, or else most contracting would fail. Nevertheless information failures are relevant to our assessment of particular markets in the face of harmful outcomes; in particular such failures serve to block justifications of a market transaction that appeal simply to the fact that it was chosen. Thus if agency is weak in surrogacy contracts, and a surrogate is now devastated by the thought of giving up the child she has borne, we will be less likely to think that we can justify enforcement of the contract simply on the basis that there was an agreement.

Although the majority of troubling markets characterized by weak agency involve extremely harmful outcomes, it is possible to be concerned by such markets even in the absence of harms. In this category would fall product markets that target young children; markets involving the production, purchase, and dissemination of information that fail to present relevant alternative points of view about a pressing political issue; and markets whose products are based on deception, even when there is no serious harm.[17]

Agency problems also arise in markets in which one of the affected parties is not directly involved in the transaction but depends on others to transact for her. In such cases we cannot be certain that the party herself actually benefits from the transaction. In the majority of cases of child labor, for example, parents are transacting on behalf of the children whose time and labor are traded. Many forms of child labor give little or no benefit to the working child and in some cases significantly interfere with the child's ability to grow up into a healthy functioning adult.[18] Other markets in which some of the affected parties are not directly involved as participants include markets in a nation's important scarce natural resources (such as timber in a rain forest), which can affect subsequent generations and others around the globe.

4. Some markets reflect the *underlying* extreme *vulnerabilities* of one of the transacting parties. Rousseau wrote that no citizen should "be wealthy enough to buy another, and none poor enough to be forced to sell himself."[19] When people come to the market with widely varying resources or widely different capacities to understand the terms of their transactions, they are unequally vulnerable to one another. In such circumstances the weaker party is at risk of being exploited. For example, when a desperately poor person agrees to part with an asset at a fire sale price, even if the exchange improves his well-being we are rightly concerned with the fact that his circumstances made him willing to accept an offer for his asset that no one with a decent alternative would ever accept. When a person enters a contract from a position of extreme vulnerability he is likely to agree to almost any terms that are offered. Other examples of markets that exploit the vulnerability of transacting agents include markets in urgently needed goods where there is only a small set of suppliers and markets where the participants have highly unequal needs for the goods being exchanged.[20]

Some markets not only *reflect* the different and unequal underlying positions of market agents but may also *exacerbate* them by the way they operate. For example, in Bangladesh a recent famine arose when the price of the main food, rice, rose very rapidly and became too expensive for the poor to purchase. By contrast, rich households were insulated from the risks of rising prices because they generally receive rice from their tenants as payment for the use of land so that they have rice for their own needs and surplus to sell.[21]

So we have two dimensions regarding the source of a market and two dimensions regarding the consequences of a market that can be used to think about the acceptability of particular markets (see Table 1).

High scores along one of these dimensions, or several of them together, can make any market appear "noxious" to us. Consider the market in diamonds, whose sale is used to fund brutal civil wars. Many people find such a market abhorrent. On the analysis offered here, the best way to understand our negative reaction to this market has to do with its *extremely harmful* outcome—prolonging a bloody civil war in which thousands or tens of thousands die, hence the term "*blood diamonds*"—and with the *weak agency* of so many who are affected by the markets that fuel that war.[22] Our discomfort with such markets doesn't seem to have anything to do with the social meaning of diamonds and little to do with the underlying income inequality of buyers and sellers.

TABLE 1. What Makes a Market Noxious?

Source: Weak Agency	*Source: Vulnerability*
Inadequate information about the nature of and/or consequences of a market; others enter the market on one's behalf	Markets in a desperately needed good with limited suppliers; markets with origins in poverty and destitution; markets whose participants have very unequal needs for goods being exchanged
Outcome: Extreme Harms for Individual	*Outcome: Extreme Harms for Society*
Produces destitution; produces harm to the basic welfare and/or agency interests of the individual	Promotes servility and dependence; undermines democratic governance; undermines other regarding motivations

At the same time, although in theory markets in any good can become noxious, markets in some goods are much more likely to score higher than others on these parameters. Consider the case of markets in goods that no one but the desperate would ever exchange. Some people think that desperation is a characteristic feature of kidney markets, a case I discuss in chapter 9.

A number of these parameters are easily incorporated within the approaches of contemporary economics; for example, concerns with harmful outcomes and information failures can be captured in the perspectives of welfare and neoclassical economics. Several authors, notably Ravi Kanbur and Michael Treblicock, have done this, showing that economic theory itself has available resources for dealing with many problematic markets. Nevertheless markets raise questions of political philosophy as well as of economics. Markets can damage important relationships people have with one another by allowing people to segment and opt out of a common condition. A central feature of most noxious markets on my approach has to do with their effects on the relationships between people, particularly the horizontal relationship of equal status. For two people to have equal status they need to see each other as legitimate sources of independent claims and they need to each have the capacity to press their claims without needing the other's permission to do so. This requires that each have rights and liberties of certain kinds as well as very specific resources, such as a level of education.

Equal status stands opposed to the ideas of caste, hereditary privilege, and unequal birthright. It insists that all individuals have an equal moral worth. Although it is perhaps possible to interpret this idea of equal status in economic terms, it is not easy to see how this would be done. Equal income and wealth by themselves do not entail equal status, as I stressed in my discussion of people with disabilities who have been marginalized from social positions and from public spaces.

Why not let people enter into labor contracts that involve bondage or contracts that grant labor bondage as remediation in the case of default? These were once common practices; later I will show that such practices are compatible with both libertarian choice theory and welfare economics.[23] But those who think that the problem with a market in bonded labor is its incompatibility with a conception of equal human status have reason to prohibit such contractual arrangements.

EQUAL STATUS IN A DEMOCRACY

Social rights in their modern form imply an invasion of contract by status, the subordination of market price to social justice, the replacement of the free bargain by the declaration of rights.[24]

The preconditions for equal status as citizens in a democracy are more demanding than those needed for people to interact in horizontal relationships based on their reciprocal self-interest and equal moral worth. According to the conception of citizenship developed by the British social theorist T. H. Marshall, citizenship not only includes formal legal freedoms, but also a set of social rights with respect to health care, education, housing, and a decent minimum of income. These latter rights, he claimed, are needed to make one a full member of one's society. I think Marshall is correct: an equal right to vote has little effective meaning if some voters are too badly educated to read a ballot; citizenship means little for the destitute if society is so structured that they have no opportunity to share in society's benefits.

According to Marshall's view, the status of equal citizenship requires that all have (1) equal basic political rights and freedoms, including rights to speech and participation in the political process; (2) equal rights and freedoms within civil society, including rights to own property; and (3) equal rights to a threshold of economic welfare and to "share to the full in the social heritage and to live the life of a civilized being according to the standards prevailing in the society."[25]

Marshall viewed citizenship as a given status, not a privilege that depends on individual virtue or achievement. Citizenship gives to all within its ambit a single set of rights, irrespective of their wealth or family origin. While markets can be supportive of equal citizenship understood in this sense, whether or not they are so depends on the background circumstances, property rights, and regulations within which they operate. Someone who is desperately poor might agree to an exchange that requires her to function as an around-the-clock domestic servant or to bond her labor to obtain a loan at usurious rates that she can never hope to repay. The fate of such a person may be little different from that of a serf under feudalism.

In thinking about the preconditions of equal citizenship, it is important to think in terms of general social practices and not acts. For example, there may seem to be no problem with allowing a single person to work for whatever wages and hours she chooses, yet the existence of minimum wages and maximum hours laws may be necessary to preserve a threshold of economic welfare "according to the standards prevailing in the society,"[26] and to enhance the bargaining power of the poorest people in society to protect them from exploitation and abuse. Or consider another example: even if it makes sense in an individual instance for a poor family to put its children to work, when child labor is adopted as a widespread social practice it drives down adult wages, making it virtually impossible for poor parents to refrain from sending their children to work. Rather than seeing a person's market choices as exogenous variables, the choices we actually have open to us may depend on other market choices being blocked.[27]

The transfer of income and wealth will not always be sufficient to maintain the conditions for citizen's equality; here the insights of specific egalitarians like Michael Walzer, Elizabeth Anderson, and Michael Sandel are important. Consider the case of distributing primary and secondary school education through a market. Lack of education is an extremely harmful outcome in terms of democratic citizenship: a very poorly educated person will be incompetent as a juror and a voter and have little or no access to the basic opportunities and liberties associated with full membership in her society. But giving money, even a great deal of money, to a child who has not been educated will not compensate for her lack of education, even if cash is what she (as an adult) now herself prefers. Not only does it not replace the personal and social development that education might have enabled for her, but it does not turn her into a citizen who can participate competently and meaningfully in democratic self-governance. (Nor can we be sure that if money were transferred to a parent he would choose to use that money to keep his children in school. While some data suggest that many parents do keep their children in school when they have enough money to feed their families, some parents are selfish or shortsighted, perhaps lacking information about education's true costs and benefits because they had little formal education themselves.)

These are all reasons for *not* distributing primary and secondary education solely through a market system, but enforcing it as a mandatory requirement. If our concern is with avoiding outcomes that undermine the conditions for citizens to interact as equals, then there is a powerful argument for guaranteeing access to a certain level of goods—education, health care, opportunities, rights, liberties, and physical security—even if some citizens would prefer to trade and sell these goods, or the opportunity to access these goods, to the highest bidder. While markets can supplement the supply of these goods in many cases, my point is that access to these goods should not depend only on individual preferences or income. The conditions for equal citizenship cannot be cashed out in terms of a generic good like money or utilitarian welfare; in addition to some level of income, they require that some goods be distributed in kind and that, in some cases, the distribution be more or less equal.

At the same time I would not defend the distribution of education or health care in terms of the idea that these goods are corrupted through sale. A public right to education is in theory compatible with the existence of a complementary or supplementary private education system.[28] Instead my argument draws on Marshall's suggestion that some goods function as prerequisites for *full inclusion* in society, for counting as an equal member. A person who lacks a certain level of education or access to medical care or physical security is not only ill-equipped to navigate her own life and values, but also faces substantial impediments to participation in the economy and to participating in public debates about social choices. Such a person is vulnerable to exploitation and manipulation by others and dependent on luck or the will of benefactors to meet her basic needs.

In addition to supplementing market distributions in goods such as education and health care, we may have reason to *block certain market exchanges altogether* if citizens are to be equals. Consider votes in a democracy. No one defends the outright sale of voting, even though it can be argued that such sale is consistent with efficiency and freedom.[29] The interesting question is why. I think there are two main answers to this question, associated with two different ideals of democratic citizenship.

The first answer points out that the regulative idea of democracy is that citizens are equals engaged in a common cooperative project of governing themselves together. Thus citizens participate with others on an equal footing in deciding on the laws and policies that will govern them. A market in votes would have the predictable consequence of giving the rich disproportionate power over others since the poor would be far more likely than the rich to sell their political power. Indeed one rationale for secret ballots is to make contracts about votes unenforceable, thus protecting the poor and vulnerable from pressure to sell. If political, regulatory, judicial, and legal decision mechanisms were literally up for sale, this would concentrate political power in the hands of a few.

A second answer pushes in a more republican direction, interpreting democracy not merely as government among equals but as a means of determining the common good.[30] On this view of democracy, *votes are acts of political co-deliberation*. Even if a vote market were not monopolized by the rich, we would still have a reason to proscribe vote trading on the grounds that voting is not about the aggregation of private interests; it is an act undertaken only after collectively deliberating about what is in the common good. Distributing votes according to preferences views citizens as consumers, not co-deliberators.

Both conceptions of democracy require that some markets be blocked and others be highly regulated. Both conceptions would block markets in votes, judicial offices, legislative offices, and voluntary slavery. Moreover, both conceptions would regulate markets governing the production and distribution of political information and markets governing access to legislative office and the opportunities associated with political influence, although to varying degrees.[31] But these two conceptions might well differ on the treatment of military service as a market good. On the republican conception of democracy, there is something deeply troubling about the ways in which today's volunteer army shares some attributes with a mercenary army. Rather than seeing military service as an obligation of citizenship, today's soldiers are drawn from a small segment of the population that is largely working class.

Just as democracies made up of equal citizens require blocks on markets in votes or people, a related argument might be made that some markets need to be blocked or highly regulated if people are to develop the *capacities* that they need to participate effectively in civil and political society. Human beings are malleable in a way that goods such as apples are not.[32] We do not usually need to worry about the noneconomic effects of a market on the apples exchanged,[33] but we do need to worry about whether a particular kind of market produces or supports passivity, alienation, or a ruthless egoism. Labor markets may be structured so as to accustom people to being pushed around and managed by others. Widespread markets in women's reproductive or sexual capacities (including quid pro quo sexual harassment contracts) might amplify gender inequalities by entrenching and deepening negative stereotypes about women.[34] Unregulated education markets are compatible with children being treated as and raised as servile dependents. We need to pay special attention to cases like these, for they pose potential threats to the stable reproduction of democratic citizenship over time. Indeed the democratic state has an interest in withholding its support from institutions that cultivate subordination and servitude, even if those institutions are not strictly illegal.

REGULATING MARKETS, BLOCKING MARKETS

How should we decide what approach to take to a noxious market? Obviously which policies it makes sense to adopt depends on the source of the market's noxiousness, which of the four parameters is in play. We need to tailor our response to the particular problems with that market. For example, if weak agency is the problem with a particular market, then we may want to undertake measures that increase information. If underlying vulnerability is a problem, we may want to redistribute income or create supplementary alternatives to market provision. Regulating a market is often the best way to address a market's noxiousness. At the same time, some problems with a market may be best addressed by closing off the ability of agents to trade in that market at all. Some markets undermine the social context in which people are able to interact on terms of equality.

In such cases we need to address not merely distributions, but also the underlying property rights of the transacting agents. To illustrate this, let's look briefly at child labor, a case I take up in more detail later in this book. In our world child labor often arises on the basis of destitution. But even in a world without destitution child labor would be problematic. Although many libertarian economists often view freedom as the freedom to participate in the market, they are often blind to the fact that individuals are not born with all the required capacities for exercising agency and making choices (including market choices) already developed. The achievement of even a minimal threshold level of decision-making powers requires support from a variety of sources, including parents and the state: nurturing, help in developing the capacities for understanding and weighing alternatives, help in developing the ability to see oneself as an agent worthy of having choices, and attaining an adequate level of education. Child labor fails to promote and often blocks the development of these capacities.

CASES: THE *TITANIC* AND TOXIC WASTE

With my framework in mind, I'd like to return to two examples invoked earlier in this book: the *Titanic*'s market in safety and Larry Summers' memo advocating a market in toxic waste.

Beginning with the *Titanic*, recall that individuals booking passage were allowed to buy tickets with or without the guarantee of access to a lifeboat in the event of an emergency. Their market choices can be understood as a function of their preferences given their resources and their information. In the case of the actual *Titanic*, there was weak agency (based on faulty information about the ship's "unsinkability") and extremely harmful individual outcomes (drowning when the ship went down). These considerations give us good grounds for treating the distribution of safety according to ticket price aboard the *Titanic* as an instance of a noxious market.

But suppose that we increased agency and redistributed income so that all could easily afford the price of a first-class ticket on the boat. Is there any reason why it might make sense to prefer a more constrained system for the distribution of safety, whereby all are prevented from making choices that they would take as individuals if those options were available? As I argued in chapter 3, I don't think that paternalism gives us a strong reason to forbid people from making decisions to forgo access to lifeboats on the *Titanic*.

A commitment to equal citizenship, however, does presuppose that there are some rights that individuals cannot contract away. This is because, if these rights were contracted away, some individuals would be subject to servitude and subordination. Employers, for example, could demand that their employees travel in the cheapest possible manner, even if that means forgoing a lifeboat. And other individuals would find themselves placed in situations where they would have to treat people as less than equal, pushing them out of the lifeboat, for example.

Note, however, that protecting people from humiliating subordination and servitude can be secured in this example by providing a floor of provision, a (literal?) safety net, compatible with large (market-generated) inequalities above the floor. As I mentioned, in his discussion of the *Titanic* example Thomas Schelling concludes that it is the *inequality* aboard the ship that is problematic, not the inadequate safety floor: "Those who risk their lives at sea and cannot afford a safe ship should perhaps not be denied the opportunity to entrust themselves to a cheaper ship without lifeboats; but if some people cannot afford the price of passage with lifeboats, and some people can, they should not travel on the same ship."[35]

Schelling seems to be suggesting that if we allow a market to distribute safety, then we must ensure that it gives the same safety to everyone, or at least to everyone within the community. We have already seen that there is an argument that connects equal provision of votes and basic political rights to democratic citizenship. But it seems puzzling to conclude that we need to equalize specific goods such as safety for the sake of such citizenship.

I can think of two basic reasons that democratic societies might want to secure the equal provision of certain specific goods. The first reason is that inequalities in some goods, such as education or political influence, sit too uneasily with the idea that we are each other's equals. For example, it may be hard to maintain that conviction if excesses of privileged schooling impose great differences on children's future lives. Education is simply too important to participation and inclusion in society's institutions, and relative inequalities can confine the worst off to occupy lowly positions. Significant educational inequalities in the quality of K–12 education do not seem fair, because they suggest that some children matter a great deal less to society than others. Of course, there are disagreements about such cases and about how much educational inequality is compatible with a democratic society. But my point is that there are instances in which inequalities in some goods affront the idea that people are the equals of their neighbors: they reek of caste like privileges. Sometimes the goods that affront equality may be conventionally determined, as Michael Walzer argued. For example, many Americans would look with great distaste on the idea of a market in positions on ticket lines at movie theaters, even if the introduction of such a market did not change their own relative position on the line.

The fact that everyone irrespective of income has to wait his or her own turn on the line for a movie is a convention that has come to symbolize our equality. (If you doubt this, just try to buy your way into the line.)

The second reason concerns the effects of markets on the aggregation of interests, an effect that we saw invoked by the republican conception of democratic citizenship. Markets enable people to opt out of relationships with particular producers and to take up new relationships, to find new ways of satisfying their preferences. Albert Hirschman used the term "exit" to describe this function that markets provide, and it is an important mechanism for enhancing freedom as well as economic improvement (because exit signals dissatisfaction, at least relative to available alternatives).[36] Hirschman counterposed "exit" with "voice," by which he had in mind trying to change another person's behavior by directly alerting him to a problem. But we might think of another function of voice; as in the case of voting, voice can play an important role in shaping and forming common interests.[37] Exit via a market might sometimes enhance common interests (as when consumers withdraw their support for a shoddy product), but it might also diminish the possibility of forming or satisfying those common interests.

Recent research by Susanna Loeb on school financing provides a good illustration of this phenomenon.[38] Among the funding models for education that she considers is one in which school districts receive a uniform per pupil funding grant from the state and then are allowed to raise unlimited additional funds. Although this system looks attractive because it allows voters to pursue their preferred spending levels while maintaining a minimum funding level for all students, Loeb argues that it may not be sustainable because the high-wealth districts may lose their incentive to support state funding. People in these districts might be rationally motivated to vote for politicians who support lower levels of state provision since much of their aid is based on their own fund-raising and local taxes. In that case the ability of those who are left to provide for public education on the basis of state provision would decline.

As this example shows, the stratification and sorting inevitably produced by a market can be especially problematic in cases where one person's prospects for attaining some important good is closely connected to another person's decisions. This is especially true in a representative form of government. For example, we may suspect that when officials can insulate their own children from the effects of poor public schooling or unsafe neighborhoods they may find it easier to support cuts to state budgets in those areas than they would if their own families were directly affected by such cuts.

In a recent paper on risk and safety and the "*Titanic* puzzle" I am concerned with here, Jonathan Wolff cites work by John Adams showing that the initial effect of mandating seatbelts for car drivers but not for passengers was an *increase* in the number of passenger deaths.[39] Because the drivers were now safer, they took more risks, which fell on others for whom the risks had not changed. Wolff points out that this analysis also applies to the case of safety aboard ships:

> If the Captain was assured of a place in the lifeboat, or even that the people he most cared about were assured of their place, then he may well have steered a riskier course than otherwise. This is an analogue to the familiar problem of "moral hazard" in insurance, reducing people's incentives to take care. This may well be why the Captain is supposed to go down with the ship, or, at least, be the last one off.[40]

When decision makers can buy private solutions for themselves in education, police protection, and even garbage collection, this may have problematic consequences for the public provision of these goods. To the extent that this is true, it may be that the best way to ensure that the public's interests are taken into account is to give both the public and the decision maker the same interests. At any rate, as this example shows, we need to be attentive to the effects of markets on motivations that affect actions. Sometimes allowing people to sort and segment into diverse groups will undermine the solidarity that is needed to provide for a public good.

Mandating the equal provision of goods is at least theoretically compatible with having those goods supplied to a large extent through regulated markets. Moreover banning a market will sometimes have costs in terms of other values people care about; there will be trade-offs. As I have repeatedly stressed, markets are engines of growth and have important roles to play with respect to our equality and freedom. In some cases the requirements of equal citizenship will push us to a floor of provision, not strict equality in the distribution of the good. In other cases that may not be so; we may care about the ceiling as well as the floor because we want to constrain the amount of inequality to maintain a healthy democracy. Often empirical considerations will be paramount, such as the effects of the inequality on the prospects of those worst off. Some markets trade in things that no democratic society can countenance; others need to be regulated, constrained, or supplemented with other mechanisms if the preconditions for a democratic society are to be maintained.

Return to the toxic waste market proposed in Larry Summers' memo that I discussed in chapter 3. Summers argued that trade in toxic waste would benefit the poor countries and indeed make both the less developed countries and the developed countries better off. The exchange appears to be a Pareto improvement. Why, then, did the public release of the memo occasion such uproar? Why did so many people view the proposed market as clearly noxious? How does the framework in this chapter throw light on the public response? There are three reasons for thinking that a toxic waste market is noxious.

In the first place, there is the unequal *vulnerability* of the bargaining positions of the rich and poor countries. Trade in toxic waste holds up a mirror to global inequality. Because of that disparity the rich countries are able to exploit the vulnerabilities of the less developed countries (LDCs). Critics might suspect that, were they not so poor, the LDCs would not consent to the transfer of toxic waste to their lands, or perhaps they would hold out for better terms.[41]

In the second place, there is likely to be *weak agency*. Many poor countries are run by corrupt governments that do not represent the interests of their citizens. When accepting toxic waste in exchange for money, the interests of these citizens, or at the least the poorest and most vulnerable citizens, might well be neglected. As Daniel Hausman and Michael McPherson note in their discussion of it, Summers' memo implicitly applies the Pareto criterion to the rich and poor nations as a whole.[42] This is, as they write, a "cheat": if we apply the Pareto criterion to individuals, some individuals, very poor individuals within the LDCs into whose neighborhoods the waste is likely to be dumped, might be made very much worse off by the trade.[43] In addition to the weak agency of the poor, the leaders of these countries (as well as the leaders of the rich countries) may not have adequate knowledge about the long-term effects of storing toxic waste.

Vulnerability and weak agency concern the *sources* of an international market in toxic waste. But we may also worry about the *consequences* of such a market. So in the third place there is the possibility for extremely *harmful outcomes to individuals*. Shipping and storing toxic waste, at least some forms of it, are likely to have very bad consequences.[44] Many people might die or suffer in terms of their health. For other forms of toxic waste there may be a risk of serious future harm. If this is so, then future generations, who are not themselves parties to the agreement, might bear the costs of extremely harmful outcomes. Additionally, if toxic waste is exported to poor countries that have less capacity to monitor and regulate pollution, this may lead to more pollution, and even more harm, overall than would be the case if the waste stayed in the developed world.

On the other hand, it is hard to *directly* connect such markets to the idea of harmful social outcomes, that is, to the undermining of equal status. At the same time, we might wonder if the readiness of country A to transfer toxic waste to country B fails to show equal concern and respect for the citizens of country B. Would citizens be as likely to transfer toxic waste to those in their own backyard, that is, to themselves? (Similar concerns, of course, can be raised about the location of toxic waste facilities in wealthy countries, which tends to be in very poor neighborhoods.)

THE LIMITS OF MY APPROACH

My account analyzes noxious market in terms of extremely harmful outcomes for individuals and for society (including the special case of equal status in a democratic society), weak agency (including incomplete information), and vulnerabilities that give some people significant power over others. It grounds a moral distinction between types of markets, but one that is not primarily based on the special nature of certain goods, but on considerations that cut across goods. (Thus on my account credit or housing markets may become more objectionable than sex markets.) But my account is also limited in certain crucial respects.

First, as I have emphasized, we cannot immediately conclude from the fact that a market is noxious that we ought legally to ban it. Even if a market interfered with or failed to promote certain values, banning it might be worse overall from the point of view of those same values. Our policy response must depend on what the alternative to a market is likely to be, as well as on the particular problematic parameters in play. Some markets are simply incompatible with securing the equality of status of individuals and should be prohibited; some are incompatible with equality of status in a democracy of equal citizens; others require regulation, including redistribution of income and property. Many markets are noxious only in a given context; instead of changing the market we might try to change the context. Even in cases where there do not seem to be good reasons in favor of allowing a particular market, it may be impractical to ban it. For example, in the case of drug markets such as for heroin and cocaine, where the transaction costs are low and the market exchange is easy to enforce,[45] a rich black market can and does exist even in the presence of state attempts to block such markets. Thus, although there will be cases in which we will want to ban the particular noxious market, in other cases it will make sense to respond to a noxious market by legislating a safety net, or by educational policies designed to increase information, or by mechanisms aimed at increasing accountability, or by tax-and-transfer schemes to reduce inequality. And sometimes we will simply want to ensure that nonmarket mechanisms for providing a good exist side by side with market mechanisms.

Second, some of the parameters I have appealed to can conflict with each other or with other values. People will have different views of the appropriate trade-offs between the different parameters, as well as between these parameters and other values. For example, people will disagree about whether to prioritize increasing agency or decreasing vulnerability.

Third, I have not settled on exactly how to operationalize these values; for example, I have not here specified a numerically precise interpretation of how much underlying vulnerability market agents must have for a market to become noxious. The characterizing parameters plainly admit of degrees, and there is room for reasonable disagreement as to when a particular market is no longer acceptable. Further, context matters a great deal for the noxiousness of any particular market. Consider large inequalities of wealth produced by a labor market. These inequalities might be blocked from translating into extremely harmful outcomes for equal citizenship in a democratic society by laws regulating the financing of political campaigns, by ensuring a fair distribution of educational resources so that wealth does not translate into a fixed intergenerational caste, and by regulations aimed at securing a high enough minimum income so that no one is impoverished.

Fourth, it should be evident that my account is sensitive to changing circumstances so that markets that are currently noxious may emerge under other conditions as perfectly acceptable (or the reverse).

Fifth, it must be admitted that other accounts of noxious markets are possible; I surveyed some of them in earlier chapters. Some may wish to question placing so much moral weight on our intuitive reactions to particular markets as I have done, pointing out that people were once horrified by the idea of life insurance. Perhaps many of our reactions are little more than an irrational repugnance at that which we dislike. Still others may find particular markets objectionable that do not seem to run afoul of any of the criteria that I have proposed, for example, a market in supermodel eggs or Nobel Prize–winner's sperm or a market in a good whose sale violates their deeply held religious values.[46] By contrast, my account focuses on widely shared values—preventing extreme harm and vulnerability—as well as considerations that democratic citizens, with differing moral frameworks and conceptions of life, have reason to find especially problematic.

My analysis in this chapter has implications for the role of markets in theories of equality. Egalitarians should focus on more than the distribution of things, but also attend to the people who have those things and their relationships with one other. Many markets are rightly celebrated as mechanisms of freedom and efficiency, yet some markets traffic in things that no decent society should allow its members to be without, some deepen objectionable hierarchies of class and privilege, and some undermine democratic values. In thinking about the scope of markets we need to pay attention not only to the distributive outcomes of different markets but also to the relationships between people that these markets enable and support.[47] Ultimately, these questions about the limits of markets are not merely questions of costs and benefits but of how we define our society, of who we are and what we care about.

Unfortunately, many proponents and critics of markets have operated on a high level of abstraction in which all markets function in more or less the same way. But different markets have particular features and raise different moral concerns. The second part of this book uses this framework to examine in more detail particular markets—in reproduction and sex, in child labor and bonded labor, and in human body parts—that many people find problematic.

PART III

5

Markets in Women's Reproductive Labor

In the past several decades American society has begun to experiment with markets in women's reproductive labor, along with markets in women's eggs. Many people believe that markets in women's reproductive labor, as exemplified by contract pregnancy,[1] are more problematic than other currently accepted labor markets. I call this the *asymmetry thesis* because its proponents believe that there ought to be an asymmetry between our treatment of markets in reproductive labor and our treatment of markets in other forms of labor. Advocates of the asymmetry thesis hold that treating reproductive labor as a commodity, as something subject to the supply-and-demand principles that govern economic markets, is worse than treating other types of human labor as commodities. Is the asymmetry thesis true? And, if so, what are the reasons for thinking that it is true? Can my account of noxious markets be useful in analyzing this case?

I believe that the asymmetry thesis both captures strong intuitions that exist in our society and provides a plausible argument against contract pregnancy. My aims in this chapter are to criticize several popular ways of defending the asymmetry thesis and to offer an alternative defense based on the idea of equal status.[2] Many feminists hold that the asymmetry thesis is true because they think it is intuitive that women's reproductive labor is a special kind of labor that should not be treated according to market norms. They draw a sharp dividing line between women's reproductive labor and human labor in general: whereas human labor may be bought and sold, women's reproductive labor is intrinsically not a commodity. According to these views, contract pregnancy allows for the extension of the market into the private sphere of sexuality and reproduction. This intrusion of the economic into the personal is seen as improper: it fails to respect the intrinsic, special nature of reproductive labor. As one writer has put it, "When women's labor is treated as a commodity, the women who perform it are degraded."[3]

Contract pregnancy provides a good test case for evaluating views about the limits of markets based on the meaning or intrinsic nature of that labor. I argue that these views are the wrong way to defend the asymmetry thesis. Although I agree with the intuition that markets in women's reproductive labor are more troubling than other labor markets, I provide an alternative account of why this should be so. My analysis has four parts. In the first part I criticize those arguments that turn on the assumption that reproductive labor is a unique form of labor. I argue that there is no distinction between women's reproductive labor and human labor that is relevant to the debate about contract pregnancy. Moreover I argue that the sale of women's reproductive labor is not ipso facto degrading. Rather it becomes problematic only in a particular political and social context.[4] In the second part I criticize arguments in support of the asymmetry thesis that appeal to the nature of parental love. Here support for the asymmetry thesis is taken to derive from a special bond between mothers and children; the bond between a mother and her child is different from the bond between a worker and his product. In response I argue that the bond between mothers and children is more complicated than critics of contract pregnancy have assumed and that, moreover, contract pregnancy does not cause parents (or the other parties to the contract) to view children as commodities. In the third part I examine concerns about contract pregnancy's potential for extremely harmful consequences for children. Although this argument has merit, I argue that its validity is still far from certain. In this section I also point out some analogies between contract pregnancy and the booming industry in reproductive services, especially in vitro fertilization (IVF), which raise similar concerns.

The first three parts of this chapter argue that the various reasons given in the literature for banning contract pregnancy on the basis of its special nature are inadequate. Nonetheless there does seem to be something more problematic about pregnancy contracts than other types of labor contract. The question is, What is the basis for and the significance of this intuition? And what, apart from its agreement with our intuitions, can be said in favor of the asymmetry thesis?

In the fourth part I argue that the asymmetry thesis is true, but that the reason it is true has not been properly understood. The asymmetry thesis should be defended on external and not intrinsic or essentialist grounds. Drawing on the theory that I developed earlier in this book, I argue that society's pervasive gender inequality is primary to the explanation of what is wrong with contract pregnancy. Markets in women's reproductive labor are troubling to the extent that they reinforce gender hierarchies—unequal status between men and women—in a way that other, accepted labor markets do not. My defense of the asymmetry thesis thus rests on the way that contract pregnancy reinforces asymmetrical social relations of gender hierarchy and inequality in American society. However, it may be that not all of the features of contract pregnancy that make it troubling concern gender. Contract pregnancy may also heighten racial inequalities and have harmful effects on the other children of the gestational mother.[5] I do not address these points in detail here. However, these considerations would have to be addressed in order to generate a complete argument against contract pregnancy.

THE SPECIAL NATURE OF REPRODUCTIVE LABOR

A wide range of attacks on contract pregnancy turns out to share a single premise: that the *intrinsic* nature of reproductive labor is different from that of other kinds of labor. Critics claim that reproductive labor is not just another kind of work; they argue that unlike other forms of labor, reproductive labor is not properly regarded as a commodity. I refer to this thesis as the *essentialist thesis*, as it holds that reproductive labor is by its nature something that should not be bought and sold.

In contrast to the essentialist thesis, recall that modern economic theories tend to treat the market as "theoretically all encompassing."[6] Such theories tend to treat all goods and capacities as exchangeable commodities, at least in principle.[7] If we accept the logic of the economic approach to human behavior, we seem led to endorse a world in which everything is potentially for sale: body parts, reproductive labor, toxic waste, children, and even votes.[8] Many people are repulsed by such a world. But what exactly is the problem with it? Defenders of the essentialist thesis provide the starting point for a counterattack: not all human goods are commodities. In particular, human reproductive labor is improperly treated as a commodity. When reproductive labor is purchased on the market it is inappropriately valued.

The essentialist thesis provides support for the asymmetry thesis. The nature of reproductive labor is taken to be fundamentally different from that of labor in general. In particular proponents of the essentialist thesis hold that women's reproductive labor should be respected and not used.[9] What is it about women's reproductive labor that singles it out for a type of respect that precludes market use?

Some versions of the essentialist thesis focus on the biological or naturalistic features of women's reproductive labor:

- Women's reproductive labor has both a genetic and a gestational component.[10] Other forms of labor do not involve a genetic relationship between the worker and her product.
- Whereas much human labor is voluntary at virtually every step, many of the phases of the reproductive process are involuntary. Ovulation, conception, gestation, and birth occur without the conscious direction of the mother.
- Reproductive labor extends over a period of approximately nine months; other types of labor do not typically necessitate such a long-term commitment.
- Reproductive labor involves significant restrictions of a woman's behavior during pregnancy; other forms of labor are less invasive with respect to the worker's body.

These characteristics of reproductive labor do not, however, establish the asymmetry thesis.

- With respect to the genetic relationship between the reproductive worker and her product, most critics object to contract pregnancy even where the so-called surrogate is not the genetic mother. In fact many critics consider "gestational surrogacy," in which a woman is implanted with a preembryo formed in vitro from donated gametes, more troubling than those cases in which the surrogate is also the genetic mother.[11] In addition men also have a genetic tie to their offspring, yet many proponents of the asymmetry thesis would not oppose the selling of sperm.
- With respect to the degree to which reproductive labor is involuntary, there are many forms of work in which workers do not have control over the work process; for example, mass-production

workers cannot generally control the speed of the assembly line, and they have no involvement in the overall purpose of their activity.

- With regard to the length of the contract's duration, some forms of labor involve contracts of even longer duration, for example, book contracts and military service agreements. Like pregnancy contracts, these are not contracts in which one can quit at the end of the day. Yet presumably most proponents of the essentialist thesis would not find commercial publishing contracts objectionable.

- With regard to invasions into the woman's body, nonreproductive labor can also involve incursions into the body of the worker. To take an obvious example, athletes sign contracts that give team owners considerable control over the athletes' diet and behavior and allow owners to conduct periodic tests for drug use. Yet there is little controversy over the sale of athletic capacities.[12] Sales of blood also run afoul of a noninvasiveness condition. In fact leaving aside the genetic component of reproductive labor, voluntary military service involves shares all the other features mentioned by critics. Do we really want to object to such military service on *essentialist* grounds?[13]

Carole Pateman suggests a different way of defending the asymmetry thesis as the basis for an argument against contract pregnancy. Rather than focusing on the naturalistic, biological properties of reproductive labor, she argues that a woman's reproductive labor is more "integral" to her identity than her other productive capacities. Pateman first sketches this argument with respect to prostitution:

> Womanhood, too, is confirmed in sexual activity, and when a prostitute contracts out use of her body she is thus selling herself in a very real sense. Women's selves are involved in prostitution in a different manner from the involvement of the self in other occupations. Workers of all kinds may be more or less "bound up in their work," but the integral connection between sexuality and sense of the self means that, for self-protection, a prostitute must distance herself from her sexual use.[14]

Pateman's objection to prostitution rests on a claim about the intimate relation between a woman's sexuality and her identity. It is by virtue of this tie, Pateman believes, that sex should not be treated as an alienable commodity. Is her claim true? How do we decide which of a woman's attributes or capacities are essential to her identity and which are not? In particular, why should we consider sexuality more integral to self than friendship, family, religion, nationality, and work?[15] After all, we allow commodification in each of these spheres. Rabbis and priests may view their religion as central to their identity, but they often accept payment for performing religious services. Does Pateman think that *all* activities that fall within these spheres and bear an intimate relationship to a person's identity should not be sold?

Pateman's argument appears to support the asymmetry thesis by suggesting that a woman's sexuality is *more* intimately related to her identity then are her other capacities. Yet she provides no explicit argument for this suggestion. Indeed at times her argument seems intended not so much to support the asymmetry thesis as to support a more general thesis against buying and selling those capacities that are closely tied to the identity of persons. But this more general argument is implausible. It would not allow individuals to sell their paintings or their book manuscripts.[16] It would prevent people who love their professions from selling their services.

The British government-commissioned *Warnock Report on Human Fertilisation and Embryology* links reproductive labor to a person's dignity, claiming, "It is inconsistent with human dignity that a woman should use her uterus for financial profit."[17] But why is selling the use of a woman's uterus "undignified," while selling the use of images of her body in a television commercial is not?

The *Warnock Report*'s argument appeals to the idea that women's sexuality and reproduction are worthy of a kind of respect. Granted, but the idea of respect alone does not entail the conclusion that reproductive labor should not be treated as a commodity. As I argued in chapter 3, we sometimes sell things that we also respect. For example, I think that my teaching talents should be respected, but I don't object to being paid for teaching on such grounds. Giving my teaching a price does not diminish the other ways my teaching has value. Giving my teaching a price does not diminish the sense in which I have value.

I believe that it is a mistake to focus, as does the *Warnock Report*, on maintaining certain cultural values without examining critically the specific social circumstances from which those values emerge. Thus the view that selling sexual or reproductive capacities is "degrading" may reflect society's attempts to control women and their sexuality. At the very least, the relations between particular views of sexuality and the maintenance of gender inequality must be taken into account. This is especially important insofar as one powerful defense of contract pregnancy rests on its alleged empowering of women.

THE SPECIAL BONDS OF MOTHERHOOD

Sometimes what critics of pregnancy contracts have in mind is not the effect of such contracts on the relationship between reproductive labor and a woman's sense of self, but their effect on her views (and ours) of the mother-fetus and mother-child bond. On this view, what is wrong with commodifying reproductive labor is that it corrupts motherhood, the relationships between mothers and their offspring. Further, it leads to a view of children as fungible objects.

Mothers and Fetuses

Critics of contract pregnancy contend that the relationship between a mother and a fetus is not simply a biochemical relationship or a matter of contingent physical connection. They also point out that the relationship between a mother and a fetus is different from that between a worker and her material product. The long months of pregnancy and the experience of childbirth are part of forming a relationship with the child-to-be. Elizabeth Anderson makes an argument along these lines. She suggests that the commodification of reproductive labor makes pregnancy an alienated form of labor for the women who perform it; selling her reproductive labor alienates a woman from her "normal" and justified emotions.[18] Rather than viewing pregnancy as an evolving relationship with a child-to-be, contract pregnancy reinforces a vision of the pregnant woman as a mere "home" or an "environment."[19] The sale of reproductive labor thus distorts the nature of the bond between the mother and the developing fetus by misrepresenting the nature of a woman's reproductive labor as a commodity. What should we make of this argument?

Surely there is truth in the claim that pregnancy contracts may reinforce a vision of women as baby machines or mere wombs. Various court rulings with respect to contract pregnancy have tended to acknowledge women's contribution to reproduction only insofar as it is identical to men's: in terms of the donation of genetic material. The gestational labor involved in reproduction is explicitly ignored in such rulings. Thus Mary Beth Whitehead won back her parental rights in the "Baby M" case because the New Jersey Supreme Court acknowledged her genetic contribution; the fact that she was the gestational mother was not decisive.[20]

However, as I will argue below, the concern about the discounting of women's reproductive labor is best posed in terms of a principle of equality. By treating women's reproductive contribution as identical to men's when it is not, women are not in fact being treated equally. But those who conceptualize the problem with pregnancy contracts in terms of the degradation of the mother-fetus relationship rather than in terms of the equality of men and women tend to interpret the social practice of pregnancy in terms of a maternal "instinct," a sacrosanct bonding that takes place between a mother and her child-to-be. However, not all women bond with their fetuses. Some women abort them.

Indeed there is a dilemma for those who wish to use the mother-fetus bond to condemn pregnancy contracts while endorsing a woman's right to choose an abortion. They must hold that it is acceptable to abort a fetus but not to sell it. Although the *Warnock Report* takes no stand on the issue of abortion, it uses present abortion law as a term of reference in considering contract pregnancy. Because abortion is currently legal in England, the *Report*'s position has this paradoxical consequence: one can kill a fetus, but one cannot contract to sell it.[21] One possible response to this objection would be to claim that women do not bond with their fetuses in the first trimester. But the fact remains that some women never bond with their fetuses; some women even fail to bond with their babies after they deliver them.

Are we really sure that we know which emotions pregnancy "normally" involves? Whereas married women are portrayed as nurturing and altruistic, society has historically stigmatized the unwed mother as selfish, neurotic, and unconcerned with the welfare of her child. Until quite recently social pressure was directed at unwed mothers to surrender their children after birth. Thus married women who gave up their children were seen as "abnormal" and unfeeling, and unwed mothers who failed to surrender their children were seen as selfish.[22] Assumptions of "normal" maternal bonding may reinforce traditional views of the family and a woman's proper role within it.

Mothers and Children

A somewhat different argument against contract pregnancy contends that markets in women's reproductive labor entail the commodification of children. Once again the special nature of reproduction is used to support the asymmetry thesis; the special nature of maternal love is held to be incompatible with market relations. Children should be loved by their mothers, yet commercial surrogacy responds to and promotes other motivations. Indeed critics argue that markets in reproductive labor give people the opportunity to "shop" for children. Prospective womb-infertile couples will seek out arrangements that "maximize" the value of their babies; sex, eye color, and race will be assessed in terms of market considerations. Having children on the basis of such preferences reflects an inferior conception of parenthood. It brings commercial attitudes into a sphere properly governed by love.

What are the reasons people seek to enter into contract pregnancy arrangements? As far as we know, most couples and single people who make use of surrogates want simply to have a child that is "theirs," which means for them genetically related to them. Furthermore, with respect to the charge of shopping, it might be pointed out that our adoption system reflects people's preferences about the race, sex, and ability of their prospective children; it is much harder, for example, for an older black child to be adopted than for a white infant. Such preferences may well be objectionable, but few argue that parents should have no choice in the child they adopt or that adoption should be prohibited because it gives rein to such preferences.[23] Instead we regulate adoption to protect the basic interests of children and we forbid the differential payment of fees to agencies on the basis of a child's ascribed characteristics. Why couldn't contract pregnancy be regulated in the same way?

Critics who wish to make an argument for the asymmetry thesis based on the nature of maternal love must defend a strong claim about the relationship between markets and love. In particular they must claim that even regulated markets in reproductive services will lead parents to love their children for the wrong reasons: love will be conditional on the child's having the "right" set of physical characteristics. But I suspect that most parents who receive their child through a contract pregnancy arrangement will love their child even if her characteristics are not what they expected.

Although I share the view that there is something problematic with the "shopping" attitude in the sphere of personal relations, it's another issue altogether as to whether we should legally block markets in which this attitude might be expressed. Individuals in our society seek partners with attributes ranging from a specified race and height to a musical taste for Chopin. Should we ban dating services that cater to such preferences?

Some critics associate contract pregnancy with baby selling. One popular argument runs thus: In contract pregnancy women not only sell their reproductive services, but also their babies. Because baby selling is wrong, this type of argument proceeds by the following syllogism: Baby selling is wrong, and contract pregnancy is a form of baby selling, therefore contract pregnancy is wrong. The *Warnock Report*, for example, makes this charge.[24]

But this argument is flawed. Pregnancy contracts do not enable fathers (or prospective mothers, women who are infertile or otherwise unable to conceive) to acquire full ownership rights over children. Even where there has been a financial payment for conceiving a child, the *child* cannot be treated as a mere commodity. The father (or prospective mother) cannot, for example, simply destroy or abandon the child. He (or she) is bound by the same norms and laws that govern the behavior of any child's biological or adoptive parents. Allowing women to contract for their reproductive services does not entail baby selling, if we mean by that a proxy for slavery.

Anderson has argued that what makes contract pregnancy a form of baby selling is the way such contracts treat the "mother's rights over her child."[25] Such contracts mandate that the mother relinquish her parental rights to the child. Furthermore such contracts can be enforced against the mother's wishes. Anderson argues that *forcing* a woman to part with her child and to cede her parental rights by sale entails treating the child as a mere commodity. Even if this is true, it does not necessarily lead to the conclusion that pregnancy contracts should be banned. Consider adoption. Adoption is frequently regulated to respect a change of mind of a biological parent within some specified time period. After that, the adoption agreement is enforced.[26] Contract pregnancy could be regulated in an analogous way, including an opt-out period to prevent harmful outcomes to a birth mother who has closely bonded with her child. It could also be structured to accord more with an open model in which all the parties to the contract retain contact with the child. Finally, pregnancy contracts could be required to increase participants' agency by providing detailed information about the emotional risks and costs associated with giving up a child.[27]

Finally, some writers have objected to pregnancy contracts on the ground that they must, by their nature, exploit women. They point to the fact that the compensation is very low, and that many of the women who agree to sell their reproductive labor have altruistic motivations. Anderson writes, "A kind of exploitation occurs when one party to a transaction is oriented toward the exchange of 'gift' values, while the other party operates in accordance with the norms of the market exchange of commodities."[28]

I have two responses to this line of argument. First, even if it is the case that all or most of the women who sell their reproductive labor are altruistically motivated,[29] it is implausible to argue that the other parties to the contract are motivated solely in accord with market values. The couples that use contract pregnancy are not seeking to make a profit, but to have a child. Some of them might even be willing to maintain an extended family relationship with the surrogate after the child's birth. Second, even if an asymmetry in motivation is established, it is also present in many types of service work; teaching, health care, and social work are all liable to result in "exploitation" of this sort. In all of these areas the problem is at least partially addressed by regulating working conditions and compensation. Why is contract pregnancy different?

THE CONSEQUENCES OF CONTRACT PREGNANCY FOR CHILDREN

The feminist philosopher Susan Moller Okin makes an argument against contract pregnancy that is based on its consequences for children. She argues that the problem with pregnancy contracts is that they do not consider the best interests of the child.[30] For Okin the asymmetry between reproductive labor and other forms of labor is based in the fact that only in the former are a child's interests directly at stake.

Okin's argument is important because it focuses on an externality of pregnancy contracts. Such contracts can affect children who are not parties to the contract. In the language of chapter 4, children are weak agents. Are these weak agents likely to be harmed? Putting aside the difficult question of what actually constitutes the child's best interests, it is not certain that a child's most basic or fundamental interests will always be served by remaining with his biological parents.[31] Some children may be better off separated from their biological parents when such parents are abusive. No one would claim that children should always remain with their biological parents. Nevertheless I agree with Okin that one problem with pregnancy contracts lies in their potential for weakening the biological ties that give children a secure place in the world.[32] If it can be shown that pregnancy contracts make children more vulnerable, for example, by encouraging parental exit, then such a consideration might contribute to the case for restricting or prohibiting such contracts. Such an argument will have nothing to do with the special nature of reproductive labor, nor will it have to do with the special biological relationship between a parent and a child. It will remain valid even where the child bears no genetic relation to its parents. Children are vulnerable and dependent, and this vulnerability justifies the moral obligations parents have toward them. Although this objection can be used to support the asymmetry thesis, it is important to note that weak agency and vulnerability are found throughout the social world; they are not unique to the spheres of the family, sex, and reproduction.

Nonetheless this objection does point out a difference between reproductive labor and other forms of labor. Does it justify prohibiting contract pregnancy? One of the difficulties with evaluating pregnancy contracts in terms of their effects on children is that we still have very little empirical evidence of these effects. The first reported case of a pregnancy contract in the United States occurred in 1976.[33] Even with the more established practice of artificial insemination, no conclusive research is available on the effects of donor anonymity on the child. Nor are we sure how different family structures, including single-parent and alternative families and adoption, affect children. We should be wary of prematurely making abstract arguments based on the child's interests without any empirical evidence. Moreover in the case of families whose life situation may be disapproved of by their community we can have moral reasons for overriding the best interests of an individual child, so long as the basic interests of the child are not harmed.[34] For example, if the child of a single or lesbian mother were to suffer discrimination that affected her child, I do not think that this would justify removal of the child from the mother.

At this point it is worth highlighting the divergent manner in which the basic interests of children are taken into account in the way that American society currently treats two other ways of making a family: in vitro fertilization and adoption. In vitro fertilization has largely followed a consumer choice model in which the decisions of prospective parents are largely seen as a private matter. This is true even in cases in which third parties are involved: sperm donors, the eggs of friends and relatives, and eggs acquired through a market. In such cases little weight is given to the interests of the child or the donor of genetic material, and society tends to view reproductive decisions as a private decision facilitated by markets and a growing industry in reproductive services. By contrast, adoption is extensively regulated, and prospective adoptive parents undergo home visits and inquiry by screening agencies, even when the baby is a newborn. It is a good question as to why decisions involved in assisted reproductive technology are assumed to be a highly private matter, despite the involvement of third parties such as gamete donors, doctors, children, and for-profit fertility clinics.[35] We seem to lack, but greatly need, a consistent approach to protecting the interests of children in the context of the changing ways of making a family.

REPRODUCTIVE LABOR AND EQUALITY

In the preceding three sections I have argued that the asymmetry thesis cannot be defended by claiming that there is something *essential* about reproductive labor that singles it out for differential treatment, nor by arguing that contract pregnancy distorts the nature of the bonds of motherhood; nor is it conclusively supported by an appeal to the best interests of the child. In addition some of the arguments I have examined tend to accept uncritically the traditional picture of the family. Such arguments take current views of the maternal bond and the institution of motherhood as the baseline for judging pregnancy contracts, as if such current views were not reasonably contested.

If we reject these arguments for the asymmetry thesis, are we forced back to the view that the market is indeed theoretically all-encompassing? Can we reject contract pregnancy, and defend the asymmetry thesis, without claiming that reproductive labor is essentially not a commodity?

I think that the strongest argument against contract pregnancy that depends on the asymmetry thesis is derived from considerations of gender equality. It is this consideration that I believe is tacitly driving many of the arguments; for example, it is the background gender inequality that makes the commodification of women's attributes especially objectionable. My criticism of contract pregnancy centers on the hypothesis that in our society such contracts will turn women's labor into something that is used and controlled by others and will reinforce gender stereotypes that have been used to justify the unequal status of women.[36]

Contrary to the democratic ideal of equal citizenship, gender has pervasive effects on a person's opportunities and achievements in our society. These effects include the unequal distribution of housework and child care that considerably restricts married women's opportunities in the workforce; the fact that despite a positive trend the ratio between women's and men's earnings remains roughly 77:100 as of 2007; the fact that divorce is an economically devastating experience for women (during the 1970s the standard of living of young divorced mothers fell 73 percent, while men's standard of living following divorce rose 42 percent); and the fact that the majority of work done by women in our society remains in a "female ghetto": service and clerical work, secretarial work, cleaning, domestic labor, nursing, elementary school teaching, and waitressing.[37]

Let me try to foreground some of the particular links between contract pregnancy and women's unequal status, links I will develop further in the next chapter, when I consider prostitution, which is currently a far more common practice than contract pregnancy. In its current form and context contract pregnancy arguably contributes to gender inequality in three specific ways.

1. Contract pregnancy gives others increased access to and control over women's bodies and sexuality. There is a crucial difference between artificial insemination by donor (AID) and a pregnancy contract. AID does not give anyone control over men's bodies and sexuality. A man who elects AID simply sells a product of his body or his sexuality; he does not sell control over his body itself. The current practices of AID and pregnancy contracts are remarkably different in the scope of intervention and control they allow the buyer. Pregnancy contracts involve substantial control over women's bodies. Such provisions include agreements concerning medical treatment, the conditions under which

the surrogate agrees to undergo an abortion, and regulation of the surrogate's emotions. Thus, in the case of Baby M, Mary Beth Whitehead not only consented to refrain from forming or attempting to form any relationship with the child she would conceive, but she also agreed not to smoke cigarettes, drink alcoholic beverages, or take medications without written consent from her physician. She also agreed to undergo amniocentesis and to abort the fetus "upon demand of William Stern, natural father," if tests found genetic or congenital defects.[38]

On my view, what makes this control objectionable, however, is not the intrinsic features of women's reproductive labor, but rather the way such control specifically reinforces a long history of group-based inequality. Consider an analogous case that has no such consequence: voluntary (paid) military service, in which men and women sell their fighting capacities. Military service, like contract pregnancy, involves significant invasions into the body of the seller; soldiers' bodies are controlled to a large extent by their commanding officers under conditions in which the stakes are often life and death. But military service does not *directly* serve to perpetuate traditional gender inequalities (although we might worry about the ways that voluntary military service tracks social class). The fact that pregnancy contracts, like military contracts, give someone control over someone else's body is not the main issue; rather the issue is that in contract pregnancy the body that is controlled belongs to a woman, in a society that historically has subordinated women's interests to those of men, primarily through its control over women's sexuality and reproduction.

Market theorists might retort that contract pregnancy could be regulated to protect women's autonomy, in the same way that we regulate other labor contracts. However, it will be difficult, given the nature of the interests involved, for such contracts not to be very intrusive with respect to women's bodies in spite of formal agreements. The purpose of such contracts is, after all, to produce a healthy child. To help guarantee a healthy baby, a woman's behavior must be highly controlled.[39]

Consider that if the pregnancy contract is a contract for reproductive labor, then, as in other types of labor contracts, compliance, what the law terms "specific performance," cannot be enforced. For example, if I contract to paint your house and I default on my agreement, you can sue me for breaking the contract, but even if you win, the courts will not require me to paint your house. Indeed this is the salient difference between even poorly paid wage labor and indentured servitude, a case I will discuss later in this book. Thus, by analogy, if the woman in a pregnancy contract defaults on her agreement and decides to keep the child, the other parties should not be able to demand performance (that is, surrender of the child); rather, they can demand only monetary compensation.[40]

This likely inability to enforce performance in pregnancy contracts may have consequences for the *content* of such contracts that will make them especially objectionable. Recall that such contracts occur over a long period of time, during which a woman may undergo fundamental changes in her willingness to give up the child. Earlier I referred to this uncertainty about future consequences of a transaction as "weak agency." The other parties to the contract will need, then, some mechanisms to ensure the surrogate's compliance. There are two mechanisms that are likely to produce compliance, but both raise concerns. (a) The contract could be set up so that payment is delivered to the woman only after the child is surrendered. But this structure of compensation closely resembles baby selling; it now looks as if what is being bought is not the woman's services but the child itself. (b) The contract could mandate legal and psychological counseling for a woman who is tempted to change her mind. Such counseling could increase the surrogate's agency, but we might worry that it could involve a great deal of manipulation and coercion of her emotions.[41]

2. The second way that contract pregnancy contributes to gender inequality is by reinforcing negative stereotypes about women as "baby machines."[42] Stereotypes are sets of beliefs in which all members of a class are considered to share a set of distinguishing characteristics. Some stereotypes are empirically based. But even in those cases in which they are consistent with observation, an important point about many stereotypes is that they are self-confirming. It is because of our widespread beliefs and expectations that individuals find it rational to conform to those beliefs and expectations. It makes little sense, for example, for a black male to invest in education and human capital if he expects that employers will not reward him for that investment.[43] In early twentieth-century America few women aspired to be doctors; their ambitions were powerfully shaped by the structure of opportunity, but also by the expectations that they and others had about their role in the household. If the practice of contract pregnancy were to become common and widespread, it might affect the way all women see themselves.

3. Finally, contract pregnancy raises the danger, manifested in several recent court rulings, that motherhood will be defined in terms of genetic material, in the same way as fatherhood. Mary Beth Whitehead won back parental rights to Baby M on the basis of her being the genetic mother. On the other hand, Anna Johnson, a gestational surrogate, lost such rights because she bore no genetic relationship to the child.[44] These court rulings establish the principle of parenthood on the basis of genetic contribution. In such cases women's contribution to reproduction is recognized only insofar as it is identical to that of men. Genes alone are taken to define natural and biological motherhood. By not taking women's actual gestational contributions into account, the courts reinforce an old stereotype of women as merely the incubators of men's seeds.[45] In fact the court's inattention to women's unique labor contribution is itself a form of unequal treatment. By defining women's rights and contributions in terms of those of men, when they are different, the courts fail to recognize an adequate basis for women's rights and needs. These rulings place an additional burden on women.

To the extent that contract pregnancy has consequences for gender inequality, I think that the asymmetry thesis is true, and that such contracts are especially troubling. Current gender inequality lies at the heart of what is wrong with pregnancy contracts. The problem with commodifying women's reproductive labor is not that it degrades the special nature of reproductive labor or alienates women from a core part of their identities, but that it reinforces (to the extent that it does) a traditional gender-hierarchical division of labor. A consequence of my argument is that under very different background conditions, such contracts would be less objectionable.[46] For example, in a society in which women's work was valued as much as men's and in which child care was shared equally, pregnancy contracts might serve primarily as a way for single persons, disabled persons, and same-sex families to have children. Indeed pregnancy contracts and similar practices have the potential to transform the nuclear family.

At the same time there are potential caveats to the acceptability of a regulated form of pregnancy contract even under conditions of gender equality: (1) the importance of ensuring that woman are not selling their reproductive labor out of extreme vulnerability; (2) the effect of the practice on other pervasive status inequalities, such as race; (3) the need to ensure the woman's participation in the overall purpose of the activity; and (4) the need to ensure that the vulnerable (children) are protected from harm. We know very little about the effects of pregnancy contracts on the psychological health of children. We know very little about the effects of pregnancy contracts on parental exit or on the other children of the birth mother. And we know very little about their effects on the security of the child-to-be. A recent article in *Slate* chronicled the effects of the financial scandal on couples who could no longer afford to pay the fees to their hired surrogates. As the author notes, "If you stop paying your surrogate, she needs to quit and find another job, just like any other worker. But surrogacy isn't like any other job. The only way to quit a pregnancy is to abort it."[47] If women do not choose to abort, but have no means to support their child once the paying couple has reneged, then the security of the child is threatened.

For this reason, even under more ideal circumstances, there is reason to be cautious about the potential use of such contracts. This can be done by allowing such contracts but making them unenforceable in the courts. Not only would banning drive such contracts underground, leaving the parties more vulnerable to one another, but many of the potential consequences of such contracts are speculative. Additionally, I believe that in the light of my previous argument, in contested cases the courts should recognize no distinction between genetic and gestational surrogates with respect to parental rights. Finally, third-party brokerage of pregnancy contracts should be illegal. These proposals aim to discourage contract pregnancy and to strengthen the position of the surrogate, who is the most economically and emotionally vulnerable party in any such arrangement.

CONCLUSION: WAGE LABOR, REPRODUCTIVE LABOR, AND EQUALITY

In this chapter I have analyzed various grounds for forbidding markets in women's reproductive labor. While I rejected most of these grounds, including the essentialist thesis, the opposing approach of market theorists misses the point that there are noneconomic values that should constrain market transactions. Market theorists ignore the role that markets have in shaping the relationships among individuals and social groups.

Libertarian-oriented market theorists may claim that my support for the asymmetry thesis entails a violation of liberal neutrality: it imposes a standard of gender equality on free exchanges.[48] Liberalism requires state neutrality among a large range of conceptions of value. This neutrality means that liberals cannot mandate that individuals converge on a single set of values. Liberals can, of course, seek to regulate exchanges so that they fall within the bounds of justice. But any argument that goes beyond justice and seeks to prohibit certain market exchanges because of a particular view of the nature of the goods being exchanged is claimed to violate liberal neutrality. Furthermore the argument that I have given is biased, distinguishing activities that harm women from those that harm everyone.

The issue of neutrality is a difficult matter to assess, for there are many interpretations of neutrality. At the very least, however, two considerations seem relevant. First, why should existing distributions serve as the standard against which neutrality is measured? I have argued that it is a mistake to assume that the realm of reproduction and sexuality is neutral; it is a product (at least in part) of the unequal social, political, and economic power of men and women. Second, most liberals draw the line at social practices such as slavery, indentured servitude, labor at slave wages, and the selling of votes or political liberties. They defend inalienable civil liberties such as freedom of conscience and association, the right to own property and to choose one's profession. Such restrictions are taken as necessary for justice. They view as suspect practices that, like systematic gender inequality, undermine a framework of free deliberation among equals. If such restrictions also violate viewpoint neutrality, the mere violation of neutrality does not seem objectionable. Indeed, on my view, if it undermines women's equal status, contract pregnancy *is* an issue of justice.

Contract pregnancy places women's bodies under the control of others and serves to perpetuate gender inequality. The asymmetries of gender, the fact of social relations of gender domination, provide the best foundation for the asymmetry thesis. I'll say more about the difference between contract pregnancy and other forms of labor that may contribute to gender inequalities, such as women being employed as domestic cleaners and preschool teachers, in the next chapter.

Not all of the potentially negative consequences of contract pregnancy involve its effects on gender inequality. I have also referred to the problematic form that such contracts will have to take to be self-enforcing, its origins in weak agency, and its shaping effects on preferences and identities. Some of these features of pregnancy contracts are shared with other labor contracts. There is an important tradition in social philosophy that argues that it is precisely these shared features that make wage labor itself unacceptable. This tradition emphasizes that wage labor, like contract pregnancy, places the productive capacities of one group of citizens at the service and under the control of another. The asymmetry thesis does not imply that there is nothing problematic about other forms of wage labor. Unfortunately there has been little attention in political philosophy to the effects of forms of gender and class inequality on the development of women's and workers' deliberative capacities or on the formation of their preferences. We have to ask, What kinds of work and family relations and environments best promote the development of the deliberative capacities needed to support democratic institutions?[49]

6

Markets in Women's Sexual Labor

The intuition that there is a distinction between markets in different human capacities is a deep one, even among people who ultimately think that the distinction does not justify legally forbidding sales of reproductive capacity and sex. I continue to probe this intuition in this chapter, focusing on the sale of sexual services. What, if anything, is problematic about a woman selling her sexual as opposed to her secretarial labor? And if the apparent asymmetry can be explained and justified, what implications follow for public policy?

My strategy in this chapter parallels that of chapter 5 on contract pregnancy. I sketch and criticize two popular approaches to the morality of prostitution. The *economic approach* attributes the wrongness of prostitution to its consequences for efficiency, the fact that it generates externalities. The important feature of this approach is its treatment of sex as a morally indifferent matter. The *essentialist approach* stresses that sales of sexual labor are wrong because they are inherently alienating or damaging to human happiness. In contrast to these two ways of thinking about the immorality of prostitution, I argue that the most plausible support for the asymmetry thesis stems from the role of commercialized sex and reproduction in sustaining a social world in which women form a subordinated social group. This parallels but also diverges from my argument about contract pregnancy. In the first place, I argue that prostitution, like contract pregnancy, is wrong insofar as the sale of women's sexual labor reinforces broad patterns of sex inequality. This might seem surprising insofar as the argument about contract pregnancy stressed perceptions of women as baby machines and prostitution seems to challenge exactly those perceptions. I present an alternative way that the practice of contemporary prostitution contributes to and also embodies the perception of women as socially inferior to men. But because many forms of labor that people do not view as especially troubling may also contribute to the socially inferior position of women—women models, maids, day care workers, and au pairs—I address the question of what makes prostitution different. In the second place, prostitution, unlike contract pregnancy, does not involve potential harms to children, nor does it necessarily involve weak agency.[1] Therefore the case against prostitution as a noxious market cannot rest on such grounds. Yet many women are harmed in forms of prostitution, and I also hope to show that there is a third party that is harmed by prostitution: the class of women.

On the basis of my analysis of prostitution's wrongness, there is no simple conclusion as to what its legal status ought to be. Both criminalization and decriminalization may have the effect of exacerbating the gender inequalities in virtue of which I claim that prostitution is wrong. Nonetheless my argument does have implications for the form of prostitution's regulation, if legal, and its prohibition and penalties, if illegal. Overall my argument tends to support decriminalization in contexts such as the United States and Western Europe, where prohibitions on abuse can be enforced and there is a social safety net to protect women from entering into prostitution under conditions of extreme vulnerability.

The argument I put forward here is qualified and tentative in its practical conclusions, but its theoretical point is not. *I argue that the most plausible account of prostitution's wrongness turns on its relationship to the pervasive social inequality between men and women.* If in fact no causal relationship obtains between prostitution and gender inequality, then I do not think that there are good reasons, at least not among the reasons I examine, for thinking that prostitution is, by itself, especially morally troubling. What would remain troubling would be the often miserable and unjust background circumstances in which much prostitution occurs.[2] In my evaluation of prostitution consideration of both the social consequences and the social origins of prostitution with respect to gender inequality play a crucial role. It follows from my analysis that male prostitution raises distinct issues and is not connected to injustice in the same way as female prostitution.

Prostitution is a complex phenomenon. I begin accordingly with the question, Who is a prostitute?

WHO IS A PROSTITUTE?

Much has been written on the history of prostitution, and some empirical studies of prostitutes themselves have been undertaken, yet the few philosophers writing on this subject have tended to treat prostitution as if the term referred to something uniform.[3] It does not. Not only is it hard to draw a sharp line between prostitution and practices that look like prostitution,[4] but as historians of the subject have emphasized, prostitution today is a very different phenomenon from earlier forms of commercial sex. In particular the idea of prostitution as a specialized occupation of an outcast and stigmatized group is of relatively recent origin.[5]

While outsiders tend to stigmatize all prostitutes, prostitution itself has an internal hierarchy based on class, race, and gender. The majority of prostitutes, especially when we consider the issue globally, are very poor. Even in the United States streetwalkers are a world apart from prostitution's upper tier. Consider these three cases:

- A fourteen-year-old girl prostitutes herself to support her boyfriend's heroin addiction. Later she works the streets to support her own habit. She begins, like most teenage streetwalkers, to rely on a pimp for protection. She is uneducated and is frequently subjected to violence in her relationships and with her customers. She receives no social security, no sick leave or maternity leave, and, most important, she has no control as to whether or not she has sex with a man. That is a decision that is made by her pimp.
- Now imagine the life of a Park Avenue call girl or a highly paid "escort" to wealthy powerful men.[6] Many call girls drift into high-class prostitution after "run of the mill promiscuity," led neither by material want nor lack of alternatives.[7] Some are young college graduates who upon graduation earn money by prostitution while searching for other jobs. Call girls can earn between $30,000 and $100,000 annually. These women have control over the entire amount they earn as well as an unusual degree of independence, greater than in many other forms of work. They can also decide whom they wish to have sex with and when they wish to do so.[8] There is little resemblance between their lives and that of the streetwalker.
- Finally, consider the small but increasing number of male prostitutes. Most male prostitutes (but not all) sell sex to other men.[9]

Often the men who buy such sex are married. Unfortunately there is little information on male prostitution; it has not been well studied as either a historical or a contemporary phenomenon.[10] What we do know suggests that, like their female counterparts, male prostitutes cover the economic spectrum. Two important differences between male and female prostitutes are that men are more likely to work only part time and that they are not generally subject to the violence of male pimps because they tend to work on their own.

Are these three cases distinct? Many critics of prostitution have assumed that all prostitutes were women who entered the practice under circumstances that include abuse and economic desperation. But that is a false assumption: the critics have mistaken a part of the practice for the whole. For example, although women who walk the streets are the most visible, they constitute only about 20 percent of the prostitute population in the United States.[11]

The varying circumstances of prostitution are important because they force us to consider carefully what we think may be wrong with prostitution. For example, in the first case the factors that seem crucial to our negative response of condemnation are the miserable background conditions of desperation, the prostitute's age, and her lack of control over whether or not she has sex with a client, as well as her vulnerability to violence at the hands of her pimp or client. In chapter 4 I referred to these factors as *vulnerability, weak agency*, and *extreme individual harmful outcome*. These conditions could be redressed through regulation without forbidding commercial sexual exchanges between consenting adults.[12] The second case of prostitution stands in sharp contrast. These women engage in what seems to be a voluntary activity, chosen among a range of decent alternatives. Many of these women sell their sexual capacities without coercion or regret. The third case rebuts arguments that prostitution has no other purpose than to exploit women.

WHAT IS WRONG WITH PROSTITUTION?

The Economic Approach

As we have seen in earlier chapters, economists generally frame their questions about the best way to distribute a good without reference to its intrinsic qualities. They tend to focus on the quantitative features of a good and not its qualities. An economic approach to prostitution does not specify a priori that certain sales are wrong; no act of commodification is ruled out in advance.[13] Rather this approach focuses on the costs and benefits that accompany such sales. An economic approach to contracts will justify inalienability rules—rules that forbid individuals from entering into certain transactions—in cases where there are costly externalities to those transactions and in general where such transactions are inefficient.

What are the costs of prostitution? First, the parties to a commercial sex transaction share possible costs of disease and guilt.[14] Second, prostitution also has costs to third parties: a man who frequents a prostitute dissipates financial resources that might otherwise be directed to his family; in a society that values intimate marriage, infidelity costs a man's wife or companion in terms of mistrust and suffering (and therefore prostitution may sometimes lead to marital instability); and sexual diseases can be spread to others. Perhaps the largest third-party costs to prostitution are "moralisms":[15] many people find the practice morally offensive and are pained by its existence. (Note that "moralisms" refers to people's preferences about moral issues and not to morality as such.)

The economic approach generates a contingent case for treating prostitution differently than we do other labor markets, focusing on prostitution's costs in terms of negative public opinion or the harms to prostitutes or others in the population (including through the spread of diseases). Consideration of which limitations on sexual freedom can be justified from a welfare standpoint can be illuminating, and it forces us to think about the actual effects of sexual regulations. Nevertheless I want to register three difficulties with this approach.

First, and most obviously, both markets and contractual exchanges function within a regime of property rights and legal entitlements. The economic approach ignores the background system of distribution within which prostitution occurs. Some background systems, however, are unjust. We might especially be worried about prostitution that arises as the only way to stave off starvation. In contrast to contract pregnancy, some of the participants in prostitution markets (especially if we consider the practice as a global phenomenon) are likely to be desperately poor and survive for all practical purposes as sexual slaves.

Second, this type of approach seems disabled from making sense of distinctions between goods, especially in cases where these distinctions do not seem to reflect mere differences in the net sum of costs and benefits. The sale of certain goods seems to many people simply unthinkable; it may be possible to justify prohibitions on slavery by appeal to costs and benefits, but the problem is that such justification makes contingent an outcome (no slavery) that we do not hold contingently. It makes little sense, phenomenologically, to describe the moral repugnance people feel toward slavery as "just a cost." Even if we are interested in tracking third party costs, as we saw in chapter 1, externalities (especially if we count moralisms as externalities) are nearly universal in practice. If we view any market that generates disapproval as producing an externality that can justify intervention, then freedom of contract is on shaky ground. We need some way of marking which costs rise to the level of justifying interference and regulation and which do not. Nothing in economic analysis helps us to do this.

Third, some goods seem to have a special status that requires that they be shielded from the market. As we saw in chapter 4, the sale of votes or political rights does not simply produce costs and benefits: it transforms the background conditions for people to interact as equals. In this sense the market is not a neutral mechanism of exchange: there are some goods whose sale reshapes the relations between the transacting parties. At best, then, the economic analysis of prostitution is incomplete. At worst it is misleading.

The Essentialist Approach

Economists abstract from the qualities of the goods they consider. By contrast, as we saw in chapter 5, some critics hold that there is something intrinsic to sex that accounts for the distinction we mark between it and other types of labor. On this view, prostitution is not wrong simply because it *causes* harm; prostitution *constitutes* a harm. Essentialists hold that there is some intrinsic property of sex that makes its commodification wrong.

Some feminist critics of prostitution argue that sexual and reproductive capacities are more crucially tied to the nature of our selves than our other capacities.[16] The sale of sex is taken to cut deeper into the self, to involve a more total alienation from the self. Recall Carole Pateman:

"When a prostitute contracts out use of her body she is thus selling *herself* in a very real sense. Women's selves are involved in prostitution in a different manner from the involvement of the self in other occupations."[17]

It seems right to say that damage to and violation of our bodies affect us in a deeper way, a more significant way, than damage to our external property. Robbing my body of a kidney is a violation *different in kind* from robbing my house of a stereo, however expensive the latter is. Distributing kidneys from healthy people to sick people through a lottery is a far different act from using a lottery to distribute door prizes, even if ultimately both such lotteries could be defended.[18]

But this point can be only the first step in an argument in favor of treating either our organs or our sexual capacities as market-inalienable. Most liberals think that individual sovereignty over mind and body is crucial for the exercise of fundamental liberties. Thus in the absence of clear harms most liberals would reject legal bans on voluntary sales of body parts or sexual capacities. Indeed the usual justification of such bans is harm to self; such sales are presumed to be "desperate exchanges" that the individual herself would reasonably want to foreclose. American law blocks voluntary sales of individual organs and body parts, but not sales of blood, on the assumption that only the former sales are likely to be so harmful to the individual that given adequate information and any reasonable alternative, she herself would refrain from such sales.

Whatever the plausibility of such a claim with respect to body parts,[19] it is considerably weaker when applied to sex. There is no strong evidence that prostitution is, at least in the United States and certainly among its higher echelons, a more desperate exchange than, say, working in Walmart. This may reflect the fact that the relationship people have with their sexual capacities is diverse: for some people sexuality is a realm of ecstatic communion with another; for others it is little more than a sport or distraction. Some people will find consenting to be sexually used by another person enjoyable or adequately compensated by a wage. Even for the same person, sex can be the source of a range of experiences.

Of course the point cannot simply be that, as an empirical matter, people have differing conceptions of sexuality. The critics of prostitution grant that. The point is whether or not, and within what range, this diversity is desirable.

Margaret Jane Radin raises a distinct worry about the effects of *widespread* prostitution on human flourishing. She argues that widespread sex markets would promote inferior forms of personhood. She says that we can see this is the case if we "reflect on what we know now about human life and choose the best from among the conceptions available to us."[20] If prostitution were to become common, Radin argues, it would have adverse effects on a form of personhood that itself is intrinsically valuable. Why should this be so? We might consider that if the signs of affection and intimacy were frequently detached from their usual meaning, such signs might well become more ambiguous and easy to manipulate. The marks of an intimate relationship (physical intimacy, terms of endearment, etc.) would no longer signal the existence of intimacy. In that case, by obscuring the nature of sexual relationships prostitution might undermine our ability to apply the criteria for coercion and informational failure.[21] Individuals might more easily enter into damaging relationships and lead less fulfilling lives as a result.

It is certainly true that prostitution usually detaches sex from intimacy. But so does casual sex. Radin's argument is best understood as an argument that widespread prostitution produces an externality. I agree. The question is, What is the nature of the externality? Radin views the externality in terms of inferior human flourishing. But even if prostitution fails to promote flourishing, there are markets in many goods we tolerate that don't promote flourishing: high-fat foods, for example. In arguing that we should assess and potentially regulate markets according to the extent to which they promote the best forms of flourishing, Radin implicitly accepts the view that the purpose of the state is to make people happy. This is a substantive claim with strong paternalistic ramifications. I have tried to make an argument about markets that does not depend on paternalism. Later I will claim that contemporary prostitution is wrong because it promotes unequal relationships between men and women, gender hierarchy, and exclusion—matters of justice—and not because it makes people less happy.[22]

An alternative version of the essentialist thesis views the sale and purchase of sex as an assault on personal dignity. Prostitution *degrades* the prostitute. Elizabeth Anderson, for example, discusses the effect of commodification on the nature of sex as a shared good, based on the recognition of mutual attraction. In commercial sex each party now values the other only instrumentally, not intrinsically. And though both parties are thus prevented from enjoying a shared good, it is worse for the prostitute. The customer merely surrenders a certain amount of cash; the prostitute cedes her body. The prostitute is thus degraded to the status of a thing. Call this the *degradation objection*.[23]

I share the intuition that the failure to treat others as persons is morally significant; it is wrong to treat people as mere things. But I am skeptical as to whether this intuition supports the conclusion that prostitution is wrong. Consider the contrast between slavery and prostitution. Slavery was, in Orlando Patterson's memorable phrase, a form of "social death": it denied to enslaved individuals the ability to press claims, to be in their own right sources of value and interest.[24] But the mere sale of the use of someone's capacities does not *necessarily* involve a failure of this kind, on the part of either the buyer or the seller.[25] Many forms of labor, perhaps most, cede some control of a person's body to others.[26] Such control can range from requirements to be in a certain place at a certain time (e.g., reporting to the office) to requirements that a person (e.g., a professional athlete) eat certain foods and get a certain amount of sleep or maintain good humor in the face of the offensive behavior of others (e.g., airline stewardesses). Some control of our capacities by others does not seem to be ipso facto humiliating, destructive of our dignity.[27] Whether or not the purchase of a form of human labor power will have this negative consequence will depend on background social macro-level and micro-level institutions. Minimum wages, worker participation and control, health and safety regulations, maternity and paternity leave, restrictions on specific performance, and the right to exit one's job are all features that attenuate the objectionable aspects of treating people's labor as a mere economic input. The advocates of prostitution's wrongness in virtue of its connection to selfhood, flourishing, and degradation have not shown that a system of *regulated* prostitution would be unable to respond to their worries. In particular they have not established that there is something wrong with prostitution irrespective of its cultural and historical contexts.

There is, however, another way of interpreting the degradation objection that draws a connection between the current practice of prostitution and the lesser social status of women.[28] This connection is not a matter of the logic of prostitution per se but the fact that contemporary prostitution degrades women by treating them as the sexual servants of men. Currently prostitutes are overwhelmingly women and their clients are almost exclusively men. In conceiving of a class of women as needed to satisfy male sexual desire, prostitution represents women as sexual servants to men. The degradation objection, so understood, can be seen as a way of expressing an egalitarian concern since there is no reciprocal ideology that represents men as servicing women's sexual needs. It is to this egalitarian understanding of prostitution's wrongness that I turn in the next section.

The Egalitarian Approach

The essentialists rightly call our attention to the different relation we have with our capacities and external things, yet they overstate the nature of the difference between our sexual capacities and our other capacities with respect to our personhood, flourishing, and dignity. They are also insufficiently attentive to the background conditions in which commercial sex exchanges take place. By contrast, I see prostitution's wrongness in terms of its relationship to gender inequality. But if this argument can be extended to cover prostitution as well as contract pregnancy, why does it not extend it to all forms of sex-stereotyped work, including secretarial labor?

The answer hinges in part on how we conceive of gender inequality. On my view, there are two important dimensions of gender inequality, often conflated. The first dimension concerns inequalities in the distribution of income, wealth, and opportunity. In most nations, including the United States, women form an economically and socially disadvantaged group based on the following factors.

- Income inequality. We saw in chapter 5 that although the gap between men's and women's earnings has narrowed, it still remains a significant one.
- Poverty. Poverty rates are highest for families headed by single women, particularly if they are black or Hispanic. In 2007 28.3 percent of households headed by single women were poor; 13.6 percent of households headed by single men and 4.9 percent of married-couple households lived in poverty.[29]
- Unequal division of labor in the family. Within the family women spend disproportionate amounts of time on housework and rearing

children. According to one recent study, wives employed full time outside the home do 70 percent of the housework; full-time house-wives do 83 percent.[30] The unequal family division of labor is itself caused by and causes labor market inequality; given the lower wages of working women, it is more costly for men to cut back from the labor market to participate in household labor and child rearing.

The second dimension of gender inequality does not concern income and opportunity, but standing in society. In many contemporary con-texts women are viewed and treated as the social inferiors of men. This inferior treatment proceeds via several distinct mechanisms.

- Negative stereotyping. Stereotypes persist as to the types of jobs and responsibilities a woman can assume. Extensive studies have shown that people typically believe that men are more dominant, assertive, and instrumentally rational than women. Gender shapes beliefs about a person's capacities; for example, women are thought to be less intelligent than their male equals.[31]
- Hierarchy. Men are able asymmetrically to sanction women; they push women around to get what they want. The paradigm case is violence. Women are subjected to greater amounts of violence by men than is the reverse: according to one (somewhat controversial) study, every fifteen seconds a woman is battered in the United States; 1.3 million women a year are physically assaulted by their male partners; on average they are assaulted 3.4 times.[32]
- Marginalization. People who are marginalized are excluded from or absent from core productive social roles in society, roles that convey self-respect and meaningful contribution.[33] At the extremes, marginalized women lack the means for their basic survival; they are dependent on male partners to secure the basic necessities of life. Less severely marginalized women lack access to central and important social roles. Their activities are confined to peripheral spheres of social organization. Although women have entered the health and legal professions in increasing numbers, they are clustered in the lower status ends of these professions. And they have made little progress in some important social positions: between 1789 and July 2009 only 2 percent of the members of Congress have been women.[34] Occupational segrega-tion by sex is extensive and pervasive; moreover it is a global phenomenon.

- Stigma. A woman's gender is associated, in some contexts, with stigma, a badge of dishonor. Consider rape. In crimes of rape the complainant's past behavior and character are central in determining whether or not a crime has actually occurred. This is not true of other crimes; mail fraud (pun intended) is not dismissed because of the bad judgment or naïveté of the victims. Society views rape differently because, I suggest, many people think that women really want or deserve to be forced into sex, treated as objects for male pleasure. Women's lower status thus influences the way that rape is seen.

These two forms of inequality, distributional inequality and status inequality, clearly interact. But they are distinct. I do not think it is plausible to attribute to prostitution a direct causal role in the first sense of gender inequality: distributional inequality between men and women. But I believe that it is a plausible hypothesis that prostitution, along with related practices such as pornography, makes an important contribution to women's inferior social status. Prostitution shapes and is itself shaped by custom and culture, by cultural meanings about the importance of sex and about the nature of women's sexuality and male desire.[35]

If prostitution is wrong it is because of its effects on how men perceive women and on how women perceive themselves. In our society prostitution represents women as the sexual servants of men. It supports and embodies the widely held belief that men have strong sex drives that must be satisfied, largely by gaining access to some woman's body. This belief underlies the mistaken idea that prostitution is the oldest profession, a necessary consequence of human (i.e., male) nature. It also underlies the traditional conception of marriage, in which a man owned not only his wife's property but also her body. Indeed until fairly late in the twentieth century many states did not recognize the possibility of "real rape" in marriage.

Why is the idea that women must service men's sexual needs an image of inequality and not mere difference? My argument suggests that there are two primary, contextual reasons.

First, in our culture there is no reciprocal social practice that represents men as serving women's sexual needs. Men are gigolos and paid escorts, but their sexuality is not seen as an independent capacity whose use *women* can buy. It is not part of the identity of a class of men that they will service women's sexual desires. Indeed male prostitutes overwhelmingly service other men and not women.

Second, the idea that prostitution embodies an idea of women as inferior is suggested by the high incidence of rape and violence against women prostitutes. Although all women in our society are potential targets of rape and violence, the mortality rates for women engaged in prostitution are roughly six times higher than that of nonprostitute women of comparable age, race, and social class.[36]

My suggestion is that prostitution depicts an image of gender inequality by constituting one class of women as inferior. Prostitution is a theater of inequality; it displays for us a practice in which women are seen as servants of men's desires. This is especially the case where women are forcibly controlled by their (male) pimps. It follows from my conception of prostitution that it need not have such a negative effect when the prostitute is male. More research needs to be done on popular images and conceptions of gay male prostitutes, as well as on the extremely small number of male prostitutes who have women clients.

The negative image of women who participate in prostitution, the perception that they are legitimate targets of violence and rape, is objectionable in itself. It contributes to an important form of inequality, unequal status, based on attitudes of superiority, exclusion, and disrespect. Unfortunately political philosophers and economists, who have focused instead on inequalities in income and opportunity, have largely ignored this form of inequality. Moreover this form of inequality is not confined to women prostitutes. I believe that the negative image of women prostitutes likely also has third-party effects: it shapes and influences the way women as a whole are seen. This hypothesis is, of course, an empirical one. It has not been tested largely because of the lack of studies of the men who go to prostitutes. Most extant studies of prostitution examine the behavior and motivations of the women who enter into the practice, a fact that itself raises the suspicion that prostitution is viewed as "a problem about the women who are prostitutes . . . [rather than] a problem about the men who demand to buy them."[37] In these studies male gender identity is taken as a given.

To investigate prostitution's negative image effects on female prostitutes and on women generally we need research on the following questions:

- What are the attitudes of men who visit women prostitutes toward prostitutes? How do their attitudes toward prostitutes compare with the attitudes of men who do not visit prostitutes?
- What are the attitudes of men who visit women prostitutes toward women generally? What are the attitudes of men who do not visit women prostitutes toward women generally?
- What are the attitudes of women toward women prostitutes?
- How do the men and women involved in prostitution view themselves?
- Does prostitution contribute to or diminish the likelihood of crimes of sexual violence?
- What can we learn about these questions through cross-national studies? How do attitudes about women prostitutes compare between the United States and countries with more egalitarian wage policies or less status inequality between men and women?

The answers to these questions will reflect social facts about our culture. Whatever plausibility there is to the hypothesis that prostitution contributes to and expresses gender status inequality, it gains this plausibility from the surrounding cultural context, the meaning of the practice in the larger society.

I can imagine hypothetical circumstances in which prostitution would not have a negative image effect, where it could mark a reclaiming of women's sexuality. Margo St. James of COYOTE (Call Off Your Old Tired Ethics) and other feminists have argued that prostitutes can function as sex therapists, fulfilling a legitimate social need as well as providing a source of experiment and alternative conceptions of sexuality and gender.[38] I agree that in a different culture, with different assumptions about men's and women's gender identities, prostitution might not have harmful effects on women in prostitution and as a group. But I think that these feminists have minimized the cultural stereotypes that surround contemporary prostitution and exaggerated their own power to shape the practice. Prostitution, like pornography, is not easily separated from the larger surrounding culture that marginalizes, stereotypes, and stigmatizes women.[39] I think that we need to look carefully at what men and women actually learn in prostitution; I doubt that ethnographic studies of prostitution would support the claim that prostitution contributes to images of women's dignity or empowerment.

If, through its negative image of women as sexual servants of men, prostitution reinforces women's inferior status in society, then it is wrong. Even though men can be and are prostitutes, I think that it is unlikely that we will find such negative image effects on men as a group. Individual men may be degraded in individual acts of prostitution; men as a group are not.

Granting all of the above, is prostitution's negative image effect greater than that produced by other professions in which women largely service men, for example, nursing or fashion modeling? What is special about prostitution?

The negative image effect undoubtedly operates outside the domain of prostitution. But there are three significant differences between prostitution and other gender-segregated professions.

First, a large number of people currently believe that prostitution, unlike housecleaning, is especially objectionable. Holding such moral views of prostitution constant, if prostitution continues to be primarily a female occupation, then the existence of prostitution will disproportionately fuel negative images of women.[40] Stigma surrounds the practice, shapes it, and is reinforced by it.

Second, prostitution represents women as objects for male use. As I indicated earlier, prostitutes are far more likely to be victims of violence than other professions; they are also far more likely to be raped than other women. A prostitute's "no" does not, to the male she services as well as to other men, mean no.

The third difference concerns a third-party harm: the effects that prostitution may have on other women's sexual autonomy.[41] Scott Anderson has recently argued that if prostitution was viewed as just another job analogous to other forms of employment, then presumably sex could be included as part of any number of jobs. Women who did not wish to have sex on demand might find that their employment options were limited and that they were less employable on the labor market. These women would now be worse off than if prostitution were illegal, and, Anderson stresses, they might feel pressured to have sex in order to get the jobs they want.

My argument has been that if prostitution is wrong, it is because the sale of women's sexual labor may have adverse consequences for achieving a significant form of equality between men and women. This argument for the asymmetry thesis, if correct, connects prostitution to stigma and unequal status. However, it is an injustice that operates in large part through beliefs and attitudes that might someday be changed. I now turn to the question of whether, even if we assume that prostitution is wrong under current conditions, it should remain illegal.

SHOULD PROSTITUTION BE LEGALIZED?

It is important to distinguish between prostitution's wrongness and the legal response that we are entitled to make to that wrongness. Even if prostitution is wrong, we may not be justified in prohibiting it if that prohibition makes the facts in virtue of which it is wrong worse, or if it has too great a cost for other important values. There are a range of plausible views about the appropriate scope of state intervention and indeed the appropriate scope of equality considerations in supporting such regulation.

It is also important to keep in mind that narrowing the discussion of solutions to the single question of whether to ban or not to ban prostitution shows a poverty of imagination. There are many ways of challenging existing cultural values about the appropriate division of labor in the family and the nature of women's sexual and reproductive capacities, for example, education, consciousness-raising groups, and changes in employee parental leave policies. The law is not the only way to provide women with incentives to refrain from participating in prostitution. Nonetheless we do need to decide what the best legal policy toward prostitution should be.

I begin with an assessment of the policy that we now have. The United States is one of the few developed Western countries that criminalizes prostitution.[42] For example, Denmark, Holland, West Germany, Sweden, Switzerland, and Austria all have legalized prostitution, although in some of these countries it is restricted by local ordinances.[43] In other countries, it is illegal to pay for sex, but not to sell it. Where prostitution is permitted, it is closely regulated.

Suppose that we accept that gender equality is a legitimate goal of social policy. The question is whether the current legal prohibition on prostitution in the United States promotes gender equality. The answer, I think, is that it does not. The current legal policies in the United States arguably exacerbate the factors in virtue of which prostitution is wrong.

First, the current prohibition on prostitution renders some of the women who engage in the practice vulnerable. Some prostitutes seek assistance from pimps in lieu of the contractual and legal remedies that are denied them. Male pimps may protect women prostitutes from their customers and from the police, but the system of pimp-run prostitution has enormous negative consequences, extreme harms, for women at the lowest rungs of prostitution.

Second, women are disproportionately punished for engaging in commercial sex. Many state laws make it a worse crime to sell sex than to buy it. Consequently pimps and clients ("johns") are rarely prosecuted. In fact in some jurisdictions patronizing a prostitute is not illegal, although prostitution is. Studies have also shown that male prostitutes are arrested with less frequency than female prostitutes and receive shorter sentences. One study of the judicial processing of 2,859 male and female prostitutes found that judges were more likely to find defendants guilty if they were female.[44]

Nor does the current legal prohibition on prostitution provide clear benefit to women as a class because the cultural meaning of the current governmental prohibition of prostitution is ambiguous. Although an unrestricted regime of prostitution, a pricing system in women's sexual attributes, could have negative external consequences on women's self-perceptions and perceptions by men, state prohibition can also reflect a view of women that contributes to their inequality. For example, some people support state regulation because they believe that women's sexuality is for the purpose of reproduction, a claim tied to traditional ideas about women's proper role.

There is an additional reason why banning prostitution seems an inadequate response to the problem of gender inequality and which suggests a lack of parallel with the case of commercial surrogacy. Banning prostitution would not by itself, does not, eliminate it. While there is reason to think that making commercial surrogacy arrangements illegal or unenforceable would diminish their occurrence, no such evidence exists about prostitution. No American city has eliminated prostitution merely through criminalization. Instead criminalized prostitution thrives as a black market activity in which pimps substitute for law as the mechanism for enforcing contracts. It thereby makes the lives of prostitutes worse than they might otherwise be, and without clearly counteracting prostitution's largely negative image of women.

If we decide to ban prostitution these problems must be addressed. If we decide not to ban prostitution (either by legalizing it or decriminalizing it), then we must be careful to regulate the practice to address its negative effects. Certain restrictions on advertising and recruitment will be needed to address the negative image effects that an unrestricted regime of prostitution would perpetuate. But the current regime of black market prostitution harms many prostitutes. It places their sexual capacities largely under the control of men. To promote women's equality, here are some suggested regulatory principles:

- No woman should be forced, either by law or by private persons, to have sex against her will. (Recall that it is only quite recently that the courts have recognized the existence of marital rape.) A woman who sells sex must be able to refuse to give it; she must not be coerced either by law or by private persons to perform.[45]
- No woman should be denied access, either by law or by private persons, to contraception or to treatment for sexually transmitted diseases, particularly AIDS, or to abortion (at least in the first trimester).
- The law should increase agency, ensuring that a woman has adequate information before she agrees to sexual intercourse. The risks of venereal and other sexually transmitted diseases, the risks of pregnancy, and the laws protecting a woman's right to refuse sex should all be generally available.
- Minimum age of consent laws for sexual intercourse should be enforced. These laws should ensure that vulnerable woman (and men) are protected from coercion and do not enter into sexual relationships until they are in a position to understand what they are consenting to.
- The law should promote women's control over their own sexuality by prohibiting brokerage. If what is wrong with prostitution is its relation to gender inequality, then it is crucial that the law be brought to bear primarily on the men who profit from the use of women's sexual capacities.

Each of these principles is meant to establish and protect a woman's right to control her sexual and reproductive capacities and not to give control of these capacities to others. Each of these principles is meant to protect the conditions for women's consent to sex—to enhance her agency, in the language of chapter 4—whether or not this sex is commercial. Each of these principles also seeks to counter the harms to women in prostitution by mitigating its nature as a form of female servitude.

CONCLUSION

If the arguments I have offered here are correct, then prostitution is wrong by virtue of its contributions to perpetuating a pervasive form of inequality: status inequality between men and women. In different circumstances, with different assumptions about women and their role in society, prostitution might not be troubling, or at least no more troubling than many other labor markets currently allowed. It follows on my account, then, that in other circumstances the asymmetry thesis would be denied or less strongly felt. Although prostitution as intrinsically degrading is a powerful intuition (and like many such intuitions, it persists even after its proponents undergo what Richard Brandt has termed "cognitive therapy," in which errors of fact and inference are corrected),[46] I believe that this intuition is itself bound up with well-entrenched views of male gender identity and women's sexual role in the context of that identity. If we are troubled by prostitution, as I think we should be, then we should direct much of our energy to putting forward alternative models of egalitarian relations between men and women.[47]

7

Child Labor: A Normative Perspective

The International Labour Organization (ILO) estimates that more than 246 million children are engaged in labor. Although the incidence of child labor has been falling globally, it is doing so unevenly, and in some areas it appears to be on the rise.[1] In many countries in South Asia and Africa the percentage of working children falls within the 20 to 60 percent range.

The widespread existence of child labor has provoked both popular outrage and legislative initiatives aimed at banning the sale of all products made by children. But developing economies, and many economists, have cautioned against universally proscribing child labor. They argue that such bans will be inefficient and will hurt poor families and their children. Some economists have voiced concern about paternalistic interference with family strategies that may have evolved rationally in the context of poverty and inadequate education systems. Others point out that because child labor is itself heterogeneous, ranging from light work delivering newspapers after school to child prostitution, uniform policies may undermine the ability to target its worst forms. There is thus considerable debate as to whether establishing and enforcing a uniform worldwide set of standards for dealing with child labor is desirable.

Against the background of this debate, this chapter explores the normative issues posed by child labor. In the first section I briefly consider the conceptual problems of defining who is a child for the purposes of identifying child labor. The second section explores several considerations that make child labor morally problematic, considerations that turn on all four of the parameters I presented in chapter 4: weak agency, vulnerability, and extreme harm to the individual child and to society.[2] Guided by these considerations I defend a position distinct from both those who argue that all child labor should be abolished immediately and those who argue that we must accommodate it. I argue that the worst forms of child labor, including child prostitution and the use of children as bonded laborers, should be unconditionally prohibited. Other types of child labor may need to be tolerated under certain circumstances, at least in the near future, even as efforts are made to eradicate them. Legal toleration, however, does not imply indifference, and states and nongovernmental organizations (NGOs) can protect and promote the interests of children in many ways. In particular they can take broad social measures to improve outcomes for children, especially by ensuring that all working children are educated.

Child labor cannot be addressed without considering our moral and political values; they are implicated in the questions we ask about child labor, in the data we seek, and in our policy design. Moreover whatever policies are adopted will involve trade-offs among different values. Policymakers need to make explicit the values they want to promote and the trade-offs they are willing to accept. In this chapter I take the most important values at stake to be preventing extreme harms to children and to society and I suggest how those values might guide policy and research.

WHAT IS A CHILD?

Many countries define childhood in terms of chronological age; others take into account social factors. In some African countries, for example, ten-year-old apprentices and brides are no longer assumed to possess all the characteristics that industrial countries bundle together into the status of "child." They may be eligible for marriage but not entitled to make decisions independently of their parents. Different countries invoke different age thresholds of adulthood; even within countries such thresholds can diverge: one age for voting, another for employment, another for military service. Finally, the category of child admits for heterogeneity: three-year-olds have dramatically different capabilities than fifteen-year-olds.

What is the normative basis of modern society's view of childhood? The concept of a child, implicit in virtually all our moral and legal practices, is that a child is a person who is in some fundamental way not developed, but rather developing.[3] Because of this undeveloped condition adult parents or surrogates are needed to act on children's behalf. Parents or surrogates are thus given special obligations, including the obligations to protect, nurture, and educate children. These obligations are paternalistic, because adults feel bound to fulfill them whether or not the children in question consent to be protected, nurtured, or educated.

Adults feel justified in treating children paternalistically because children have not yet developed the cognitive, moral, and affective capacities to deliberate and act competently in their own interests.[4] At the same time children have legitimate claims to have their interests considered; they are not simply tools. Children are not yet full persons, but they are persons.

NORMATIVE DIMENSIONS OF CHILD LABOR

What are the normative dimensions of child labor? Child labor raises moral concerns because of the weak agency of children (and sometimes of their parents), its connections to underlying vulnerabilities, and especially its potential for extremely harmful outcomes for children themselves, and for society.

Weak Agency

Children cannot be assumed to have full agency. They lack the cognitive, moral, and affective capacities of adults, and they seldom have the power in the family to make decisions about how to allocate their time.[5] Parents are usually the primary decision makers for children, especially very young children, exercising authority and control over most aspects of their children's lives.

Consider the contrast with ideal labor markets, in which workers and employers are fully rational agents who transact on their own behalf with perfect information. As Jane Humphries has pointed out, there is no *infans economicus* responding to market signals; most children are put to work by their parents.[6] This gap between chooser and chosen for in the labor market for child labor opens up the possibility that those children's interests will be discounted. Surrogate decision making is a morally fraught arena, especially in the case of young children, who often cannot even articulate their own interests. Moreover such surrogate agency sometimes breaks down, as in the case of parents who lose custody of children they have abused, exploited, or neglected. Families are not homogeneous entities but intimate associations whose members have heterogeneous interests. We cannot simply assume that the head of household functions as a benevolent dictator in the interests of the family as a whole.

Child labor also differs from ideal labor markets in that the decision maker may lack important information regarding the consequences of his or her choice. The costs of child labor can extend far into the future, having, for example, long-term adverse effects on the child's health. It is not clear that these costs are taken into account, even by well-meaning parents. Lack of information may be especially important if the parents are themselves from very poor or despised social groups. As Dreze and Gazdar point out, "The ability of parents to assess the personal and social value of education depends, among other things, on the information they have at their disposal. If their entire reference group is largely untouched by the experience of being educated, that information might be quite limited."[7] It is noteworthy that children in bonded labor tend to have parents who were also bonded laborers.[8]

In calculating the costs and benefits of children's labor for their families, we should note that children are not analogous to other resources that might be exchanged on the market. Children's market value to their families is not only exogenously determined by supply and demand, but is also determined by the choices parents make. Parents decide how much of their own resources to devote to their children, affecting the skill level and productivity of child laborers. And children affect their own net cost; as adults, they make choices about their commitments to their aging parents.

Agency problems (surrogate decision making, ignorance, uncertainty about the future costs and benefits of educating one's children) may be typically associated with child labor. But even if those choosing child labor were fully informed and chose voluntarily, child labor would not necessarily be morally justified. If the background circumstances and options poor children and their parents face are unjust, the option chosen does not by some mysterious process suddenly become just. A key input for the moral assessment of an action depends on one's views about the moral legitimacy of the socially available choices an agent faces. In other words, whether a choice confers legitimacy depends on other conditions besides its being voluntary. I now turn to consider those other conditions.

Asymmetric Vulnerability

Child labor may be particularly objectionable because of the vulnerabilities that underlie it. These vulnerabilities may be present in exchanges between children and their employers or in the situation of the family itself. The family's vulnerability is likely to be a factor in child labor markets; the majority of parents of child laborers are in a precarious position, often one step away from destitution. They are also likely to be uneducated and illiterate. Child labor then appears as a symptom of an objectionable degree of vulnerability. In some countries caste and ethnic divisions may compound these vulnerabilities.

Child labor can also produce, reflect, and perpetuate unequal vulnerability *within* families. Some families may sacrifice a working child for the sake of other children or family members. They may, for example, keep girls out of school to care for younger children while the mother works outside the home.[9] This extreme bias in favor of some children within a family over others is morally troublesome.

Child labor may also reflect power and resource inequalities between mothers and fathers. A growing body of evidence suggests that mothers have a stronger preference than fathers for investing in their children's welfare, including education.[10]

Extremely Harmful Outcomes

The nature of the damage generated by child labor markets depends on the form of child labor. Many international protocols (including the ILO's Worst Forms of Child Labor Convention 182 and the Sanders Amendment, considered by the U.S. Senate in 1997) view forced labor as one of the worst forms of child labor. But forced labor is not a useful category for distinguishing the most harmful forms of child labor from others. Parents make paternalistic decisions on behalf of their children that can include "forcing" children to go to school. Given the weak agency of children, it follows that almost all child labor (and child education) is forced. It is therefore not possible to identify what is harmful about child labor without a fuller theory of children's interests.

Children have two kinds of interests, which, following Amartya Sen, I referred to earlier as *welfare interests* and *agency interests*.[11] As I defined them in chapter 4, welfare interests concern a person's overall good; agency interests concern his ability to set and pursue his own goals and interests. Both children and adults have these interests, but they possess them in different ways and to different degrees.

Consider welfare interests first. A child's present welfare interests include shelter, food, health, education, bodily integrity, and a stable, loving relationship with his or her parents (or other caregivers). Children need parents to protect and provide for these interests because they cannot yet provide for them themselves. Because of a child's vulnerability and weak agency, the state needs to play a crucial role in serving as a backstop to protect children against parental abuse and neglect. Of course, the state must do more than serve as a backstop against abuse because parents cannot provide all of the things that their children need by themselves, for example, a clean environment. The well-being of children, like that of adults, depends in good measure on the nature of social institutions.

An adult's welfare interests are different. First, adults are not dependent on others in precisely the same way children are. Given appropriate background conditions and institutions, adults are assumed to have the capacity to make choices that enable them to provide for their own welfare: to obtain nourishment, health, and shelter; to find gainful employment; and to exercise a range of their capabilities. Second, adults' welfare is shaped by their own values, by what they care about and how they want to live. An adult's welfare cannot be viewed as completely separable from her conception of value and purpose. An atheistic adult, for example, will likely get little welfare from mandatory religious instruction.

Very young children have few immediate agency interests.[12] But unlike other dependent and vulnerable people (e.g., people with severe cognitive disabilities), in reasonably favorable conditions children will develop the capabilities to set goals for themselves and to choose and act in accordance with their own values. As they develop, children's interest in exercising their agency grows, although given their lack of competency and experience societies still reasonably set legal bounds on it.

Adults, by contrast, have a significant interest in exercising their agency, in being participants in decisions that affect their lives. They reasonably find it offensive to be treated as children. They willingly allow others, such as political leaders, to make decisions on their behalf only with their consent. Corrupt and despotic institutions, which prevail in many of the world's poorest states, are serious obstacles to the achievement and exercise of adult agency.

Although the interests of children and adults differ, children are also developing into adults. Any theory of children's interests must look at those interests dynamically, as contributing to the development of their interests as adults.

On the individual level, harms can be defined in terms of negative effects on a child's present or future (adult) agency and well-being interests. In particular one can define a level of *basic* agency and well-being interests, the failure to satisfy which would be abusive to children or stunt the development of crucial adult capabilities. Child labor that violates children's basic interests would constitute extreme harm.

It is important to distinguish this "basic interests" standard from the "best interests" standard that some children's advocates have proposed for judging child labor. The best interests standard suffers from two major problems. First, because there is no widely shared view of exactly what constitutes a child's *best* interests, parents can interpret the standard in radically different ways.[13] Broad consensus is much more likely to be reached on a basic interests standard.[14]

Second, the best interests standard assumes that parents (which in practice usually means mothers) are mere instruments for optimizing their children's interests and do not count independently. From a moral point of view, this is just wrong. There is no inherent injustice in family structures that assume that children must make some contribution to the well-being of their families as a whole or to other family members. Some trade-offs among interests within the family are acceptable and are, at any rate, inevitable. Work performed by children might thus be acceptable under certain conditions and given certain restrictions.[15]

On the social level, child labor can also generate extreme harms. No society can be indifferent to how children are raised and educated because these factors affect the nature of its future members. Uneducated, illiterate, and passive adults will not be able to contribute much to social development or play a role in responding to social problems. The presence of child labor may inhibit the long-term productive development needed to help the poor move out of their desperate circumstances or to raise up the wealth of a nation.

Child labor can undermine the possibility of a society of equals. Uneducated, illiterate adults will often form a servile social caste, excluded from participating in society's main institutions. Indeed Myron Weiner has argued that in India child labor is itself a symptom of objectionable hierarchy and not poverty; because most of India's labor force come from the lower classes and is involved in performing menial tasks, the upper-class elite has not thought that education for poor children was necessary. Moreover uneducated children grow up to be adults who cannot demand their rights.[16]

In the language of chapter 4, the case for viewing child labor as a noxious market rests on all four of my parameters: weak agency, vulnerability, extreme individual harm, and extreme social harm. Child labor is also likely to have dynamic effects that shape and perpetuate individuals and societies of a certain type where some people are simply used and discarded by others. It is worth underscoring that the children caught up in child labor and who live in extreme poverty around the globe are innocent. They have done nothing to deserve their situation.[17]

POLICY IMPLICATIONS

What should be the response to child labor that scores poorly along these normative dimensions, manifesting weak agency on the part of children or their parents, vulnerability within and between families, or extremely harmful outcomes for children or society? One approach, taken by some activists and NGOs, is to define *all* child labor as a violation of the rights of the child and to call for its immediate abolition. In this framework drawing distinctions between kinds of child labor— hazardous versus nonhazardous, bonded versus non bonded, part time versus full time—is considered pointless because anything short of full-time formal education for children is seen as a threat to children's basic interests.[18]

Although this approach offers little guidance on how it could be implemented—a serious concern in the context of weak states and a weak global order—it nevertheless has an important policy function. Rights, especially legal rights, create, legitimate, and reinforce social understandings about what people deserve.[19] Articulating rights for children may thus have positive effects on children's welfare by reinforcing the idea that children have a claim on the state, society, and ultimately on the international community for their protection.

Assessing the practicality of abolishing child labor by strictly enforcing legal sanctions is difficult because we do not really know whether there are cases in which child labor is an unavoidable reality for some poor countries. Debate continues over the extent to which child labor is caused by poverty and underdevelopment or by policy failures, including failures arising from social and political inequality.

Children's education, rather than child labor, has been linked to economic development. China, the Republic of Korea, and Taiwan (China) all made rapid economic progress while promoting basic education. *Banning child labor and thus restricting the labor market may raise the wages of adult workers enough to make children's work unnecessary.*[20] If this is true, then allowing child labor may make many poor families worse off than an available alternative. We do not yet know the limits of the possible in poor countries themselves or what the industrial countries might do to eradicate child labor if they really had the will.

Given resource constraints and the likely need for trade-offs between values, blanket prohibitions on child labor face two important challenges. First, in some contexts bans on all child labor may drive families to choose even worse options for their children. Children are better off attending school part time than not at all; they are presumably better off working in factories than as prostitutes or soldiers. Policymakers must thus take care to combine legislation or efforts to ban all child labor markets with policies designed to protect children from worse outcomes on the black market.

The second objection to immediate bans on all child labor stems from the recognition that child labor is often a symptom of other problems that will not be eliminated simply by banning child labor. Such problems include poverty, inadequate education systems, discrimination within families, ethnic conflicts, inadequately protected human rights, and weak democratic institutions. Blanket legislation against all child labor may do nothing to address the underlying problems. Additionally many children who do not work do not attend school. Many of these "nowhere" children are likely to be girls who work in the home, helping with chores and child rearing.[21] A focus on enforcing legislative solutions banning child labor may not solve the problems that such children face and may direct scarce resources away from other methods of improving children's lives.

The framework I adopt provides the basis for a somewhat different approach. When we examine children's labor from the perspective of weak agency (especially in the form of parental ignorance and adaptive preferences), vulnerability, and extreme harms, not all work performed by children is equally morally objectionable. Some work, especially work that does not interfere with or undermine their health or education, may allow children to develop skills they need to become well-functioning adults and broaden their future opportunities. Indeed in some countries, given the deficiencies of the public education system, some children work to earn the tuition for private education.[22]

Child labor is most objectionable where it clearly violates children's basic interests. The miserable conditions of abuse that children suffer in some kinds of work cannot be seen as being in a child's basic interests, present or future. According to the most recent study by the ILO, 171 million working children—two-thirds of all working children—are routinely exposed to health risks, violent abuse, and probable injuries. Millions of children are beaten, raped, harassed, and abused, suggesting that more than economic motivations are driving employers (often the children's parents). Indeed children's lives might be much better if only the bloodless impersonal economic motives of an ideal market were at issue. An estimated 8.4 million children are caught in what the ILO refers to as "unconditional worst" forms of labor, including slavery, trafficking, debt bondage, participation in armed conflict, prostitution, and pornography.

Eliminating these forms of child labor should be the highest priority. Even if under some circumstances children have to work, at least in the short term, there is no reason they should suffer the kind of abusive treatment that underlies such practices. No state, NGO, family, lending agency, or consumer can justify participating in activities in which the basic interests of children are completely disregarded, in which children are treated with contempt, their lives disposed of as carelessly as the contents of a trashcan.

Two other considerations should also be used to determine how harmful a child labor practice is. First, children who work and do not go to school will likely lack the capacities that they need—literacy, numeracy, broad knowledge of personal and social alternatives, communication skills—to effectively exercise their agency as adults. One central benefit of education is the ability of an educated person to choose in a more informed way. Education thus deeply influences the quality of a person's life. For example, the ability to read documents and newspapers can help oppressed people demand their rights; it can be especially important to women. Empirical investigations by Murthi, Guio, and Dreze indicate that female literacy is a crucial variable in empowering women in the family and lowering birth rates.[23] Thus even child labor that is not immediately harmful can be very harmful in terms of the child's future well-being and agency interests as an adult.

Second, significant third-party harms can result from child labor. Child labor can lead to an illiterate and minimally productive workforce, reduce adult wages, undermine health, and lead to a passive and ignorant citizenry. It can lead to some people being put in circumstances in which they are entirely dependent on others for basic survival and thus vulnerable to abuse, exploitation, and contempt. It props up a world of servility and humiliation, where the lowly cower and the mighty are arrogant and disdainful. All of society is harmed by such outcomes.

These two types of harm—to the child's future interests as an adult and to society as a whole—are costs that parents may not take into account in making their decisions about how to allocate their children's time. This is especially so in the case of harms to society; few people may be aware of these implications, and even if they are they may not give such considerations much weight in the context of their individual decision making. The discrepancy between parents and children's short-term interests and children's and society's long-term interests suggests two main routes for intervention.

First, where child labor reflects the weak agency of children or their parents, action could be to taken to try to increase both parties' agency. This could be accomplished by providing more information to parents about the true social and individual costs of child labor and the benefits of education, strengthening the intrafamily decision-making process to bolster the mother-child axis (since data suggest that mothers are more likely to attend to their children's interests than are fathers), or requiring that parents sign agreements with their children's employers about the limits on the terms of work, agreements backed up by law.

Second, interventions could aim at changing the external context of family decision making, tackling head-on the underlying poverty that leads to child labor. A widely cited example of a promising intervention is Mexico's Programa de Educación, Salud y Alimentación, which provides cash transfers to mothers whose children attend school. Other strategies include strengthening the education system, restricting children's work days to a limited number of hours so that they can attend school at least part time, encouraging measures (training, organizing) to raise adult wages, and providing credit to poor families.[24]

It is worth reflecting on the environment in which much child labor thrives: crushing poverty, weak states, poor education systems, ethnic conflicts, massive inequalities, and lack of democratic institutions. How much of South Asia, which has the highest absolute numbers of working children, has functioning labor markets? How much of the economy is characterized by bonded labor, serfdom, debt peonage, and the near monopoly pricing of unskilled labor?

Even if one grants that in some circumstances children must work, there is no doubt that children are vastly worse off than they would be if laws created and enforced genuinely free markets, including the right to exit from employment and restrictions on monopoly and monopsony, with perhaps the state stepping in as a source of credit to poor families. Developing and strengthening democratic political and economic institutions is likely to be an essential component in the process of ending child labor.

In the absence of broad changes in policy and commitment, different interventions will lead to different trade-offs between values. For example, imposing a uniform and egalitarian educational system in a country may discriminate against children who are at greatest social and economic disadvantage. Some families may simply not be able to afford to send their children to school full time. But allowing some children to attend school part time undermines a commitment to educational equity and perhaps perpetuates caste and geographic inequalities. Tolerating child labor in some countries will give rise to worries about unfair competition in the international context. When considering various policy tools it is thus extremely important to be explicit about which values are being favored.

CONCLUSIONS

In this chapter I have used my framework to argue for a position between the absolutists who want to immediately abolish all forms of child labor and the contextualists who seek to accommodate it.[25] Trade-offs among different values are inevitable, but there is good reason to draw some bottom lines. Child labor that is abusive to children—prostitution, bondage, slavery, and the employment of children as soldiers—threatens the core of their lives and should not be tolerated. There are other ways for children to provide income for their families that do not involve such extreme harm. But trade-offs between different values above this line need to be weighed in working to eliminate other forms of child labor that score especially high along one or more of the normative dimensions.

Although different people, organizations, families, and states will draw those trade-offs in different ways, it is important to keep the focus on what different policies do to individual children, not to aggregates. Limits should be placed on the costs that policies impose on children in the name of future familial or societal benefits. Children are not mere things, to be used and discarded. Contextualism must be guided and regulated by the universalist standards we are trying to realize.

In a sense the normative perspective proposed here is broadly humanitarian, giving priority to the securing of a decent minimum level of capacities and resources for all children. But the content of this humanitarianism is itself tied to a conception of equality: providing children with the resources they need to be independent adults. As Walzer described this conception of equality, "No more bowing and scraping, fawning and toadying; no more fearful trembling; no more high and mightiness; no more masters, no more slaves."[26] Additionally insofar as liberal democratic institutions are instrumental to that humanitarian goal, promoting them must be part of overall strategies for addressing child labor. Indeed gradualist approaches to ending child labor are more likely to succeed in the context of accountable political entities. The poor are undoubtedly better off when governments do not devote themselves to theft or ethnically based spoils systems but to providing health clinics, primary schools, roads, and communications. Diminishing certain kinds of social inequality may also lead to better outcomes for the most vulnerable and least advantaged.

The state of the world may justify the use of some gradualist measures, but we need to be attentive to the trajectory of societies using child labor. It makes a great deal of difference whether child labor is a transitional strategy that can deliver future benefits to the child or a strategy of exploitation, propping up the profits of ruthless merchants, selfish parents, or corrupt governments or satisfying the whims of sadistic employers. It is thus crucial to establish benchmarks for progress in educating children. These benchmarks can foster accountability and allow tracking of what is actually happening over time to children's interests. If children's interests are to be realized, NGOs and lending institutions need to hold the parties they work with—parents, local villages, corporations, national governments—accountable for what happens to children.[27]

More data and empirical research are needed to identify which gradualist policies should be favored in which contexts. For example, although the claim is sometimes made that children benefit from child labor under some circumstances, insufficient attention has been paid in the empirical literature to the question of whether the child who is working is the *same* child who benefits.

Data are also needed (although difficult to come by) on intrahousehold trade-offs between children and between adults and children. It makes a great deal of difference whether all the children in a family work a little but all go to school or whether daughters are pulled completely out of school so that sons need not work. It is therefore important to continue to gather data on lower levels of analysis to assess the relevance of gender and other factors. Collecting these data could help policymakers formulate effective interventions. They could reveal, for example, that the focus should be on informing parents and teachers about the importance of educating girls or that, if this could be effective, lending agencies should make some of their loans conditional on achieving gender equity in education.

Too much of the data we currently have are underinclusive. In particular very few studies provide data on girls working at home who do not attend school. Indeed the ILO does not include such girls in its statistics on child labor. This limitation on who counts as a working child may be behind the category of nowhere children, children who are neither at work nor at school. Although it may be extremely difficult to obtain survey data on girls working at home, those data are critically important for assessing the effectiveness and the normative adequacy of different policies.

Attention also needs to be paid to children who combine work and school. Subsidy programs may draw children into school without reducing the family's need for the child's labor. Kabeer has noted the implications of this "double burden" for children's achievements and well-being.[28] Studying this group of children is especially important insofar as gradualist strategies for combating child labor are adopted.

Good empirical projects are needed to investigate how and why some states and governments have made substantial progress in educating their children. Poor countries do differ in what they provide to their children. In India, for example, states with similar levels of poverty have dramatically different levels of educational performance. In Uttar Pradesh only 32 percent of rural twelve- to fourteen-year-old girls have ever attended school, about a third as many as in Kerala, where 98 percent of girls this age have attended school.[29] What factors explain this difference in outcomes?[30]

Child labor was once prevalent in what is now the industrial world. Eliminating it in poor societies may not be feasible on the basis of the resources and institutions of those societies. But a key difference between historical and contemporary cases of child labor is that today the industrial world exists. Increasing development aid, ending protectionist policies that close off markets to poor countries, encouraging multinationals to pay higher wages to adult workers, facilitating partnerships in the research and development of products needed by the poor (vaccines, drugs), empowering democratic institutions around the world, and transferring technology may all make a difference. The need for a well-funded global initiative on basic schooling, stressed by the United Nations, is also clear. Child labor may be understandable in parts of the world as a response to poverty. But different distributions of wealth and power would undercut the need for child labor. Much depends on whether these alternative distributions can be realized.[31]

8

Voluntary Slavery and the Limits of the Market

Most anyone ought to know that a man is better off free than as a slave, even if he
did not have anything. I would rather be free and have my liberty. I fared just as
well as any white child could have fared when I was a slave, and yet I would not
give up my freedom.

—*Reverend E. P. Holmes, 1883*

One of the most momentous achievements of modern Western capitalism was the transition from a system of bonded labor, indentured servitude and forced work to a system of formally free contractual labor. Fifty years ago it might have been assumed that just as indenture and bondage declined in the industrial world, it would eventually disappear everywhere with capitalism's globalization. But bondage has not faded away. In parts of the world today labor bondage and similar practices persist under other names (e.g., debt peonage, attached labor, serfdom, debt slavery). In a bonded labor arrangement "a person is tied to a particular creditor as a laborer for an indefinite period until some loan in the past is repaid."[1] In practice this indefinite period can last a lifetime. Bonded workers are often completely servile, forced to exhibit deference and subordination to their employers both on and off the job.[2] Even those who have defended the economic rationality of such relationships have noted the "ugly power relations" involved in the phenomenon.[3] The International Labour Organization estimates that some 12.3 million people, many of them children, are held as bonded laborers around the globe.[4]

Although bonded labor is considered by many to be a paradigm of unfree labor and is often analogized to slavery, it is generally contracted voluntarily. Indeed while slavery itself is usually rooted in an initial act of coercion, it is not necessary for even slavery to originate in violence and force. Slavery has been reported to be voluntary in a number of important historical instances.[5]

How might labor bondage arise voluntarily? Because poor peasants have no assets, they have no formal collateral. The wages they receive tend to vary with the agricultural seasons; they are lower during the lean seasons when unemployment is high and higher during the peak growing seasons when unemployment is low. In many cases peasants' survival from one harvest season to the next will depend on borrowing for consumption during the lean seasons; they simply do not earn enough during peak seasons to save.

Consider the case of a landlord who offers credit in exchange for a laborer's agreement to pledge his future services as collateral for the loan. In so doing the landlord increases his power to enforce the agreement because he can directly deduct the amount due from the worker's wages during peak season. And the laborer now has access to credit that might not otherwise have been available to him. From the perspective of contract theory, it is not evident that there should be any legally imposed limits on competent adult landlords and laborers who seek to enter such contracts. For if agents are rational and can foresee the future consequences of their contractual provisions, there is no reason not to allow borrowers the freedom to commit to providing indentured services to lenders should they lack the resources to repay their loans.

In this chapter I examine the ways that two different frameworks with different underlying normative assumptions view the phenomenon of bonded labor: libertarian laissez-faire theory and Paretian welfare economics. Libertarians believe that consensual agreements between competent adults should be respected.[6] Paretians endorse exchanges that leave both parties better off in terms of their preferences. Each theory gives us reasons for endorsing many, if not most instances of the practice of bonded labor, reasons that are intuitively plausible. But each theory also ignores or dismisses other considerations, such as those that I raised in earlier chapters, that might lead us to view *these very same* instances of labor bondage more critically.

I argue that neither theory fully accounts for our objections to bonded labor, objections that are codified in the laws of developed capitalist countries. In the United States, for example, there are important restrictions on labor contracts: the state does not enforce voluntary slavery contracts, debt slavery, specific performance as a remedy for breach, or contracts that are considered "unconscionable." Libertarianism and Paretianism do not adequately account for these restrictions. Moreover their failures to do so are *interesting;* they support my claim that we cannot rely on abstract concepts of freedom, equality, and externality to evaluate market exchanges.

In considering the adequacy of these theories to account for our objections to bonded labor, I distinguish between two important dimensions of bonded labor: the background circumstances in which bonded labor arises (ideal versus nonideal markets) and the nature of the agent whose labor is bonded (adult laborer versus child laborer). With respect to the first dimension, bonded labor arrangements tend to arise in desperate circumstances, where they exploit the vulnerabilities of the most vulnerable and make some people utterly dependent on the will and whims of other people.

Even in more ideal circumstances, where there are no market failures and no dire poverty, we still have reasons not to enforce labor bondage agreements. Beginning with the case of children, I build on my argument in chapter 7, arguing that bondage of children's labor can stunt the development of the capacities they will need to be able to stand as social equals. Bondage prepares children for a life of servility based on "misunderstanding one's rights . . . (or) placing a comparatively low value on them."[7] I then suggest that my argument about children can provide a lever to mount an objection to binding the labor of adults; perhaps if the capacities to stand as an equal can be stunted by bonded labor arrangements, they can also be lost. I draw on some empirical evidence to suggest that the capacity for autonomy is, as John Stuart Mill put it, "in most natures a very tender plant, easily killed, not only by hostile influences, but by mere want of sustenance; and in the majority of young persons it speedily dies away if the occupations to which their position in life has devoted them, and the society into which it has thrown them, are not favorable to keeping that higher capacity in exercise."[8]

The central idea I defend here is that where certain competitive markets undermine or block egalitarian relationships between people, there is a case for market regulation, even when such markets are otherwise efficient or arise on the basis of individual rational choice.[9]

LIBERTARIANISM

Libertarians believe in the principle of freedom of contract within the bounds of justice. If two or more rational adults agree to an exchange, then, provided that they are actually entitled to the goods they are exchanging and that no one else's rights are thereby violated, the government (and other agents) ought not to interfere. In Robert Nozick's pithy formulation, libertarians do not forbid "capitalist acts between consenting adults."[10] Whereas economists typically value free market exchange as an instrument of efficiency, the ability to freely exchange one's own property is seen by libertarians as closely connected to the freedom and inviolability, the separateness and sanctity, of the individual person.[11]

In evaluating the permissibility of a particular bonded labor contract, a libertarian will consider whether the goods and services to be exchanged were acquired by legitimate means and whether or not the exchange was voluntary. If these conditions are met, then according to the libertarian the exchange should be allowed. In *Anarchy, State and Utopia* Nozick claims that respect for the principle of freedom of contract entails that individuals even have the right to sell themselves into slavery.[12]

Because the libertarian justification of the freedom to participate in bonded labor or slavery contracts refers to the idea of voluntary choice, its application seems to depend on an understanding of what makes an act of exchange voluntary as opposed to coerced.[13] What coercion consists of, however, is an elusive matter; the distinction between offers that are coercive and those that are not is notoriously difficult to draw. As I noted in chapter 1, coercion rarely takes the form of direct compulsion that deprives individuals of all choice. Even when a gunman threatens "Your money or your life," what makes the offer coercive is clearly not that you have no power to choose.

On Nozick's account, what makes an offer coercive is that it decreases an agent's position with reference to her legitimate baseline situation.[14] Even though an individual confronted with a gunman's threat might well decide freely to hand over her money, she is coerced given that the gunman has no right to her money and that by taking it he impermissibly worsens her situation with respect to her legitimate entitlements.

Nozick's point is that coercion is essentially a normative concept.[15] Two people can agree on all the facts about an exchange and still reasonably disagree as to whether one party to the exchange was coerced by the other. Whether or not they each find an offer coercive is dependent on their prior determination as to whether the coerced party had a legitimate entitlement that was violated. The reason that the extreme constraints an agent faces due to poverty, lack of education, and so forth would be said to render her action coerced is if she has a right, of some kind, not to be in such circumstances.

Libertarians of course do not generally think that the state has any affirmative duty to improve the background circumstances of an individual, no matter how bad these circumstances are. In thinking about the legitimacy of bonded labor contracts, then, a main issue between libertarians and their egalitarian critics concerns the nature of agents' underlying entitlements: the morally acceptable baseline for agreeing to (or threatening not to) contract.

What kind of underlying entitlements, particularly with respect to property, do libertarians think people have? Libertarians tend to think that property rights rest on something like the rights of first claimants.[16] As long as a landlord was the first to produce goods on the land or acquired property in land via a voluntary transfer from the first claimant, libertarians will grant the landlord an exclusive right to determine how this land is used. On the libertarian view, the state acts unjustly if it prevents the landlord from using his land and the surplus that it generates as he wishes. If an individual landlord wishes to loan some of his surplus to others, then he should be free to decide the terms under which he is willing to forgo the private use of some of his own resources. It is the landlord's piece of good luck if he finds others willing to accept his highly unequal terms, but, on the libertarian view, this good luck generates no injustice.[17]

Although libertarianism is often seen as the theory most compatible with a pure form of capitalism, it can also embrace and justify a system of voluntary feudalism that includes serfdom.[18] Indeed if a feudal lord acquired his land by first title and offered employment on his land to only those who wished to live under his protection and accept his terms, a libertarian like Nozick would condemn state intervention to limit his power. This means that at least some versions of libertarianism are compatible with the permanent direct subjection of one individual to another.[19]

A libertarian who puts great weight on initial just acquisition would point out that in fact much of the lord's initial acquisition during feudalism was based on plunder, fraud, and violence. Libertarians do not accept as legitimate agreements based on force or fraud. If the agreements reached between a landlord and a bonded laborer had dirty origins—if they are based in employer malfeasance or maintained only by physical violence—then this is a reason for not respecting these agreements.[20]

Not all libertarians worry about the origins of property rights; some emphasize the importance of respecting individual rights in property, however these rights have been erected.[21] But even these libertarians recognize *some* limits on private property rights.[22] As we shall see below, even Nozick argues that a person cannot legitimately acquire all of the water in the world. Some libertarians might argue that individuals have a nonalienable right to self-ownership, so that they cannot contract themselves into permanent slavery, although everything short of permanent slavery is acceptable.[23]

Let's consider in more detail the example of a very poor laborer who has agreed to bond himself to a landlord in order to attain a loan. In theory a state can set limits on the private property rights involved in this transaction in a number of very different ways:[24]

1. The state can accept that it has an affirmative duty to give the laborer subsistence income or other employment choices to enlarge her background alternatives. If she still enters into the bonded labor contract, it can refuse to enforce the contract.

2. The same as (1), except that if the laborer under improved circumstances still enters into the bonded labor contract, the state will now enforce the contract.

3. Although it has no affirmative duty to improve the background options of the laborer, the state can refuse to enforce the bonded labor contract in any fashion, even if the laborer defaults.

4. The state can refuse to enforce the bonded labor contract and make it a crime for anyone to solicit voluntary servitude arrangements with workers. It can prosecute the landlord.

5. The state can enforce the contract through specific performance and require the laborer to work for the lender until his debt is repaid but alter the substantive terms of the exchange to make it less lopsidedly favorable to the landlord. For example, the state can set legal limits on the amount of interest that a lender can charge for a loan.

6. The state can refuse to enforce the contract through a specific performance decree but give the employer some other sort of monetary or equitable remedy (e.g., allowing the employer to garnish the wages of the employee when she goes to work for someone else).[25]
7. The state can enforce the contract as written through a specific performance decree, and in the event the employee fails to comply with it, prevent her from working for anyone else.
8. Same as above, but the state can enforce the decree by jailing the employee if she defaults on her loan.

Which of these scenarios is a libertarian committed to accept? Libertarians do not generally hold that the state has any affirmative obligation to improve the background circumstances of a laborer, and hence they tend to reject (1), (2), and (5). Libertarians believe that treating individuals with respect precludes the state from compelling them to transfer any of their resources to others, even if those others are in dire need. But in practice almost no libertarian would go all the way to either (7) or (8). Nozick, for example, doesn't; when faced with some de facto monopolistic markets, such as a monopoly over water in a desert, he won't even go as far as (6).[26]

In *Anarchy, State and Utopia* Nozick defends a version of the "Lockean proviso," which argues that to be legitimate an initial act of appropriation must not leave anyone worse off than he would have been had there been no appropriation at all.[27] This appeal to the Lockean proviso, and to welfare-based restrictions on the principle of freedom of contract, sits uncomfortably within the confines of libertarian theory.[28] After all, the libertarian's commitment to freedom of contract is supposed to be justified *independently* of its consequences for human welfare. For once we admit that the welfare consequences for individuals can form a basis for evaluating other people's entitlements, why should we not contrast the property regime embraced by libertarians with other alternatives, such as a redistributive welfare state that limits background property rights and redistributes income? Perhaps a poor landless peasant would be better off under some alternative form of ownership than he would be under a libertarian regime of private property. At the very least the peasant might be better off if his background assets were more equal to his employer's.

It is striking how strongly Nozick's version of the Lockean proviso resembles the Pareto efficiency criterion appealed to by welfare economists.[29] However, even if we admit some version of the Lockean proviso, it won't necessarily kick in with respect to bonded labor arrangements. What if the employer's monopolizing power is based not on appropriated natural resources such as land, but simply on social power and capital? Nozickean libertarians would deny the application of the proviso at all in that situation.

Of course the fact that libertarians think that people can legitimately enter into bonded labor agreements does not itself entail that they think that the state is *required* to enforce such agreements in any particular way (or even to enforce them at all. Nozick himself says surprisingly little about the enforcement of rights). My point, however, is that there is nothing in Nozick's libertarian theory that *rules out* the state's demanding that a laborer comply with the terms of his contract by specific performance or imprisoning him if he fails to perform his part of the agreement. Further it would seem that for Nozick the state may have a duty to refrain from interfering with the private enforcement of these contracts, which implies its recognition of them.

A libertarian might yet have another objection to press against at least some bonded labor arrangements. As we saw in chapter 7, most children who work are put to work by their parents. Libertarians might claim that parents are not entitled to bond the labor of their children, at least not into adulthood. To the extent that the libertarian defense of the principle of freedom of contract rests on the idea that individuals are voluntarily contracting on their own behalf, or for others who have (voluntarily) designated them to act on their behalf, there is room for libertarian criticism of practices that involve parents using their children's labor as collateral for their own loans.

Like most libertarians (and to be fair, most political philosophers), Nozick says little about children's positive rights.[30] In fact some libertarians argue that although it would be a good thing if parents cultivated their children's abilities, they have no obligation to do so. Their only obligation is not to harm their children.[31] Of course to identify "harm" to children we have to know the appropriate baseline for comparison. There are tricky issues here for libertarians because young children cannot provide for their own needs but require *others* to do so for them.[32] Do children have substantive rights over the time and caring labor of their parents?

Whatever baseline of entitlement we take young children to have will be closely connected to the entitlement of their parents. If children have a right not to starve, then the best way to ensure that right may be to improve the background circumstances of their adult parents. Again this is a strategy that libertarians generally reject.

Moreover, as I emphasized in chapter 7, children are not born with all the requisite capacities for making choices, acting justly, and supporting themselves. The development of an independent individual depends on, among other things, nourishment, education, information, and favorable social circumstances. In particular children raised to be servile laborers tied to a single employer for a lifetime will likely lack the habits and dispositions that enable them to see themselves as rights bearers and independent sources of moral claims. Indeed children whose parents are bonded laborers may find their own self-conceptions shaped by the relations of domination and subordination around them. If this is so, there is a long-term instability to a libertarian regime that does not prevent the bondage of children's labor: it will fail to reproduce itself because it will create people who lack the dispositions and capacities to sustain libertarian values and conceptions of the self.[33]

With the exceptions of malfeasance and children, then, many libertarians have no principled objection to even lifelong bonded labor arrangements, as long as the baseline entitlements of the contractors are legitimate and the contracts freely entered into. They have no principled objections to feudal serfdom arrangements, so long as these were established by contract rather than by birth or conquest. Ironically, far from being the natural ideology for a capitalist society, libertarianism has difficulty representing capitalism as a *moral* advance over feudalism, to the extent that its rise depended on curtailing feudal property rights over labor.[34]

PARETIAN WELFARE ECONOMICS

Welfare economics evaluates institutions in terms of whether they make people better or worse off. Typically, as we have seen, welfare economists operate with a view of human welfare (or well-being) that identifies it with the satisfaction of preferences.[35] Unfortunately the extent to which the preferences of different individuals are satisfied is difficult, if not impossible, to compare. Recall, however, that welfare economists do have a way of comparing social states without comparing individual preferences: by using the concept of a Pareto optimum.

There is a large literature that argues that under certain assumptions, the practice of labor bondage is a Pareto improvement, even if it is not Pareto optimal. A Pareto improvement is a change in a social state that leaves at least one person better off and no one worse off. Bardhan shows that landlords have incentives to offer such long-term contracts to avoid costly recruitment of workers in the peak season.[36] He also argues that such contracts can provide risk-averse laborers with insurance against income fluctuations through varying seasons and risk-neutral landlords with assured cheap labor during peak season.[37] Braverman and Stiglitz analyze how labor-tying contracts can give incentives for agricultural laborers to work more productively in the slack season.[38] Srinivasan argues that attempts to reduce the landlord's power by restricting his credit activities will lower agrarian output and make tenants worse off.[39]

Of course the Paretian evaluation of bondage as *an improvement* depends on, among other things, the assumption that the parties to an agreement are rational and have adequate information. But a peasant who agrees to borrow from a lender at the interest rate of 20 percent per month may not understand what he is actually agreeing to. A positive evaluation also depends on the absence of significant transaction costs.

What about under more ideal conditions, where there is adequate knowledge and no transaction costs? In such a world wouldn't Paretians have to reject restrictions on the freedom to contract as inefficient? Doesn't prohibiting a landlord and peasant from contracting as they wish stand in the way of obvious gains from trade?

Not necessarily. When an individual acts so as to maximize his welfare, we should not assume that he does so within a set of constraints that is exogenously defined. The set of choices that an agent faces is often endogenous. Allowing laborers the option to bond themselves to their creditors may make alternative options (that the laborers would actually prefer) unavailable to them.[40]

Recall the example of child labor. For an individual family, child labor may look to be the family's best option. At the same time, however, the widespread availability of child labor can serve to drive down the wages and skills of the adult laborers, thus making child labor necessary for every family. The institution of child labor thus restrains the set of alternatives available to poor families so that they now have no better choice than to send their children to work. This is an important point of "moral mathematics" stressed by Derek Parfit. Our evaluation of a set of acts need not be the same as our evaluation of each act contained within the set.[41] *Although an individual act (token) of child labor may be Pareto improving when we consider its consequences for a single poor family, the practice (type) of child labor may make other families worse off by changing the range of options that are open to them.*

When evaluating social policies about markets it is also important to recognize that there are often multiple equilibria, all of which are Pareto optimal. For example, for a given society, there can be one optimum with child labor and low adult wages and another optimum with high adult wages and no child labor. Which one is reached depends on the background entitlements that agents have, the rules of the game, so to speak. Those rules make some outcomes more likely than others.

The fact that Pareto optima are rarely unique reveals some interesting limits of the Paretian justification of labor bondage. First, by revealing the ways that the set of choices an agent faces are endogenously determined, we undercut one classic defense of the market. That is, the recognition of the endogenous nature of choice sets leaves open the question of institutional evaluation. If two different systems create and satisfy different preferences, on what grounds should we choose between them?

Second, the endogeneity of choices shows us that the distinction between a voluntary choice and an imposed form of servitude is not so clear. Powerful agents often act to restrict the set of choices open to less powerful agents, who then choose the best option that is now available. (Indeed the choices of poor peasants are inevitably made against a background of property rights and market institutions that they are not able to choose.) Permitting child labor is in the interests of some employers because it provides them with a cheaper source of labor than adults. Such employers may seek to manipulate the choice environment.

Third, the endogeneity of agents' preferences and choice sets in bonded labor suggests that in some exchanges the parties themselves—their culture, their values, and their preferences—might be partly constituted by the exchange itself. This insight—that certain kinds of exchanges not only distribute things but also distribute power and shape the kind of people we become—is missing from the conventional welfare economist's approach to markets.[42] If we incorporate the idea that our preferences and capacities are not fixed into our economic models, then we cannot ignore the ways that a set of social arrangements is likely to change us.

Of course, there is no reason that welfare economists must limit themselves to Paretianism. As we saw, there are other conceptions of *efficiency*, in particular the idea of *potential* Pareto improvements: Kaldor-Hicks efficiency. As we saw earlier, this idea is behind cost-benefit analysis. In theory, if banning child labor raised the productivity of adult labor enough (perhaps by stimulating increased employer inputs into developing adult skills) so that winners could compensate the losers, then the ban would be justified.

There are also other conceptions of *welfare*: one could move away from the assumption that preference satisfaction is the correct measure of welfare. Amartya Sen's view describes certain basic functionings, "beings and doings," that an individual needs to achieve a certain quality of life. These basic functionings include nourishment, literacy, life expectancy, satisfying work, and the ability to appear in public without shame. Well-being, understood as quality of life, does not consist exclusively in a person's level of subjective preference satisfaction but is primarily a matter of the objectively defined functionings that she actually achieves. If we accept Sen's view, we might try to rank alternative equilibria in terms of the important functionings that they actually make open to people. We might also want to include such considerations as whether the contracting parties live at the mercy of their creditors, and whether they have a role in determining the choice sets they face.[43] This will take us beyond considerations of welfare.

WHY BONDED LABOR IS NOXIOUS

Although bonded labor can be the product of an agreement and although it can improve an individual worker's welfare, it has other features that make it noxious.

Vulnerability

Labor bondage arises in circumstances in which some people lack the resources to protect themselves against life-threatening hunger due to crop failures or seasonal unemployment. Lenders take advantage of the vulnerability of workers in these situations, offering credit on terms that are well below what people who were less desperate would accept.[44] The background desperation behind this agreement arouses our suspicion that the exchange is unfair. Perhaps in more ideal circumstances we could imagine bonded labor that did not arise on the basis of a desperate exchange and that was not exploitive. But this consideration certainly underwrites our moral repugnance at the existing practices of labor bondage.

Weak Agency

Most people who enter into bondage are innumerate and illiterate. It is not plausible to think that they understand the terms of the loans that they are accepting.[45] Although most bondage arrangements allow for the termination of the contract once the debt is repaid, in practice these arrangements often last a lifetime. Bonded laborers are not free to leave their employment, even when they can obtain employment on better terms (and thus accelerate repayment of their debt). Agricultural workers in India and Pakistan, where labor bondage is a frequent occurrence, rarely pay off their debts in their own lifetime. When they die before their debts are repaid, their children and grandchildren are sent to work in their place.

If they have the information, why shouldn't people be able to contract themselves to an employer for a lifetime? I think that no one should be able to bind her future self in such a manner because people have what I have called a basic agency interest, which includes maintaining some arena for choice and decisions. Moreover bondage not only involves a surrender of decision making, but it gives this power to another person. I have argued that any society is harmed by the dependency and servility of its members. But even those who disagree and think that maintaining minimal autonomy is not a basic interest, or deny that relational equality is an important value, should be concerned that such arrangements have the potential for very harmful individual outcomes. Not only does an individual lack complete knowledge about her future self—what I have been calling weak agency—but her conditions are likely to change in ways that she cannot now predict and in which, having surrendered her independence, she may be very badly off. Given the potential for extreme harm it makes sense from a regulatory standpoint to set down guidelines (e.g., no lifetime contracts without exit) that minimize the risk of future serious harm.

Extreme Individual Harms

In practice bonded workers lack the freedom to disobey their employer's commands, no matter how arbitrary, humiliating, or personally costly such commands are. Workers are expected to answer to their employer's demands around the clock both in the fields and in their own homes. Although poor peasants retain some formal control over their bodies and their labor, in bonded labor arrangements they most often lack any meaningful substantive control. Like the worker in a company town, the bonded laborer lives in complete dependence on his employer, vulnerable to the employer's whims and abuse.

Research shows that labor bondage is not only a contractual phenomenon, but also a psychological one. In a study of workers held in debt bondage in northeastern Brazil, subject workers referred to their employers as men (*homens*) and to themselves as goats (*cabras*), perhaps indicating their social subordination.[46] Studies have also reported on the role of social norms in preparing women and lower-caste men for lives of submissiveness and compliance. Women who have been abducted as sexual slaves and children who have been repeatedly sold sometimes return to their owners when freed.

Consider the example of Baldev, a bonded laborer who managed to free himself through a windfall inheritance from a relative. Two years later, lacking any preparation for freedom, he reentered bondage. In an interview, he explained:

> After my wife received the money, we paid off our debt and were free to do what-
> ever we wanted. But I was worried all the time—what if one of our children got
> sick? What if our crop failed? What if the government wanted some money? Since
> we no longer belonged to the landlord, we didn't get food everyday as before.
> Finally, I went to the landlord and asked him to take me back. I didn't have to
> borrow any money, but he agreed to let me be his halvaha [bonded plowman]
> again. Now I don't worry so much; I know what to do.[47]

Baldev places little value on his ability to make decisions, exhibiting a condition that, following the philosopher Thomas Hill, I will call *servility*.[48] A servile person not only refuses to press his rights in certain cases, but does not see himself as having rights in the first place. Even when he is able to walk away from bondage his mind is unfree, shaped by a world in which others have always made decisions for him.

For workers who have been bonded for decades and whose employers constantly reinforce their inferiority and the preordained nature of their bondage, it can be frightening to contemplate disobedience or flight. Bonded workers are often purposely isolated from nonbonded laborers so that their horizons remain narrow and their aspirations low. In such circumstances they may well come to believe that their servility is the way things must be, inevitable and right.[49]

These aspects of labor bondage are reasons not to enforce or support such arrangements even where they arise through an agreement and represent subjective welfare improvements. Baldev may be happier as a bonded laborer since this is the life he has been prepared for. But the state has good reasons not to lend its support to arrangements that depend on the exploitation of the vulnerabilities of the most vulnerable, permanently bind one person to another, give one person inordinate power over another, or undermine the capacities of individuals to stand in society as equals. Arguably several of these reasons are relevant to the desperate and nonideal circumstances under which bondage arises. But the example of Baldev also directs our attention to the need for society to produce and reproduce certain capacities in its members.

Every society depends on its members having the capability to behave in ways that realize that society and reproduce it in their actions, preferences, and habits of mind. In particular democratic societies depend on the ability of their citizens to operate as equals. This means not only that in such societies people have equal rights, but also that they *see themselves* as having equal basic rights, *understand* and act on the requirements of justice, and *accept that they and others are* self-authenticating sources of claims who do not need to ask permission to have and make demands.

Work occupies a large fraction of most adults' time and attention. The idea that work is a source of personal development has received support in experimental studies. Researchers have found, for example, that the way work is organized has a real and substantial impact on psychological functioning.[50] Studies have measured the effect of work organization on workers' capacities for independence, attitudes toward conformity, self-concept, and sense of moral responsibility.

In thinking about labor markets our evaluative frameworks will miss important normative dimensions of such markets if we think only in the terms of libertarianism or Paretianism. As the classical economists understood, in free labor markets not only are *preferences* created, but also certain *skills and capabilities* are enabled while others are hindered or eroded.[51] If egalitarians are to embrace the aim of ensuring that people have the ability to stand in society and relate to one another as equals, then they cannot be indifferent about the effects of institutions on skills and capabilities. Our evaluation of institutions, including markets, thus needs to consider their possible effects on human motivations, aspirations, and capabilities.

WHAT'S SO SPECIAL ABOUT LABOR BONDAGE?

Most labor contracts involve at least one of the parties surrendering some aspects of control over herself. Furthermore many unskilled workers who retain the formal ability to exit from their employers have no realistic alternative options. Finally, it is unclear whether the practice of bonding labor is inherently hostile to the capacities needed for independence and equal social relations. Aren't there forms of contract that, while enacting "specific performance" or restrictions on a worker's ability to exit, are perfectly compatible with equality of social relations? What about professional sports players tied to a particular team, or soldiers?[52]

Undoubtedly many of the problems associated with bonded labor have to do not with the bondage per se, but with extreme poverty, lack of education, imperfect information, incomplete credit markets, and lack of decent alternatives for the poor. These considerations are important for the assessment of the practice, just as they are important for the assessment of prostitution and contract pregnancy. But I do not believe that they exhaust our reasons to be concerned with employment contracts. Some labor contracts are affronts to the equal standing of the agents by their overt content. In this category would likely fall slave contracts and contracts that allow an employer to sexually harass his employees in exchange for a wage. Other contracts may be objectionable because of their scope. People frequently enter into agreements that bind their future selves (that's what most contracts do, after all), but we have reasons to reject what are effectively *permanent* labor-tying contracts. To the extent that we value allowing people to form, revise, and act on their conceptions of value, we have strong reasons to allow people to retain the legal right to exit (at some point) from their employment relationships with other adults and not to make irreversible permanent agreements. To the extent that we seek to place limits on the power that one person can exercise over another to maintain the conditions for individual freedom and equality, we have strong reasons not to enforce permanent labor-tying contracts even when they offer fair remuneration and are the products of an agreement.

Reflecting on what is special about bonded labor prompts us to consider (again) the meaning of equality. Labor movements have long recognized the centrality of concerns about the social bases of self-respect in negotiating contracts.[53] Workers have struck not only over wages and hours, but also for the right to organize and for the establishment of limits on the non-job-related discretionary power of their employers. More generally, liberal societies have typically placed limits on the authority that one person has over another; they do not enforce "specific performance" in the majority of contracts, they do not enforce contracts whose terms are considered unconscionable, and they do not throw people into prison for nonpayment of a debt. Such societies also recognize the right of people to divorce one another, even after they have pledged lifelong fidelity.

CONCLUSION AND IMPLICATIONS

Two important schools of thought, Paretian welfarism and libertarianism, are committed in theory to an ideal market without limits. Neither theory would condemn bondage contracts, or indeed voluntary slavery contracts, in principle. Instead such arrangements are condemned insofar as they generate externalities, reflect imperfect information, are the effects of incomplete markets, or are based on physical force or theft.

Ironically neither theory has the resources to fully appreciate capitalism's advance over its feudal predecessor. Capitalist markets are not facts of nature, but are shaped by social preconditions, including underlying entitlements and social norms. In order to transform feudal relations, capitalism had to limit property rights and transform the ways people related to one another, conceived of one another, and indeed conceived of themselves. To appreciate the magnitude of this transformation, contrast the idea of equal citizenship with Augustine's idea of natural servitude:

> It is you [the Catholic Church] who make wives subject to their husbands . . . by chaste and faithful obedience; you set husbands over wives; you join sons to their parents by a freely granted slavery, and set sons above their parents in pious dom-ination. . . . You teach slaves to be loyal to their masters. . . . You bind all men together in the remembrance of their first parents, not just by social bonds, but by some feeling of their common kinship. You teach kings to rule for the benefit of their people; and you it is who warn the people to be subservient to their kings.[54]

This conception of servility as the cement of society is completely alien to our own moral and political universe in the West. But millions of people in the developing world have no rights against employer violence, little political voice, and few civil rights and are routinely exploited, sexually abused, traded to others, or simply disposed of. Bonded labor thrives in societies without compulsory education (either in law or, more typically, in practice), with weak rule of law, weak formal credit and labor markets, and weak rights of exit and where caste-like social divisions and conflicts are common.[55] That's not capitalism, that's feudalism.

9

Ethical Issues in the Supply and Demand of Human Kidneys

Societies sometimes ban the sale of goods whose supply they actually wish to support or encourage.[1] Examples include bans on markets in votes, children, and human organs. In the United States sales of organs such as kidneys are currently illegal, and those needing transplants must rely on altruistic donation. From an economic perspective, an organ ban appears inefficient, as it seems likely that payments to donors would elicit greater supply, thereby reducing chronic shortages. From a libertarian perspective, a ban on organ sales is an illegitimate infringement on personal liberty; allowing people to sell their own body parts is merely a way of recognizing their legitimate sphere of control.[2] Nonlibertarian proponents of a market in human organs also argue that a ban on sales is morally dubious because lives would be saved by the increased supply.

The idea of establishing a kidney market is now attracting unprecedented support among those involved in transplantation, as well as among economists and medical ethicists. This chapter examines the values at stake in the debate about organ markets, drawing on the framework I developed in chapter 4. But I also raise a distinct consideration that is relevant to these markets: the link between markets and motives. Unlike the cases of child labor, bonded labor, sex, and surrogacy, we have an interest in motivating people to act in ways that increase the supply of transplant organs.

BRIEF BACKGROUND: THE STATUS QUO SYSTEMS OF KIDNEY PROCUREMENT

Despite the prima facie case for organ markets just noted, kidney selling is currently illegal in every developed society in the world.[3] The United Nations and the European Union have instructed their member countries to prohibit the sale of body parts. The World Health Organization has interpreted the Universal Declaration of Human Rights as prohibiting the sale of organs. Indeed most of the globe's countries have enacted legal bans of such sales, although states differ dramatically in their enforcement capacity, and a black market thrives in many countries.

In the United States people can donate their kidneys after death or while they are alive only out of altruism. The Uniform Anatomical Gift Act, drafted in 1984 (the same year the National Organ Transplantation Act was enacted), made it illegal for anyone to receive any payment, or "valuable consideration," for providing an organ. Instead those who need kidneys must rely largely on individual or social exhortation to induce people to donate. The result is that most live donations come from close relatives or intimates, with parents entrusted to make decisions about whether a child can serve as a donor for a sibling or relative. Individuals have a right to donate their kidneys to loved ones, but not a right to sell them.

Cadaver organs in the United States come from two main groups: those who explicitly consented to have their organs used after their death, whether through a living will or indicating a wish to be a donor on a driver's license, and those who are *presumed* to have consented. More than fifteen states rely on presumed consent laws, whereby someone who undergoes a mandatory autopsy (often in the context of a homicide) is presumed to have consented to the use of some of his organs unless he explicitly objected to such donations prior to his death.[4] (In the United States presumed consent laws are limited to bodies under the authority of the coroner or medical examiner.)

Individuals also have the right *not* to donate their organs; *no* society makes kidney donation mandatory. Current U.S. law protects living persons from having their organs taken from them without their consent, even in cases in which another person's life is at stake.[5] If exhortation fails to secure an organ, the person needing the donation has no (legal) recourse but instead must wait his turn on the transplant list.[6] Currently there are long queues for obtaining a kidney. In the United States alone there were more than fifty thousand Americans on the waiting list for a kidney in 2003. That same year there were twelve thousand donors.[7] This means that thirty-eight thousand people were carried over onto the 2004 waiting list, along with the year's new additions to that list. Many people wait years before an organ becomes available. Several thousand people die each year in the United States alone while waiting for an organ transplant.[8] Some of these people would not have died had an organ been available for them at the time they needed it most.[9]

A number of European societies rely on an opt-out system of organ procurement rather than the opt-in system used in the United States. In many nations—including Austria, Belgium, Denmark, Finland, France, Italy, Luxemburg, Norway, Singapore, and Spain—all individuals are presumed to consent to allow their organs to be used after their death for the benefit of others. In an opt-out system the default position is that every individual's organs are available on her demise, although each individual is permitted to rebut the presumption (to opt out), usually signaled by an explicit notation on a driver's license.[10]

Moving toward an opt-out baseline allocation system could be a justified social policy if it saved lives, but it does not appear to solve the shortage of organs needed for transplant. Shortages remain in many European countries, including in those that rely on opt-out allocation systems.[11] In fact some studies suggest that the choice of opt-out systems over opt-in systems often makes little difference to the ultimate numbers of organs procured.[12] This result might seem counterintuitive, but there are three reasons why changing the default starting point might not increase the yield of organs. First, many countries with opt-out systems give relatives a right of refusal with respect to cadaveric donations, even when the deceased indicated support for such donations. And relatives frequently choose to forgo donation for religious or personal reasons. Second, many procured organs are simply not suitable for transplantation; the deceased may have been very old or very sick or not found in time for his organs to be useful after death.[13] And the ability to effectively procure an organ, to safely and quickly remove it and deliver it for transplantation, seems to depend crucially on institutional factors.[14] Third, given burgeoning rates of obesity and diabetes and longer life spans, the numbers of people needing kidney transplants continues to grow at a faster rate than do increases in the supply.

ANTI-MARKET CONSIDERATIONS

As we have seen, the free market has considerable appeal: freedom of contract is taken to promote liberty; competitive markets are supposed to pay each input what it deserves (its marginal product); and markets tend to be extremely efficient mechanisms for the production and distribution of goods. Given the shortages in available kidneys and the strong interests at stake, it is not surprising that when a kidney was offered for sale on eBay the bidding reached $5.8 million before being shut down by the administrators of the site because the sale would violate U.S. law.[15]

Despite such considerations, I think there are reasons to be wary of jumping on the growing bandwagon for a market in human kidneys. Some of these reasons turn on nonideal features in a nonideal world and can be addressed through regulation; some of these reasons would hold in any realistic world.

Does a Market Ban Necessarily Decrease the Supply of Available Organs?

In his famous study, *The Gift Relationship*, Richard Titmuss argued that a purely altruistic system for procuring blood is superior to a system that relies on a combination of altruistic donation plus a market.[16] Comparing the American and British systems of procuring blood, he demonstrated that a system of donated blood (the British system) is superior in quality to a system that also uses purchased blood (the American system), in part because blood sellers have a reason to conceal their illnesses, whereas altruistic blood donors do not. Furthermore Titmuss claimed that offering financial incentives for blood leads those in need of money to supply too frequently, endangering their own health. According to Titmuss, an altruistic system is not only more ethical, but it also produces a blood supply of higher quality.

Titmuss also argued, to the surprise of many economists, that a system that relied only on altruistic donation might be more *efficient* than a market system for blood. He claimed that, with respect to blood, the introduction of markets "represses the expression of altruism [and] erodes the sense of community."[17] If blood is treated as a commodity with an associated price tag, some people who would have donated when doing so bestowed the "gift of life" now decline to donate. Therefore blood supply would not necessarily be increased by the addition of a market; indeed Titmuss hypothesized that the net result of introducing a market for blood in England would be *less* blood of inferior quality.

This might seem surprising. Insofar as we are simply adding a new choice (i.e., selling blood) to a set of existing options, why should any of the existing options (i.e., donating blood), or their attractiveness to altruistic individuals, change?[18] Why should policies that appeal to self-interest also lead people to act in a less public-spirited way?

Consider the following real-life experiment, which illustrates the market effect that Titmuss conjectured on motivation. Faced with parents who habitually arrived late to pick up their children at the end of the day, six Haifa day care centers imposed a fine for such parental lateness. They hoped that the fines would give these parents a self-interested reason to arrive on time. The parents responded to the fine by *doubling* the amount of time they were late.[19] Even when the fine was revoked three months later the enhanced lateness continued. One plausible interpretation of this result is that the fine undermined the parents' sense that they were morally obligated not to take advantage of the day care workers; instead they now saw their lateness as a commodity that could be purchased.

This result has been replicated using carefully designed experiments. The experimental economist Bruno Frey and others have examined circumstances where *intrinsic motivation* is partially destroyed when price incentives are introduced.[20] An action is intrinsically motivated when it is performed simply because of the satisfaction the agent derives from performing the action. Whereas conventional economic analysis assumes that offers for monetary compensation will increase the willingness to accept otherwise unwanted projects, Frey found that support for building a noxious nuclear waste facility in a neighborhood actually *decreased* when monetary compensation to host it was offered. His study suggests that in cases where individuals are civically minded, using price incentives will not increase but can actually decrease levels of support for civic actions. For an intrinsically motivated agent, performing an act for money is simply not the same act when it is performed for free.[21] The presence of monetary incentives can crowd out a person's intrinsic reasons for performing the given action, changing the attractiveness of the options he faces. For example, in the nuclear waste example, citizens may feel bribed by the offer of money. In the case of timely day care pickup, altruistic concern for the teachers may be replaced by self-interested calculation about the worth of avoiding the fine.

This kind of crowding-out altruism result is not inevitable; the market can also be harnessed in a socially beneficial and more *altruistic* direction. A study of the introduction of a market wherein people purchased access to express carpool lanes in San Diego found that the program's initiation correlated with increased overall traffic in the express lanes, decreased traffic in the main lanes, and a significant *increase* in carpooling levels. (Carpoolers have access to the express lanes but do not have to pay for this access.) The author hypothesizes that the most likely explanation for the increase in carpoolers is that new drivers were attracted to carpooling by a *relative* monetary benefit: they felt better about getting for free what others pay for.[22]

If these case studies are illustrative, markets can change social norms. And if introducing a market does affect intrinsic motivations, we cannot a priori predict in which direction the net change of behavior will go. In the nuclear waste example we get less prosocial behavior, but the reverse is true in the carpooling example. Of course, kidney markets and blood markets are different from markets in access to faster commuting. Donations of organs and blood often involve questions of life and death, not simply convenience, and so it may well be that different motivations are invoked in those performing altruistic actions, motivations that are more likely to be vulnerable to crowding out.

Would the introduction of a kidney market actually serve to reduce supply by crowding out those with altruistic motivations? Even if kidney markets drove out altruists, it is still possible that the net supply of kidneys would be increased. Maybe there are more potential extrinsically motivated donors than donors who are only, or primarily, intrinsically motivated. Furthermore if the amount of organs procured through a market remained inadequate, increasing the price of organs would likely lead to more nonaltruistic donors. In Friedrich Dürrenmatt's splendid tragedy, *The Visit of the Old Lady*, an incredibly rich woman who had been wronged in her youth by her lover now offers the residents of her hometown $1 million to kill him. At first the offer is angrily rejected by the citizens as deeply immoral, but the woman induces them to raise their consumption and take on debts. Finally as they accommodate themselves to their new level of comfort, they decide to kill the lover who refused to accept paternity for her child so many years ago. Perhaps in the cases Frey and others examined the monetary rewards were simply insufficient to motivate people or offered before people had a chance to get used to the idea.[23]

It is also important to consider whether, if there are crowding-out effects on people with altruistic motivations, it is the case that *all* extrinsic rewards for giving up a kidney—including rewards to one's heirs after one's death, lifetime medical benefits, and payment of funeral costs—would have the same crowding-out effects as cash.[24]

Perhaps legalizing kidney sales decreases altruistic donation and at the same time increases the net supply of organs, at least if the price is right.[25] Whether or not it does so is an especially relevant consideration if a person's support for or opposition to organ markets rests solely on the effects of such markets on supply. Because the positive case for organ markets does largely rest on such grounds, it is clearly relevant to whether that case is a good one; moral motivations may be more fragile than we often assume. But whether the introduction of markets increases or decreases supply may not be decisive for some opponents of kidney markets; some people believe that kidney selling is wrong even if it increases supply.

Vulnerability

For some a kidney sale is objectionable because it is a paradigmatic *desperate exchange*, an exchange no one would ever make unless faced with no reasonable alternative. A kidney is, in the words of one organ market critic, the "organ of last resort."[26] Many people object to organ markets precisely because they believe that these markets would allow others to exploit the desperation of the poor. This objection to desperate exchanges is often associated with a paternalistic concern that sellers would actually be harmed by the sale of their organs, but that given their desperation they would sell their organs if it were legal.

A defender of organ markets might argue that the worries about exploitation could be addressed through regulation: by eliminating organ brokers who capture much of the price of the organ; by allowing open competition that is precluded by the black market; and by enforcing the terms of contracts. To address this concern, it might also be argued that organ donation should be legal only in contexts in which people are not likely to be desperately poor.[27]

Weak Agency

Whereas ideal markets involve fully informed participants, we have seen in this book that many markets do not, and in fact cannot, function on that basis. This is sometimes because market transactions involve consequences that can be known only in the future. Kidney transplants involve surgical operations and, like all surgical operations, entail risks. In a careful study of India's kidney sellers, 86 percent of the participants in the study reported a marked deterioration in their health following their nephrectomy.[28] Although one kidney is capable of cleansing the blood if it is functioning well, the removal of a kidney leaves the seller vulnerable to future problems if the remaining kidney becomes damaged or if its filtering capability declines. (In fact the decrease in filtering capacity is a normal byproduct of aging.) Needless to say, the poor in the developing world who sell their kidneys have no health insurance and no claim on an additional kidney if their remaining one fails to function properly. Moreover, although most studies of kidney transplants have reported few adverse effects for the donors, these studies have been overwhelmingly conducted in wealthy countries; we simply do not know whether people in poor countries do as well with only one kidney as those in rich countries. Health risks are likely to be greater in places where people have little access to clean water or adequate nutrition and often are engaged in difficult manual labor.

Two other findings in the study of Indian kidney sellers relate to concerns with weak agency. First, an overwhelming majority of those interviewed (79 percent) said that they regretted their decision and would not recommend that others sell a kidney. Second, a majority of sellers interviewed (71 percent) were married women. Given the weak position of women in Indian society, the voluntary nature of the sales is questionable. The most common explanation offered by wives as to why they and not their husbands sold their organs were that the husbands were the family's income source (30 percent) or were ill (28 percent). Of course, as the authors of the study point out, most of the interviews of women were conducted in the presence of their husbands or other family members, so they may have been reluctant to admit to being pressured to donate.

Weak agency is a serious problem for those who wish to base their defense of the market in organs on the right of a person to make her own decisions with respect to her body parts, and this is especially true when the weak agency is connected to significant harm. The fact that most organ sellers would not recommend the practice suggests that potential sellers would be unlikely to sell a kidney if they were better informed about the outcomes of their sale.[29] Perhaps it is difficult to imagine what it means to lose a kidney before one actually experiences the loss. When we couple the information problems with the lack of benefit, the case for allowing a kidney market is thereby weakened.[30]

A defender of organ markets might reply that the appropriate response to the diminished agency of sellers is simply to make sure they are better informed about the likely consequences of their transactions. For example, organ sellers could be required to take classes dealing with the risks of live organ donation and to demonstrate that they understand the likely consequences of giving up a kidney. However, given the horrific poverty that many sellers face, and perhaps their lack of education, it is unclear to what extent they will refrain from undertaking the transaction simply because of the risks. Additionally, in poorer countries regulatory institutions are weak and underfunded.

Note, however, that the argument from weak agency—lack of information about how a seller will feel in the future about her kidney sale—might lead us to discourage altruistic organ donations as well as paid donations. That is, weak agency doesn't really single out what is problematic about the kidney *market*.[31] If the potential health risks for donors are substantial, then perhaps all such transfers from living donors should be banned. (And it is doubtful whether altruistic donation is really made from the vantage point of full information and in the context of a range of choices. Family members are often under enormous pressure to donate and, as we have seen, parents are free to donate the organs of their own children.)

It is also important to consider just how substantial the potential harms are to organ donors and sellers. Currently we allow people to engage in risky occupations (e.g., work in nuclear reactor plants); we do not prohibit markets enabling people to engage in risky behaviors such as cigarette smoking and skydiving; and we rely on financial incentives in military recruitment, which also exposes individuals to grave risks. So, to the extent that the argument from weak agency is compelling because it is predictive of harm, it is important to consider whether or not the potential harms are worse than from other sales that we currently permit.[32]

Equal Status Considerations

Current black markets in kidneys certainly reflect the different market situations of buyer and seller. Most sellers are extremely poor; most buyers are at least comparatively wealthy. It has been keenly noted that international organ markets transfer organs from poor to rich, third world to first world, female to male, and nonwhite to white. Indeed the fact that there is increasing pressure to allow kidneys to be bought and sold itself arguably reflects the fact that those who seek to purchase them tend to have the cash to be able to do so.[33] Contrast this with the situation of poor people whose health needs currently go unmet. Despite the fact that urgent health needs are shared by millions (billions?) of desperately poor people, poor people have little cash. Therefore their health needs tend to get far less attention than the health needs of the comparatively wealthy.

A system that relied on a kidney market of individual buyers and sellers for procurement and distribution would have the consequence that poor people would disproportionately be the organ sellers of the world and rich people the likely recipients.[34] By contrast, a procurement system that relies on donation is much more likely to have suppliers that come from all classes of people. Indeed Titmuss found just such a contrast between the American and British systems of blood donation.[35]

In his haunting novel *Never Let Me Go*, Kazuo Ishiguro imagines a world in which human clones are created to serve as organ donors for others.[36] Before these created humans are middle-aged, they start to donate their vital organs. At the end of the novel these purposely created humans "complete," that is, give up the last vital organs they have for transplantation into others, and then die. Along these lines critics of proposed organ markets have charged that such markets will effectively turn desperately poor people into "spare parts" for the rich. In her response to the argument that such organ markets nevertheless transfer money to the poor, Organs Watch founder Nancy Scheper-Hughes caustically quips, "Perhaps we should look for better ways of helping the destitute than dismantling them."[37]

There is surely something disturbing about the picture of poor people supplying the rich with vital organs, just as the world Ishiguro portrays, where some are created to supply others with needed organs, is unsettling. Still, it is important to realize that there are many services that the poor of this world already provide for the rich that are not reciprocally provided by the rich for the poor. Few, if any, wealthy people take hazardous jobs in mines or work in nuclear power plants or are employed cleaning other people's latrines. Societies justify such tasks by pointing out that they are socially necessary and that what is important is that those who perform these tasks are justly compensated under conditions that meet health and safety standards. Given that, the inequality between suppliers doesn't pick out what is especially objectionable about a kidney market.

At the same time I think the critics raise the legitimate concern that kidney markets might actually *worsen* existing inequalities based on class. Such markets could expand inequality's scope by including body parts in the scope of things that money gives a person access to. There are people who have little or no money currently waiting on kidney transplant lists. To a large extent the selection of the person who receives a kidney for transplant is independent of his ability to pay. By contrast, a kidney market might mean that kidneys go to the highest bidders. But shouldn't kidneys be allocated on the basis of need, length of time waiting, and medical suitability and not on the basis of ability to pay?

Theoretically, of course, a legalized organ market could be regulated to ensure that rich and poor have access to kidneys, with the government providing funding for the organ purchases of poor buyers. Through subsidy and insurance the government *could* seek to make the demand for kidneys independent of the wealth of the buyer. Additionally the government might devote itself to finding donors for poorer patients.[38] From an egalitarian viewpoint, these regulations are desirable. Indeed the government might create a monopsony in which it was the *only* legal buyer of organs. And it could buy these organs using a future market, in which people are paid for their organs only after their death as a way of staving off coercive ploys. However, even if a government took such measures, it remains difficult for any government with limited resources and other priorities to make kidney allocation via a market completely independent of the wealth of the donor. Establishing a maximum price for kidneys under a monopsony might re-create the shortages that the kidney market was designed to overcome, especially if the availability of subsidized kidneys created a moral hazard problem.[39]

THE INTEGRITY OF THE BODY

Three of the concerns that I have detailed thus far—weak agency, vulnerability, and the possibility that poor people will become suppliers of organ parts for the rich—can be dealt with through regulating the kidney market rather than blocking it. The concern about whether or not markets will increase supply is different: markets may decrease altruistic donation of organs under any realistic background social conditions, even in the context of regulation.

There is an additional consideration about kidney markets, a consideration that came out in my discussions of bonded and child labor: the way that adding a choice to a choice set changes the other choices that are available to the agent. I want to consider the ways that the existence of kidney markets might make some poor people worse off than they would otherwise be. Although this consideration isn't decisive—the banning of kidney markets makes others in desperate need of a kidney worse off than they would otherwise be—I think it has been missing from the current enthusiasm for organ markets and needs to be addressed. This consideration prompts us to think about the ways that a person's internal resources can differ from their external resources, a point that will resonate with specific egalitarian approaches.

The idea I want to explore here is that even if restrictions on kidney sales are beneficial from the point of view of an individual seller, they may be harmful to others. This is because allowing such markets as a widespread practice, as a pattern of repeated and regular exchanges backed up by laws, has effects on the nature of the choices that are available to people. While proponents of kidney markets usually focus on individual transactions within given environments, the introduction of markets can change environments (including, as we have seen, by possibly altering motivations). Consider that where the practice of kidney selling is widespread, kidneys are viewed as potential collateral and moneylenders acquire incentives to seek out additional borrowers as well as to change the terms of loans. The anthropologist Lawrence Cohen found that in areas of India where kidney selling was relatively common, creditors placed additional pressures on those who owed them money.[40] Cohen notes, "In the Tamil countryside with its kidney belts, debt is primary. . . . Operable *women are vehicles for debt collateral.*"[41]

Cohen's finding suggests that if kidney selling became widespread, a poor person who did *not* want to sell her kidney might find it harder to obtain loans.[42] Ceteris paribus, the credit market allocates loans to people who can provide better collateral. If a kidney market exists, the total amount of collateral rises, which means that those without spare kidneys or those that refuse to sell them, will get fewer loans than before, assuming that the supply of loanable funds is more or less fixed. In other words, these people are made worse off by the kidney market. If this is so, then although allowing a market in kidneys expands a single individual's set of choices, if adopted in the aggregate it may reduce or change the available choices open to others, and those others will be worse off. They will have less effective choices insofar as they will no longer be able to find reasonable loan rates without mortgaging their organs. Once we see the effects of a kidney market on those who are not party to the transactions, we can no longer say that such markets have no harmful consequences.

Of course this argument is true of other linked markets; many markets generate pecuniary externalities. Recall that a pecuniary externality is an effect of production or transactions on outside parties through prices and not through direct resource allocations. For example, the introduction of a market in second homes in a rural community may price some first-time buyers out of the housing market in that community. But people who find kidney markets troubling do not necessarily find markets in second homes troubling. So my point about the effect of a kidney market on other people's choice sets does not settle the issue of whether that market should be blocked. Instead it leads us to ask, Should people have to pay a cost for their unwillingness to sell their organs? And if not, why not?

If we view kidneys as resources analogous to other resources we have, whether money or apples, it is unclear why we should not have to part with that resource if we wish to secure credit. But many people resist this analogy. They seem to tacitly believe, following Ronald Dworkin, that we have good reason to draw a "prophylactic line" around the body, a line "that comes close to making [it] inviolate, that is, making body parts not part of social resources at all."[43] I concur that there is something to this line of thought, and indeed that a horror at the thought of the conscription of our bodies by others may lie behind the repugnance people feel toward kidney markets, but my endorsement of it as a reason to block kidney markets is a bit tentative because it does not take into account the person who may be dying for lack of a kidney. Nevertheless it is worth stressing that whether or not this line of argument is ultimately successful, it offers a different perspective on kidney markets from one that focuses on the fact that a trade entered into out of desperation is also a trade that is likely to be exploitive, overreaching, or otherwise extremely unfair.[44] That is, this objection holds even if we think that the terms of trade are fair and that the choice made by the seller is not one of desperation.

POLICY

I've analyzed the discomfort people feel with kidney markets in terms of vulnerability, weak agency, harmful outcomes, inequality, and motivations, looking at the case for curtailing such markets based on these considerations under both existing and more ideal circumstances. Many problems with kidney markets arise precisely because such markets are not likely to be ideal markets, but rather markets in which there are widespread market failures: weak agency, significant pockets of monopoly power, and human desperation leading to exploitation and inadequate pricing. Much of the repugnance that people feel toward kidney markets arises from the potential for harm stemming from the circumstances in which sellers are found: poverty, lack of clean water and basic health care, and grueling labor. Market regulation may go some way to mitigating the problems along the dimensions of weak agency, although it is unlikely to make the problem of desperate world poverty go away. It is also possible that any potential harms from giving up a kidney can be addressed by mandating appropriate follow-up care, ensuring access to a replacement organ if needed, and perhaps banning the international trade of kidneys. But again, in parts of the world this may be difficult to enforce. One way of mitigating the possibility of harmful outcomes for sellers would be to have purchased organs taken only after the seller's death—a kind of futures market in organs.

Even with the ban on kidney markets and even with little follow-up or no care, people who are desperate are likely to resort to the black market. If the state is too weak to enforce the ban or not particularly inclined to do so, a black market in organs will thrive, as it does in parts of India, Pakistan, and Brazil. According to many observers, the sale of organs on the black market has reached alarming proportions in the third world, especially as advanced medical technology spreads. Regulating a legalized kidney market rather than relying on a black market would arguably go some way in redressing the worries about exploitation and one-sided terms of sale. If properly regulated, an organ market might be structured to discourage sales from extremely poor donors.

But this is where the argument from pecuniary externalities becomes relevant. Allowing the desperately poor to sell their organs as a social practice will have an effect on the choices that are open to those who do not want to participate in such a market. Some may think that it is inappropriate to make people pay a cost for exercising their choice not to sell their kidney. This issue also needs to be considered in policy design.

The problem of inequality, of turning poor people into "spare parts" for the rich, can also be addressed, at least in part, by regulation. Instead of relying on a competitive market we might create a monopsony, with the state the only legal buyer, and distribute on the basis of medical need. We might provide for the state to purchase organs for poor recipients. Nonetheless if there is a market there is likely to be greater stratification by wealth in organ donors and recipients than is currently the case. This may be significant for many reasons, not least of which is that it might "repress the expression of altruism and erode the sense of community."

Reflecting on the values at stake in different kinds of markets helps us to see why kidney markets are different from apple markets. Some of the values that I have discussed are internal to the functioning of markets: perfect information is assumed by the efficiency theorems of welfare economics; if the introduction of a market actually serves to decrease supply, then there is no social cost to banning it. Some of these values are external to the functioning of markets—in matters of life and death urgent needs should trump ability to pay—but widely shared. Some of these external values are more controversial: the list of goods that no one should have to pay a price for refusing to sell.

I want to conclude by briefly considering how a number of recent proposals for kidney markets, some of which are now being debated among policymakers, fare along the dimensions I have set out: vulnerability, weak agency, harmful individual outcomes, and harmful social inequality. The proposals I consider are (1) competitive markets governing supply and demand, in other words, treating kidneys like apples; (2) competitive markets governing supply only and distributing either on the basis of need or supplementing market distribution with subsidized

TABLE 2. Evaluating Alternative Methods of Organ Allocation

Market/Allocation	Weak Agency	Vulnerability	Individual Harm	Harmful Social Inequality
Competitive market in supply and demand	Yes, although could be mitigated by informed consent	Yes	Yes: harm to very poor seller; externalities to other poor	Yes
Competitive market in supply only; government monopsony	Yes: see above	Yes	Yes: see above	No
Futures markets	No	No, unless this gives people an incentive to hasten the death of future donors	No	No
Matching-in kind exchanges	Possible: see above	No	No	No
Altruistic donation	Possible: see above	No	No	No

distribution to the poor; (3) competitive futures markets with organs given up only after death; and (4) matching-in kind exchanges, where a patient with a willing donor who has an incompatible blood type can trade with another such incompatible patient-donor pair.[45]

A *yes* in table 2 indicates a problem along a dimension; a *no* indicates a relatively low (but not necessarily unproblematic) score.[46] As can be seen from this schematic, a pure competitive market in kidneys appears to be the most problematic, scoring fairly high on all parameters. By contrast, a market in apples would not normally score high along all these dimensions. Given the imperfect information, the potential for harmful outcomes, and the inequality in access to urgently needed goods (kidneys), I think we should view this market as morally unacceptable.

On my view, the greater the extent to which the concerns raised along the various dimensions can be addressed, the more acceptable is the market. Even for those who worry about the pecuniary effects of such markets—changing the terms of trade for those who do not want to participate in such markets—the question is whether mechanisms can be found that would prevent kidney sales from entering into other kinds of contracts, for example, as loan collateral or as a means of eligibility for social services.

And if these considerations cannot be adequately addressed, whether through information dissemination, regulation, income transfer, or some other means, other possibilities need to be considered, including increased exhortation to donate. I do not want to lose sight of the fact that in addition to the potential for harm to the seller from a kidney market, there is also the potential to extend the life of a person who would otherwise die. Much more could be done to encourage the altruistic donation of organs. Meanwhile, given the desperation on both the buyer and seller sides of the equation, the search for solutions to the shortage of transplantable organs is likely to be with us for a long time to come.[47]

Conclusion

Without commonly shared and widely entrenched moral values and
obligations, neither the law, nor democratic government, nor even the
market economy will function properly.

—*Vaclav Havel,* Meditations on Politics, Morality and
Civility in a Time of Transition

The overestimation of the market's ability to self-correct surely had a
role in the financial crises that have recently shaken the United States. In
particular the largely unsupervised and unregulated buying and selling
of credit derivatives, instruments that Warren Buffett has called "financial weapons of mass destruction," contributed to the pandemic that
has now spread around the globe.

The market in credit derivatives has some of the features that characterize a noxious market.[1] First some terminology. Credit derivatives
were adopted as a way for banks to diffuse risks; they involve the sale of
risks of default on an obligation to pay. If a party makes a loan to a risky
borrower, he can protect himself by buying credit protection for a percentage interest on the notional principle. If the borrower defaults, the
protection entitles the lender to a lump-sum payment.

Derivatives allowed lenders who took unwise risks to pass off the
financial assets to third parties—third parties who are remote from
the original transaction and often have little information about them.
The derivatives served thereby to weaken *agency*. In addition these
financial instruments encouraged banks and other financial organizations to take on riskier loans than they should have. If I know that I
can sell a loan that I have just made within weeks (or sometimes days),
I have little reason to be concerned if the borrower will not be able to

repay the loan in twenty years: it's not my problem. However, the buying and selling of these risky loans not only led many banks that people depended on to be threatened with collapse, but also led to extreme harms to the borrowers who believed that they were actually qualified for the loans they took out, and to third parties who depend on the economy to more or less correctly price the assets and productivity of the nation. There are important regulatory lessons here with respect to credit markets, lessons that were clear to Adam Smith hundreds of years ago but seem to have been lost until quite recently.

It should be apparent that the invisible hand of the market does not operate alone: markets *depend on* background property rights, the availability of information, and an array of nonmarket institutions such as courts, regulatory agencies, and schools. And they depend on social trust and other motivations that go beyond a narrow self-interest. This book has also stressed the converse proposition: that markets can *affect* property rights, information, nonmarket institutions, and socially oriented motivations. This is because markets can have not only economic effects but also political and cultural effects. Particular markets can crowd out altruism, enable hierarchical relationships between market agents, and even undermine the conditions for a democratic society.

When we look to evaluate markets there is a broad array of values that we should consider. I have argued that four values are critically important to our assessment of noxious markets: weak agency, vulnerability, extreme harms to individuals, and extreme harms to society. The economists' generic view of externality is not fine-grained enough to allow us to distinguish the markets that score high on one or more of these parameters from other markets with third-party effects.

In addition to laying out four values that serve as parameters for evaluating markets, I have defended what might be termed a social democratic thesis: that certain goods need to be provided outside the market if citizens are to be equals. Equality in these goods is *necessary* for democratic citizenship; thus in democratic countries there are no markets in votes or basic political or civil rights. Other necessary goods for citizenship can be supplied (unequally) by markets, in part, but also require nonmarket provision; for example, American society allows parents to buy private education for their own children but also guarantees education as an entitlement to all children. A democratic society has strong interests in the production of adults who are capable of participating in the political structures of society and in ensuring that all children receive an education sufficient to allow them to become adults capable of independent functioning, of standing as an equal citizen.[2] Such a society also has an interest in drawing its leaders from all walks of life, an interest that places limits on the extent of acceptable educational inequality. Too much inequality in what public and private education provides also threatens a society of equals.

Other goods need to be protected from markets because when the exchange of these goods is adopted as a social practice (in markets) they reinforce significant inequalities of bargaining power and sometimes of political power that lead to extreme harms. In this book I have discussed the example of child labor as an illustration of the way that a market exchange that may be Pareto improving in a single case can be problematic when undertaken by large numbers of people. An analogous argument might be made about minimum wage laws. One way of thinking about minimum wage laws is as a means to induce firms to adopt strategies based on enhancing the quality of labor inputs through improvements to worker health and safety and through training and skill development. If this is so, then we might justify restrictions on voluntary exchanges (between those willing to work for below the minimum wage and those willing to pay them) by their endogenous effects on the development of workers' capabilities, including those needed for full participation in society's institutions.

My social democratic account stands in contrast to the views of those I termed, following James Tobin, *general egalitarians* insofar as I insist that equality must have a much broader metric than income and wealth. Although I agree that a certain amount of income and wealth, and perhaps a certain level of equality in the distribution of income and wealth, are necessary for social equality, they are not sufficient. Some noxious markets are problematic for social equality independently of the way they distribute income.[3] But the general egalitarians are surely right about one thing: in a world in which one billion people, one sixth of the world's population, are destitute we should not expect noxious markets to go away.

I agree with the *specific egalitarians* about the need to differentiate kinds of markets, but I disagree with many of the reasons they offer for making that differentiation. I have tried as far as possible to steer clear of arguments that appeal to particular views about human flourishing or the meaning of goods. My argument has rested on what I take to be widely shared concerns, such as the need to avoid extreme harms and to protect the most vulnerable. I have also stressed the importance of thinking about the effects of different markets on our democracy. These considerations can cut across different kinds of goods.

I have also been reluctant to endorse blanket prohibitions on markets that have troubling characteristics. The moral concerns that I have argued are deeply implicated in assessing when markets are appropriate do not deliver simple answers. There are multiple factors to be considered, many values in play. The fact that a market is noxious does not tell us whether we should ban it or attempt to regulate it. Which policy response is appropriate will often, although not always, rest on messy empirical details. But sometimes our basic values as a society are at stake.

When I began thinking about this topic, I never assumed I would wind up writing a book that focused on markets so closely connected to the human body: sex, kidneys, labor, and pregnancy. But I came to realize that these markets brought into sharp focus the main issue that interests me: the ways that certain markets influence our capacities and our self-conceptions, including our capacities for independence and equal relations. There are, however, other markets in which this influence seems likely to be as present: markets in political influence (campaign contributions, professional lobbyists), in information (media), in education, in child care, and in health care.

Beyond these cases there are many more examples of particular markets that continue to arouse debate and concern: carbon markets, markets in life-saving drugs, school vouchers, private prisons, and markets in international weapons. I hope that my framework is helpful for·thinking about them, but I do not expect that I will have the last word. My hope is to prompt a conversation about the heterogeneity of markets, the kinds of considerations that we should use to assess them—including considerations about their effects on motivations and human capacities—and especially the kind of society in which we want these heterogeneous markets to function.

Notes

Introduction

1. Over the past twenty years a number of pollutants have become tradable commodities. Companies that emit less than their assigned limits (or caps) of a pollutant can sell their residual allowances on the open market, or bank them for the future. Those facilities with higher pollution levels can then either buy these banked allowances and continue releasing the same pollutant or clean up their own emissions, whichever is cheaper.

2. For a related view see Bowles, "What Markets Can and Cannot Do."

3. Marshall, "Citizenship," 122.

4. Walzer, *Spheres*, xiii.

5. See Bowles, "What Markets Can and Cannot Do."

6. See Pettit, *Republicanism*, for discussion of the liberal idea of freedom as non-domination.

7. Tobin, "On Limiting."

8. For related discussion, see Kanbur, "On Obnoxious Markets"; Treblicock, *The Limits of Freedom of Contract*. I am particularly indebted to Kanbur's discussion of these issues. I discuss some differences with their approaches and mine in chapters 4.

9. Thanks to Josh Cohen for noting the way my parameters fall into sources and effects.

10. I borrow from Kanbur's terminology here; see "On Obnoxious Markets," 45–52.

11. See ibid., 56.

Chapter 1

1. There is, for example, no definition of a market in Hal Varian's widely used *Intermediate Microeconomics*. It is striking how little discussion there is about the features of a market in economics, despite the fact that this is the central institution that economists study.

2. Friedman, *Capitalism and Freedom*, 13–15.

3. See Nozick, *Anarchy;* Wertheimer, *Coercion.*

4. I consider the question of voluntariness in more detail in chapter 8, in my discussion of bonded labor.

5. See Kanbur, "Obnoxious Markets," 42.

6. *New Shorter Oxford English Dictionary*, 1699.

7. Might markets have a natural basis? Adam Smith thought so. So did Hayek. But both thinkers were also well aware of the market's evolved dependence on rules of property, social conventions, and state enforcement.

8. Mnookin and Kornhauser, "Bargaining."

9. See Lindblom, *The Market System*, 4.

10. A. Buchanan, *Ethics*, 2.

11. Gordon, *Ants at Work*, x.

12. This concept is named after Vilfredo Pareto, an Italian economist who used the concept in his studies of economic efficiency and income distribution. For discussion, see Amartya Sen, *On Ethics and Economics* (Oxford: Basil Blackwell, 1987), 30.

13. "Obvious" does not mean true. For criticisms of the Pareto principle, see G. A. Cohen, "The Pareto Argument"; Philips, *Which Equalities Matter?* See also G. A. Cohen, *Rescuing Justice and Equality*.

14. Sen, *On Ethics and Economics*, 32.

15. Lionel Robbins, quoted in Sen, *On Economic Inequality*, 81.

16. Sen, *Development as Freedom*, 25–30.

17. Marx, "The Communist Manifesto," 476.

18. Smith, *An Inquiry*, vol. 1, book III, chap. 4, paragraph 4, p. 412, my emphasis.

19. This dependence was secured by both the lord's possession of force as well as an ideology that made hierarchical relationships seem natural.

20. See the discussion of Smith's view of markets in chapters 2.

21. See Putterman, "On Some Recent Explanations."

22. Smith, *Wealth of Nations*, 27.

23. For discussion, see Hirschman, *Exit*.

24. But see Marglin, "What Do Bosses Do?," for arguments about the persistence of hierarchy in the capitalist firm.

25. I discuss bonded labor arrangements in chapter 9.

26. See Marglin, *The Dismal Science*.

27. See McMillan, *Reinventing the Bazaar*. I am indebted to McMillan's excellent discussion of the background institutions and norms presupposed by the market system.

28. Some property rights are distributed among different individuals or entities.

29. See also the discussion of the conventional nature of ownership in Murphy and Nagel, *The Myth of Ownership*.

30. See McMillan, *Reinventing the Bazaar*, chap. 4, p. 45.

31. Akerlof, "The Market for 'Lemons'"; Arrow, "Uncertainty."

32. See Kahneman and Tversky, "Prospect Theory."

33. See Bowles, "Mandeville's Mistake."

34. Hirschman, *The Passions*.

35. See Taylor, *Anarchy and Cooperation;* Ostrom, *Governing the Commons*.

36. As I mentioned earlier, markets have coexisted with political regimes that have denied basic liberal freedoms. Pinochet's Chile and Nazi Germany are prominent examples.

37. Recent work recognizes that market failure may be more widespread than previously supposed, due to transaction costs, information failures, and strategic actions by the parties.

38. Economists also consider the effects of a market transaction on the relative prices of goods for others, effects referred to as "pecuniary externalities." Such effects are also omnipresent, and I discuss their significance in later chapters.

39. Herzog, "Externalities."

40. The canonical statement of the harm principle is in John Stuart Mill's *On Liberty* (Harmondsworth, England: Penguin, 1984).

41. One might try distinguishing between a person's moral judgment and his happiness or utility, but such a distinction seems at best unmotivated from within the framework of economics, which tends to view moral judgments in terms of preference functions.

42. Elizabeth Anderson notes of the theory of market failure that it is "a theory not of what is wrong with markets, but of what goes wrong when markets are not available" (*Value*, 192).

43. The "complete markets" model assumes away the problems of contract enforcement. This assumption is actually hugely misleading, because once we assume that there is trade occurring extended over time, then it may not be in the economic interest of agents to fulfill their contract. This means that we have to rely on norms or other mechanisms to secure compliance: the other mechanisms may interfere with efficiency.

44. Robbins, *An Essay*.

45. Tobin, "On Limiting," 269. Of course, it is possible to argue that vote selling creates externalities, but I won't pursue that argument here because I find it unpersuasive. But see http://gregmankiw.blogspot.com/2007/11/on-selling-votes.html.

46. Basu, "Economics."

47. This condemnation has found its way into international law. Article 47 of the Protocol Additional to the Geneva Conventions of 12 August 1949 and Relating to the Victims of International Armed Conflicts states, "A mercenary shall not have the right to be a combatant or a prisoner of war."

Chapter 2

1. A theorist's overall vision can matter more than her grasp of the empirical facts or the details of her overall argumentation. Many of the great political theorists of the past—Locke, Rousseau, Hobbes, and Smith—are remembered largely because they bequeathed to us new *ways of seeing* ourselves and society. As a somewhat tongue-in-cheek illustration of the importance of vision, Albert Hirschman recounts the following parable. The rabbi of Krakow interrupts his prayers with a wail that he has just seen the death of the rabbi of Warsaw two hundred miles away. A few days later some Jews from Krakow happen to travel to Warsaw, where to their surprise they see the Warsaw rabbi in good health. After the Jews return to Krakow rumors spread among the Krakow rabbi's congregation, and there is criticism and snickering among the skeptical. A few of the rabbi's disciples, however, rush to his defense, claiming that although he was wrong on the details, "Nevertheless, what vision!" (*Passions*, 117).

2. Polanyi, *The Great Transformation*.

3. Hirschmann, *Rival Views*.

4. C. F. Alexander, "All Things," 3.

5. Hobbes, *Leviathan*.

6. Smith, *Wealth of Nations*, vol. 1, 412.

7. The theoretical possibility of mobility differed in different feudal societies, since in some of these societies the peasant's obligations were contractual and in others it was coerced. Indeed there is controversy as to exactly what the defining feature of feudalism is. Here I understand feudalism as a social order based on hierarchical status and serfdom. See Bloch, *Feudal Society*. Recent historical scholarship has questioned whether or not serfdom is essential to feudalism.

8. Smith, *Wealth of Nations*, 420.

9. Marx, *Capital*, vol. 1, 280. Of course, Marx immediately notes that in the realm of production, this freedom, equality, property, and Bentham are anything but evident.

10. See E. Anderson, "Ethical Assumptions."

11. Rodbertus, quoted in Bohm-Bawerk, *Capital*, 332.

12. Smith, *Wealth of Nations*, 157–58.

13. Ibid., 83.

14. Ibid., 725.

15. See also Rothschild, *Economic Sentiments*, for a fascinating history of Smith's assimilation into the normative frameworks of more conservative economists.

16. Smith, *Wealth of Nations*, 143, emphasis added.

17. For changes in the rules of labor contract in the United States, see Steinfeld, *Coercion*.

18. Smith, *Wealth of Nations*, 781–82.

19. Smith, *Wealth of Nations*, 782. This striking admission of the limited nature of industrial workers in a capitalist economy was later developed by Hegel and Marx in their ideas of the alienation of labor.

20. Smith, *Wealth of Nations*, 28–29.

21. Smith, *The Theory of the Moral Sentiments*, 189–90.

22. Smith, *Wealth of Nations*, 356–57.

23. Amartya Sen discusses Smith's rationale in *Development as Freedom*, 124–25.

24. Smith, *Wealth of Nations*, 781.

25. Ibid., 785.

26. Ibid., 785–86.

27. J. Baldwin, "A Talk to Teachers," p. 326.

28. Smith, *Wealth of Nations*, 785.

29. To see this, think about the effects of education on a person's preferences. If education changes preferences, as it presumably does, when we judge an education system, should we use the person's ex ante or ex post preferences? When policies and institutions change preferences, we face a problem of circularity. A defender of markets might reply that she is not interested in the content of preferences or how those preferences came about. She is interested only in satisfying *as many of an agent's preferences as possible*, and markets do better on this quantitative dimension than alternatives. But this

does not address the circularity problem, and the circularity problem attacks the link between preferences and welfare. Which preferences should we use to judge an agent's welfare?

30. See Sen, *Development as Freedom*, for discussion of the importance of people's real freedoms.

31. See Satz, "The Limits."

32. Smith, *Wealth of Nations*, 67.

33. Blaug, *Economic Theory*, 75–82.

34. Ricardo, "An Essay on Profits," 21.

35. Like Adam Smith, Ricardo thought of rent as payment for the "use of the original and indestructible powers of the soil." Ricardian rent is therefore restricted to land and does not include any interest on capital improvements such as buildings. Ricardo, *On the Principles*, 69.

36. Ibid., 74.

37. For an excellent discussion of the implications of Ricardian rent theory for American progressive legal and social thought, see Fried, *The Progressive Assault*.

38. See Ibid., 120–123.

39. Marx, *Capital*, vol. 1, chap. 10, sec. 3, p. 240.

40. Ibid., 933.

41. Ibid., 280.

42. Marx, "Economic and Philosophic Manuscripts of 1844."

43. See Marx, "Critique of the Gotha Program."

44. There is what might be called a "second wave" of criticism of the assumption of perfect markets, with attention paid to nonclearing markets, information and enforcement problems, and the endogenous effects of institutions.

45. Jevons, *The Theory of Political Economy*, 267.

46. For difficulties with the cost of production theory, see Blaug, *Economic Theory*.

47. See discussion in Fried, *The Progressive Assault*, 131.

48. Fried, *The Progressive Assault*.

49. See Veblen, *The Theory of the Leisure Class*.

50. Fried, *The Progressive Assault*.

51. They were also attacked by economists writing at the same time as, or soon after, the first marginalists: Thorstein Veblen, Leonard Hobhouse, and John Commons, among others.

52. Ricardo, preface to *On the Principles*, 5, my emphasis

Chapter 3

1. See Tobin, "On Limiting."

2. Ibid., 264.

3. In Arthur Okun's famous book, *Equality and Efficiency: The Big Tradeoff*, he assumes that equality must be traded off against efficiency, and the question is to decide how to make that trade-off. For a different and less antagonistic view about the relationship between efficiency and equality, see Birdsall, "The World."

4. Or if not a strictly equal division, advocates believe the distribution of such goods should be sensitive to egalitarian considerations.

5. The example of the *Titanic* was first suggested to me by Andrew Williams. Thomas Schelling discusses *Titanic* cases in *Choice and Consequence*. Jonathan Wolff has also discussed the implications of Schelling's example in several of his papers. See "Market Failure." See also Bernard Williams's treatment of this example in his review of Schelling's book in *Economics and Philosophy*.

6. See Sen, *Inequality Reexamined*, 1.

7. R. Dworkin, *Sovereign Virtue*, 1. Actually, in most of *Sovereign Virtue* Dworkin formulates his requirement in terms of "equal concern," as opposed to his earlier formulation of "equal concern and respect." I am, for present purposes, assuming nothing much follows from this change. Thanks to Zosia Stemploskowa for pointing this out to me.

8. Will Kymlicka also defends the idea that all contemporary theories of justice are egalitarian in his book *Contemporary Political Philosophy*, 4–5.

9. R. Dworkin, *Sovereign Virtue*, 12.

10. Ibid., 66.

11. See Bennett, "Ethics and Markets."

12. As Ronald Dworkin himself notes in "What Is Equality," 285. Of course, we could manipulate the size of the piece of land people receive, but we would still need a way to determine when two pieces of unequal size were of equal value.

13. Ibid., 289.

14. Dworkin uses an auction to approximate the results that would be achieved in an ideal market.

15. The model abstracts from information problems, transaction costs, and externalities. In the presence of such factors we cannot assume that markets will clear. So in nonideal markets Dworkin's view allows for intervention to correct for distortions.

16. R. Dworkin, "What Is Equality," 287, n. 2.

17. Thus for Dworkin *ex ante* equality (after the auction but before market trading begins) renders *ex post* inequalities fair. As we will see, I attach far less importance to ex ante equality than Dworkin and more importance to ex post equality.

18. R. Dworkin, *Sovereign Virtue*, 78–79. This assumption is clearly a second-best one on Dworkin's view. Ideally we would have information about just how much insurance each individual was willing to purchase when reasoning under counterfactual conditions of ignorance about his own levels of talent and ability. I'll come back to this point later in this chapter.

19. Ronald Dworkin himself raises this as a potential objection. See *Sovereign Virtue*, 70, 159–61.

20. See Bennett, "Ethics and Markets," 201. The authenticity and stability of many of our preferences is a particular problem when we consider the ways that various institutions—education, cultural institutions, and media—influence and shape our preferences from childhood to adulthood. To be sure, Dworkin's hypothetical insurance market operates under informationally impoverished circumstances and so can correct for "endowment effects" and other distortions on our evaluations. But it gives us little handle on which of our preferences can underwrite fair market distributions.

21. See Frank, *Luxury Fever*.

22. R. Dworkin, *Sovereign Virtue*, 159. Dworkin does argue that people should not be held accountable for their mere "cravings." See also 82, 293.

23. Ibid., 239–242.

24. Dworkin does say that equality of resources condemns evaluations of goods and services that are based on racial prejudice. But he does not develop the criteria for his auctioneer to use when attempting to rule out various preferences as inappropriate.

25. For criticisms of Dworkin's view of disability, however, see Tremain, "Dworkin on Disablement"; MacLeod, *Liberalism*, 79–109. Tremain faults Dworkin for conceiving of disabilities as features of an individual, rather than as an interaction between features of an individual and the world. For example, whether or not having little use of my legs is disabling depends largely on features of the environment; a wheelchair and accessible spaces can make this particular disability less disabling.

26. Rawls, *A Theory of Justice*, 64.

27. For discussion of the problems with using a model of compensation to redress disabilities, see Wolff, "Addressing Disadvantage."

28. See Tremain, "Dworkin on Disablement." Many theorists have rightly stressed the importance of "recognition" and its independence from "redistribution." See Fraser and Honneth, *Redistribution or Recognition?*

29. I do not deny that material resources have a role to play in the inclusion of people with disabilities. Some resources, such as hearing aids for those who need and desire them, cost money. But the interest of the disabled is not in generic money per se, but in resources that allow them to participate in society as equal and full members. Money is no substitute for accessible voting booths to a person in a wheelchair. (Unless the idea is to enable the wheelchair user to hire people to carry him up the stairs? But that puts to the side the question of why spaces aren't designed to provide access for these members of the community as well as the question of what happens if the resources allocated aren't used for inclusion, perhaps because the costs of inclusion are greater than are those of individual compensation.)

30. See Okin, *Justice*.

31. See A. Williams, "Dworkin on Capability." See also E. Anderson, "Against Desert."

32. Dworkin gives this response to Andrew Williams in R. Dworkin, "Sovereign Virtue Revisited," 137.

33. Extrapolating from race to gender may give Dworkin more leverage to deal with cases of gender inequality within his theory of equal resources than I have assumed here. See Browne and Stears, "Capabilities," for one argument as to how Dworkin's theory might be developed in ways to deal with gender inequality.

34. E. Anderson, "What Is the Point of Equality?," discusses such choices. See also E. Anderson, "Against Desert."

35. Dworkin does note in passing, "We may have paternalistic reasons for limiting how much an individual may risk" (*Sovereign Virtue*, 75).

36. Recently there have been interesting debates about the extent of aid that should be forthcoming to climbers undertaking especially risky climbs. See William Yardley, "Alpines vs. Armchairs," *New York Times*, February 25, 2007.

37. In a recent paper considering Dworkin's view of equality, Elizabeth Anderson asks us to consider a person who assumes a risky occupation, such as a coal miner or firefighter. She claims that Dworkin's insurance model would allocate the costs for such risks to these individual workers, even though society has an interest in having people make such career choices. Of course, there are socially positive externalities when an individual chooses to be a firefighter. So Anderson's point must be that Dworkin would assign all the costs of such risks to the individual firefighter—beyond those that are assumed by the public for the benefit that is produced for them. See E. Anderson, "Against Desert."

38. R. Dworkin, *Sovereign Virtue*, 75.

39. See ibid., 334–38, for an incisive discussion of unemployment insurance.

40. Ibid., 287.

41. Thanks to Rob Reich for suggesting I separate the backward- and forward-looking aspects to my criticisms of relying on individual preferences for guidance about what we owe one another.

42. Blocking a role for such preferences is one important purpose of antidiscrimination laws.

43. My discussion has been concerned with Dworkin's use of a market to model initial equality of resources. But one can also press criticisms on his use of the market as a distributional mechanism after the auction has taken place. For example, why should we allow some people to reap huge benefits simply from owning land? As I noted in chapter 2, this was a question that preoccupied Ricardo and his followers. Or why should we assume that the price a person gets for his labor on the market is his alone, given all the other social inputs that have gone into it? See Freeman, "Rawls," for discussion.

44. Dworkin's auction is meant to mimic the properties of an ideal market. Thus he too would favor correction of inequalities due to externalities, imperfect information, and so forth, in addition to favoring intervention to correct for differences in innate talents and abilities.

45. It is important not to overstate the efficiency benefits of general egalitarianism over specific egalitarianism. There are pragmatic limits on the redistributive use of taxation and cash transfers. Rational economic actors, faced with taxes on their earnings, may change their preferences between work and leisure, as well as their selection of occupations. As Tobin notes, "We have yet to conjure the reality of the economist's dream tax—the lump sum tax that no one can avoid or diminish by altering his own behavior" ("On Limiting," 265).

46. Schelling, *Choice and Consequence*, 4–5.

47. See Roemer, "Egalitarianism," arguing that egalitarians should not be committed to the "nanny state."

48. And, as I discuss above, Dworkin largely rejects such interventions.

49. See Sunstein and Thaler, "Libertarian Paternalism."

50. This is not to say that the only obligations that the state has to its members is their urgent needs. I return to this in chapter 4.

51. Tobin, "On Limiting," 264.

52. Walzer, *Spheres*. The argument traces back at least to Karl Marx's discussion of money in "Economic and Philosophic Manuscripts of 1844."

53. Nonetheless I may accept compensation for those goods and entertain wrongful death suits. Acceptance of such compensation in the case of injury, for example, does not imply that I believe that the value of my limbs is equivalent to money.

54. Kant, *Groundwork*, 42–43.

55. I discuss Titmuss's argument in chapter 9. See also Healy, *Last Best Gifts*.

56. Dworkin makes this argument quite forcefully in his review of Walzer's book in "To Each his Own," *New York Review of Books*, April 14 1983, 4–6.

57. E. Anderson, *Value*.

58. Sandel, *What Money Can't Buy*.

59. Radin, *Contested Commodities*.

60. Lawrence Summers, quoted in *The Economist*, February 8, 1992, 66. Dan Hausman and Michael McPherson discuss Summers' memo in *Economic Analysis*. Ravi Kanbur refers to it as well in his paper "On Obnoxious Markets." Lant Pritchard has claimed to be the actual author of the memo.

61. *The Economist*, 66.

62. Schelling, *Choice and Consequence*, 116.

63. Indeed Schelling has argued that poor people should be able to patronize airports and airlines that offer a lower level of safety than rich people require, since they might prefer the savings that lower quality travel allows.

64. See Bowen and Bok, *The Shape*, 341.

65. In discussion, Steve Darwall pointed out that unlike the case of taking risks on the *Titanic*, mountain climbing and skydiving involve the pursuit of certain excellences. Though I find this suggestive, I do not pursue this way of distinguishing the cases here.

66. G. Dworkin, "Paternalism," 120–23.

67. See Wolff "Market Failure," for discussion.

Chapter 4

1. See also Kanbur "On Obnoxious Markets," for discussion of the distinction between abstract and particular markets.

2. Calabresi and Bobbitt, *Tragic Choices*.

3. The rationale for intervention in the case of market failure is only prima facie: a little market inefficiency might be preferable to a lot of bureaucratic red tape.

4. See Gauthier, *Morals*.

5. While most economists concentrate on designing an efficient market, their approach does not preclude arguments in favor of the state's redistribution of wealth for equity or other reasons. There may nevertheless be a tension between the two approaches, given that all actual tax systems impose inefficient distortions on taxpayer behavior.

6. See also Treblicock, *The Limits*; Kanbur, "On Obnoxious Markets." Treblicock's approach to markets stresses externalities, information failures, and coercion; Kanbur's account stresses extreme individual outcomes, weak agency, and distributional inequality, where extreme outcomes and inequality are characterized in terms of welfare economics.

7. This appeal to moral and political rationales for limiting markets makes my approach distinct from those of Michael Treblicock and Ravi Kanbur. Although I draw on some of their insights in formulating my parameters, I offer a particular way of thinking about harmful outcomes and externalities that is tied to a theory of equality.

8. Of course, as I have stressed, many markets *promote* access to goods and services, decreasing their price and making them more available to more people than do other systems of distribution.

9. Kanbur, "On Obnoxious Markets," 44.

10. Sen, *On Ethics and Economics*.

11. Shue, *Basic Rights*, 18. The language of human rights tries to capture the idea of some universal basic interests whose protection is especially urgent.

12. Adam Smith stressed this point in his famous remarks on the human tendency "to truck, barter, and exchange":

> When an animal wants to obtain something . . . it has no other means of persuasion but to gain the favor of those whose services it requires. A puppy fawns upon its dam, and a spaniel endeavors by a thousand attractions to engage the attention of his master who is at dinner, when it wants to be fed by him. Man sometimes uses the same arts with his brethren, and . . . endeavors by every servile and fawning attention to obtain their good will. . . . But man has almost constant occasion for the help of his brethren, and it is in vain for him to expect it from their benevolence only. He will be more likely to prevail if he can . . . show them that it is for their own advantage to do for him what he requires of them. . . . It is not from the benevolence of the butcher, the brewer, or the baker that we expect our dinner, but from their regard to their own interest. We address ourselves, not to their humanity, but to their self-love. . . . Nobody but a beggar chooses to depend chiefly upon the benevolence of his fellow-citizens. (*Wealth of Nations*, 118–19)

Elizabeth Anderson's article "Ethical Assumptions" reminded me of the importance of this quotation.

13. Tobin, "On Limiting," 269.

14. In Milton Friedman's words, "The possibility of coordination through voluntary cooperation rests on the elementary—yet frequently denied—proposition that both parties to an economic transaction benefit from it, *provided the transaction is bilaterally voluntary and informed*" (*Capitalism*, 13).

15. Kanbur, "On Obnoxious Markets," discusses agency failures.

16. I discuss commercial surrogacy in chapter 5.

17. Industry spending on advertising to children under the age of twelve has exploded in the past decade, increasing from a mere $100 million in 1990 to more than $2 billion in 2000. See www.media-awareness.ca/english/parents/marketing/marketers_target_kids.cfm.

18. See chapter 7.

19. Rousseau, *Social Contract*, 34.

20. See White, *The Civic Minimum*, for an illuminating discussion of market vulnerability.

21. See Crow, *The Diversity of Markets*.

22. Again, see Kanbur, "On Obnoxious Markets," for illustrations.

23. I write "compatible with," not "entailed by," because welfare economists need not embrace bonded labor. But insofar as a libertarian thinks that all rights are alienable, the permissibility of labor bondage may well be entailed by it.

24. Marshall, "Citizenship," 122.

25. Ibid., 78. I discuss the implications of Marshall's view of citizenship for education in Satz, "Equality."

26. Marshall, "Citizenship," 78.

27. If there is paternalism involved in such cases, it is a form of *collective paternalism*: we restrict the choices open to us in order to maintain the choices that we need to protect ourselves from serious harm to our society.

28. Vast inequalities in education, however, may undermine democratic society. See Satz, "Equality," for discussion.

29. Perhaps some libertarians would gladly engage in vote buying and selling, but they are unlikely to find many followers.

30. See Sandel, *What Money Can't Buy*, for discussion of a republican view of democracy.

31. See Rawls, *Theory of Justice*, for discussion of the *fair* distribution of political liberties. See also, Brighouse, "Egalitarianism and Equal Availability."

32. Labor markets may be highly constitutive in their effects on the parties involved. As we saw, Adam Smith conjectured that a worker who spends her life engaged in menial, servile tasks in which she has no voice or authority is not likely to develop the capacities she needs to function as an active citizen. (Nor is she likely, given the chance, to be a loyal employee. Indeed a large body of research shows that high worker effort and loyalty require substantial departures from the treatment of labor as a pure commodity.)

33. Although see Pollan, *The Omnivore's Dilemma*, on the effects of large-scale industrial food production on the quality of the food that is produced.

34. See chapters 5 and 6.

35. Schelling, *Choice and Consequence*, 115–16.

36. Hirschman, *Exit*.

37. Wolff, "Market Failure."

38. Loeb, "Estimating."

39. Adams, *Risk*, 121.

40. Wolff, "Market Failure."

41. See also Kanbur, "On Obnoxious Markets," 52.

42. See Hausman and McPherson, *Economic Analysis*, 200.

43. Ibid., 201.

44. Kanbur, "On Obnoxious Markets."

45. Such markets are easy to enforce because market exchange is close to instantaneous in time, and there are effective private sanctions for noncompliance.

46. Eric Rakowski raised the example of supermodel eggs in conversation. A Web auction site purported to sell the eggs of beautiful female models to the highest bidder. Although the website was later exposed as a fraud, the site got bids of up to $42,000, proving that some people were willing to be part of such a market.

47. It is important to keep in mind that many allocative decisions are shaped neither by government nor by the market. These include distribution through gift, lottery, merit, the intrafamily regulation of work and distribution, and other principles such as seniority and need.

Chapter 5

1. I use the terms *contract pregnancy* and *pregnancy contract* in place of the misleading term *surrogacy*. The so-called surrogate mother is not merely a surrogate; she is the biological and/or gestational mother. In this chapter I do not make any assumptions about who is, and who is not, a "real" mother.

2. See E. Anderson, "Is Women's Labor a Commodity?"; Overall, *Ethics*; Warnock, *A Question of Life*; Field, *Surrogate Motherhood*; Corea, *The Mother Machine*; Pateman, *The Sexual Contract*; Radin, *Contested Commodities*.

3. E. Anderson, "Is Women's Labor a Commodity?," 75.

4. I believe that my argument can also be applied to the case of prostitution, which I discuss in the next chapter.

5. See A. Allen, "Surrogacy"; Overvold, *Surrogate Parenting*; Kane, *Birth Mother*.

6. Radin, "Market-Inalienability," refers to this view as "universal commodification."

7. The theoretical assumption that everything is commodifiable characterizes a range of modern economic theories. As discussed in earlier chapters, it is found in both liberal welfare economics and in the conservative economics of the Chicago School. See Becker, *The Economic Approach*. For criticisms of the application of Walrasian equilibrium theory to certain domains, see Stiglitz, "The Causes"; Putterman, "On Some Recent Explanations"; Bowles and Gintis, "Contested Exchange."

8. See Nozick, *Anarchy*, 331.

9. See E. Anderson, "Is Women's Labor a Commodity?," 72.

10. In cases of in vitro fertilization, reproductive labor is divided between two women.

11. See Katha Pollitt, "When Is a Mother Not a Mother?," *The Nation*, December 31, 1990, 843.

12. See Patterson, *Slavery*, for comparisons between slaves and athletes.

13. In the case of military service, of course, once you volunteer you are committed for your term whether you want to remain or not. But in the case of contract pregnancy, as with other labor contracts, it may be possible to opt out by aborting (at least until the end of the second trimester) or by refusing to perform in the sense of refusing to hand over the newborn child. I discuss the importance on bans on "specific performance" below.

14. Pateman, *The Sexual Contract*, 207.

15. Perhaps Freudian theory, with its emphasis on "natural" drives, might give us such reasons, but Pateman does not explicitly endorse such a theory.

16. For an interesting approach that argues for limits on the commodification of housing, see Radin, "Residential Rent Control."

17. Warnock, *A Question of Life*, 45.

18. E. Anderson, "Is Women's Labor a Commodity?," 81.

19. See Orange County Superior Court Judge Richard Parslow's ruling in *Johnson v. Calvert*, 851 p.2d 776 (1993), in which he referred to surrogate birth mother Anna Johnson as a "home" for an embryo and not a "mother." See also Seth Mydams, "Surrogate Denied Custody of Child," *New York Times*, October 23, 1990, A14. The Maryland Supreme Court referred to a gestational surrogate as a "gestational host" in *In re Roberto B*, 923 A2d 115, 117 (2007).

20. *In the Matter of Baby M*, 537 A.2d 1227 (N.J. 1988). Other cases in which a gestational surrogate's maternity claims have been denied include *In re Roberto B*, 923 A 2d 117 (2007), in which the Maryland Supreme Court ruled that even in the absence of an intended mother, the name of the gestational surrogate need not appear on the birth certificate.

21. Michael Bratman suggested to me that the analogy between abortion and contract pregnancy might break down in the following way. In contract pregnancy a woman gets pregnant with the intention of giving up the child. There is presumably no analogous intention in the case of abortion; few women, if any, intentionally get pregnant in order to have an abortion. Critics of contract pregnancy might claim that *intentionally* conceiving a child either to give it up for money or to abort it is immoral. I am not persuaded by such arguments and, at any rate, from a policy point of view pre-conception intention is impossible to verify. My own view is that the best argument in favor of the right to abortion makes no reference to intentions, but concerns the consequences of abortion restrictions for women, restrictions that, moreover, directly burden only women. But I do not pursue that line of thought here.

22. See Rich, *Of Women Born*.

23. Although see Fogg-Davis, "Racial Randomization."

24. Warnock, *A Question of Life*, 45.

25. E. Anderson, "Is Women's Labor a Commodity?," 78.

26. Of course, in adoption no one is directly paid for surrendering her child. So there is a disanalogy between adoption and contract pregnancy. Indeed insofar as payment for adoption would weaken parent-child ties (and raise equality considerations) and lead to harm to children, there is reason to prohibit it. I discuss harm to children below. Thanks to Samuel Freeman for pressing this issue.

27. I owe this suggestion to Rachel Cohon.

28. E. Anderson, "Is Women's Labor a Commodity?," 84.

29. Parker, "Motivation." See also Aigen, "Motivations."

30. Okin, "A Critique."

31. See Elster, *Solomonic Judgments*, for a discussion of the difficulties of ascertaining the best interest of the child. Elster is also skeptical of the idea that the best interest of

the child should necessarily prevail in custody disputes. I discuss fundamental interests in chapters 7. For now, recall the discussion in chapters 4 of basic interests in well-being and agency.

32. E. Anderson, "Is Women's Labor a Commodity?," 80, raises this point as well.

33. D. Gelman and E. Shapiro, "Infertility: Babies by Contract," *Newsweek*, November 4, 1985.

34. Elster, *Solomonic Judgments*, 134–150.

35. See Satz, "Remaking Families."

36. Of course, pregnancy contracts also give another woman, the adoptive mother, control over the body of the surrogate mother. The important point here is that in a society characterized by gender inequalities, such contracts put women's bodies at the disposal of others.

37. On the differential in men's and women's earnings in 2007, see www.bls.gov/opub/ted/2008/oct/wk4/art03.htm. In 2008 the average median weekly earnings of women working full time were 79.9 percent of men's (www.bls.gov/opub/ee/empearn/2009.01.pdf). On divorce's effect on standard of living, see Weitzman, *The Divorce Revolution*, 323. But see also Peterson, "A Re-evaluation."

38. See Bartels, *Beyond Baby M*, "Appendix: Baby M Contract."

39. There is already legal precedent for regulating women's behavior in the "best interests" of the fetus. A Massachusetts woman was charged with vehicular homicide when her fetus was delivered stillborn following a car accident. See Eileen McNamara, "Fetal Endangerment Cases on the Rise," *Boston Globe*, October 3, 1989, cited in Tribe, *Abortion*. See also Campbell, "Women as Perpetrators," 463.

40. This analogy may be complicated by the fact that the other parties to the contract may have at least some biological relationship to the child.

41. E. Anderson also makes this point in "Is Women's Labor a Commodity?" 84.

42. See Corea, *The Mother Machine*.

43. See Loury, *The Anatomy*, for discussion.

44. Anita Allen in "Surrogacy, Slavery and the Ownership of Life," has pointed to the disturbing possibilities contract pregnancy poses for racial equality. In cases like *Johnson v. Calvert*, where the gestator (surrogate) Johnson was a black woman and the Calverts were respectively white and Filipina, it is difficult to imagine a judge awarding the baby to Johnson. For example, there are almost no adoption cases in which a healthy white infant is placed with black parents. In his ruling in *Johnson v. Calvert*, Judge Parslow referred to Johnson as the baby's "wet nurse." Any full assessment of contract pregnancy must consider the implications of the practice for women of color.

45. The medieval church held that the male implanted into the female body a fully formed homunculus (complete with a soul). See Ehrenreich and English, *Witches*.

46. Of course, under different conditions the importance of genetically based ties between parents and children might decline.

47. Saletan, "Fetal Foreclosure."

48. In *Birthpower* Carmel Shalev develops a powerful defense of contract pregnancy that draws on considerations of liberty, welfare, and liberal neutrality. She argues that it is a matter of the "constitutional privacy" of individuals to define legal parenthood in

terms of their prior-to-conception intentions; that contract pregnancy will empower women and improve their welfare by unleashing a new source of economic wealth; and that the market is neutral between competing conceptions of human relationships.

49. A much earlier version of this chapter appeared as Satz, "Markets in Women's Reproductive Labor."

Chapter 6

1. Although it sometimes does. See below.

2. That is, if there were gender equality between the sexes, but a substantial group of very poor men and women were selling sex to survive, this would indeed be troubling. We should be suspicious of any labor contract entered into under circumstances of desperation, what I have referred to as the underlying vulnerability of transacting agents. This is the case with much prostitution around the globe.

3. Laurie Shrage, "Should Feminists Oppose Prostitution?," is an important exception. See also her book *Moral Dilemmas of Feminism*.

4. The fact that monetary exchange plays a role in maintaining many intimate relationships is a point underscored by George Bernard Shaw in *Mrs. Warren's Profession*.

5. See Walkowitz, *Prostitution and Victorian Society*; Rosen, *Prostitution in America*; Hobson, *Uneasy Virtue*.

6. See Danny Hakin and William Rasbaum, "Spitzer Linked to a Sex Ring as a Client, Gives Apology," *New York Times*, March 11, 2008, late ed., A1.

7. Decker, *Prostitution*, 191.

8. See Greenwald, *The Elegant Prostitute*, 10.

9. For discussion of male prostitutes who sell sex to women, see H. Smith and B. Van der Horst, "For Women Only—How It Feels to Be a Male Hooker," *Village Voice*, March 7, 1977. Dictionary and common usage tends to identify prostitutes with women. Men who sell sex to women are generally referred to as "gigolos," not "prostitutes." The former term encompasses the sale of companionship as well as sex.

10. Male prostitutes merit only a dozen pages in John Decker's monumental study of prostitution. See also Drew and Drake, *Boys for Sale*; Deisher, "Young Male Prostitutes"; Sereny, *The Invisible Children*. I am grateful to Vincent DiGirolamo for bringing these works to my attention. See also D. Allen, "Young Male Prostitutes."

11. P. Alexander, "Prostitution." A recent economics paper suggests that the portion of prostitution carried out by streetwalkers is declining because of the Internet. See Cunningham and Kendall, "Prostitution 2.0."

12. Moreover to the extent that the desperate background conditions are the problem, it is not apparent that outlawing prostitution is the solution. Banning prostitution may only remove a poor woman's best option; it in no way eradicates the circumstances that led her to such a choice. See Radin, "Market-Inalienability," on the problem of the "double bind."

13. For an attempt to understand human sexuality as a whole through the economic approach, see Posner, *Sex and Reason*.

14. Although two-thirds of prostitutes surveyed say that they have no regrets about choice of work. See Decker, *Prostitution*, 165–66. This figure is hard to interpret, given the high costs of thinking that one has made a bad choice of occupation and the lack of decent employment alternatives for many prostitutes.

15. See Calabresi and Melamed, "Property Rules."

16. Prostitution is, however, an issue that continues to divide feminists. On the one side, some feminists see prostitution as dehumanizing and alienating and linked to male domination. This is the view taken by the prostitute organization WHISPER (Women Hurt in Systems of Prostitution Engaged in Revolt). On the other side, some feminists see sex markets as affirming a woman's right to autonomy, sexual pleasure, and economic welfare. This is the view taken by the prostitute organization COYOTE (Call Off Your Old Tired Ethics).

17. Pateman, *The Sexual Contract*, 207, emphasis added.

18. Thus Richard Posner errs when he claims that the "prohibition against rape is to the sex and marriage market as the prohibition against theft is to explicit markets in goods and services" ("An Economic Theory," 1199). For discussion of analogies and disanalogies between body parts and external things, see Harris, "The Survival Lottery"; Fabre, *Whose Body*.

19. See chapter 9 for discussion.

20. Radin, "Market-Inalienability," 1884.

21. An objection along these lines is raised by Margaret Baldwin in "Split at the Root." She worries that prostitution undermines our ability to understand a woman's capacity to consent to sex. She asks, Will a prostitute's consent to sex be seen as consent to a twenty-dollar payment? Will courts determine sentences in rape trials involving prostitutes as the equivalent of parking fine violations (e.g., as another twenty-dollar payment)? Aren't prostitutes liable to have their fundamental interests in bodily integrity discounted? I think Baldwin's worry is a real one, especially in the context of the current stigmatization of prostitutes. It could be resolved, in part, by withholding information about a woman's profession from rape trials.

22. Radin does try to give a fairly abstract account of what makes people flourish, one that may be filled out in various ways. So perhaps her account is less controversial than more specific accounts.

23. E. Anderson, *Value*, 45.

24. Patterson, *Slavery and Social Death*.

25. Actually the prostitute's humanity is a part of the sex transaction itself; that is why few people are interested in nonhuman sexual substitutes. Indeed the prostitute's humanity (and gender) may be crucial to the john's experience of himself as superior to her. See MacKinnon, *Toward a Feminist Theory*.

26. Scott Anderson, however, has recently argued for the special importance of sexual autonomy, over and above other forms of autonomy. See his "Prostitution." I return to this idea below.

27. Although Arlie Hochschild has found that the sale of "emotional labor" by airline stewardesses and insurance salesmen distorts their normal responses to pain and frustration. See *The Managed Heart*.

28. I owe this point to Elizabeth Anderson, who stressed the need to distinguish between different versions of the degradation objection and suggested some lines of interpretation.

29. See www.npc.umich.edu/poverty/.

30. Rix, *The American Woman*. Rix notes that the time women spend doing housework has not declined since the 1920s, despite the invention of labor-saving technologies (e.g., laundry machines and dish washers). See also Bianchi et al., "Is Anyone Doing the Housework?," reporting that women still do twice as much housework as men.

31. Haslanger, "Gender and Race."

32. "Full Report of the Prevalence, Incidence and Consequences of Violence against Women: Findings from the National Violence Against Women Survey," November 2000, p. 26, Washington, D.C: National Institute of Justice and the Centers for Disease Control and Prevention.

33. I am indebted here to Iris Young's discussion in *Justice and the Politics of Difference*.

34. See www.cawp.rutgers.edu/fast_facts/levels_of_office/congress.php.

35. Shrage, *Moral Dilemmas of Feminism*, argues that prostitution perpetuates the following beliefs that oppress women: (1) the universal possession of a potent sex drive; (2) the "natural" dominance of men; (3) the pollution of women by sexual contact; and (4) the reification of sexual practice.

36. See Potterat et al., "Mortality." See also Silbert, "Sexual Assault," for a study of street prostitutes in which 70 percent of those surveyed reported that they had been raped while walking the streets.

37. Pateman, "Defending Prostitution," 563.

38. See also Schwartzenbach, "Contractarians."

39. It is of course possible, albeit difficult, for a group of people to change the meaning of a social practice. Consider the contemporary controversy around the social meaning of marriage.

40. I owe this point to Arthur Kuflik.

41. S. Anderson, "Prostitution."

42. In the United States prostitution is legalized only in several jurisdictions in Nevada.

43. These countries also have more pay equity between men and women than is true in the United States. This might be taken to undermine an argument about prostitution's role in contributing to income inequality. Moreover women's status is lower in some societies that repress prostitution (such as those of the Islamic nations) than in those than do not (such as those of the Scandinavian nations). But given the variety of cultural, economic, and political factors that need to be taken into account, we need to be very careful in drawing hasty conclusions. Legalizing prostitution might have negative effects on gender equality in the United States, even if legal prostitution does not correlate with gender inequality in other countries. For skepticism about the link between pornography and gender inequality, see Richard Posner, "Obsession," *New Republic*, October 18, 1993, 31–36.

44. Lindquist et al., "Judicial Processing." Several state laws banning prostitution have been challenged on equal protection grounds. These statistics support the idea that prostitution's negative image effect has disproportionate bearing on male and female prostitutes.

45. See Sunstein, "Neutrality."

46. Brandt, *A Theory*, 11–12, 126–27, 333.

47. An earlier version of this chapter appeared in *Ethics*. See Satz, "Markets in Women's Sexual Labor."

Chapter 7

1. Fallon and Tzannatos, *Child Labor*.

2. See also Kanbur, "On Obnoxious Markets."

3. The fact that children have not yet developed important capacities makes their situation different from that of adults who have developed these capacities but whose capacities are in some way deficient, for example, they (the adults) make bad choices. See Schapiro, "What Is a Child?"

4. Children should not be seen as merely passive "patients" whose opinions never need be consulted. Clearly the extent of children's agency increases over time, so that three-year-olds differ dramatically from sixteen-year-olds in terms of their level of effective rational agency. The fact that children's agency is lower than that of adults does not denigrate the contributions children make to their own well-being or to the well-being of others.

5. Children orphaned by AIDS or civil wars and older children who have fled abusive homes do make decisions on their own behalf. But even in these cases, to the extent that their powers of decision making remain undeveloped, they cannot generally be seen as full agents.

6. Humphries, "Cliometrics."

7. Dreze and Gazar, "Uttar Pradesh," 86.

8. Burra, *Born to Work*.

9. There is evidence that in many countries girls are systematically undervalued by their families. Such discounting helps explain why, as Amartya Sen has dramatically phrased it, "more than 100 million women are missing," mainly in South Asia and China. See also Jejeebhoy, "Family Size."

10. See Haddad, Hoddinott, and Alderman, *Intrahousehold Resource Allocation*. See Agarwal, *A Field*, for evidence that land allocation to women rather than men results not only in higher productivity in agriculture but also in better outcomes for children.

11. Sen, "Well-being." I introduced the two types of interests in chapter 4.

12. Here I draw on Brighouse, "What Rights."

13. This was an objection I raised earlier against Margaret Jane Radin's attempt to use the best conception of human flourishing as a lever with which to move certain markets into the blocked or regulated zone.

14. What if a state rejects the existence of these core interests? One could, for example, appeal to certain physiological and psychological needs that people have

regardless of their cultural circumstances, or draw on the choices people make for themselves when they are in a position to make meaningful choices.

15. Given that in the family parents' interests are likely to prevail over children's interests, there are practical reasons to adopt an approach to child labor that focuses on what happens to the children in a family.

16. Weiner, *Child and State*.

17. I am not of course assuming that the millions of extremely impoverished adults around the globe deserve their situation either.

18. Kabeer, "Deprivation," 4.

19. Kahneman, Knetch, and Thaler, "Fairness."

20. Basu, "Child Labor."

21. Bhatty, "Educational Deprivation."

22. D. Brown, Deardorff, and Stern, "Child Labor."

23. Murthi, Guio, and Dreze, "Mortality."

24. See Grootaert and Kanbur, "Child Labor," for additional suggestions.

25. Contextualists should be distinguished from relativists, who deny universal standards as such. Contextualists recognize the pull of such standards but also recognize that it may not be possible to implement them given current conditions.

26. Walzer, *Spheres*, xiii. I quoted this earlier, in my introduction.

27. The international lending institutions should not repeat the policies of the past, in which corrupt dictators such as Mobutu Sese Seko were repeatedly given new loans for development that did nothing to improve the lives of Zaire's people. See Easterly, *The Elusive Quest*.

28. Kabeer, "Deprivation."

29. Ibid.

30. Economic analyses of child labor tend to treat the marginal productivity of a child as a property of the child, given a fixed technology of household production. As I mentioned earlier, children are not analogous to other economic products; their benefits and costs are not only exogenously determined. Parents can, for example, assign household duties in different ways, such as by challenging gender norms and giving more productive jobs to girls. Vivianna Zelizer, *Pricing*, argues that a variety of cultural forces rather than changes in the structure of the labor market changed the view of children in the United States during the nineteenth century.

31. An earlier version of this chapter appeared as Satz, "Child Labor: A Normative Perspective."

Chapter 8

The epigraph quotes Reverend E. P. Holmes, a black clergyman, testifying before a congressional committee in 1883. Quoted in Foner, *Nothing but Freedom*, 7.

This chapter was presented at the Equality and Markets Conference at Stanford University, at BAFFLE, at the University of Toronto Law School, at the NYU School of Law Colloquium on Law, Economics and Politics, and at a conference in Tel Aviv on labor rights. I have benefited from written and verbal comments from Barbara Fried and from

Josh Cohen, Yossi Dahan, Rob Reich, Seana Shiffrin, Elizabeth Anderson, Elizabeth Hansot, Paul Gowder, Marc Fleurbaey, Meir Dan-Cohen, Eric Rakowski, Andrew Levine, Lewis Kornhauser, Liam Murphy, Jonathan Wolff, and many other members of the audiences.

1. Bardhan, "Labor Tying."

2. Schaffner, "Attached Farm Labor."

3. Bardhan, "A Note."

4. International Labour Organization, "A Global Alliance."

5. See Patterson, *Slavery*, chap. 4.

6. Some libertarians will be willing to regulate transactions that have external third-party effects.

7. Hill, *Autonomy*, 12.

8. Mill, *Utilitarianism*, 14. Mill himself considers any defense of voluntary slavery to be self-defeating: it is self-contradictory to say we should be free not to be free. See his discussion in *On Liberty*. This argument faces some serious problems, as Mill is defending liberty as noninterference and there is nothing paradoxical about giving someone the ability to enslave in the absence of interference. Of course in the case of enforcement in the face of default, there will be interference, but this is true of other contracts.

9. See Mistry, *A Fine Balance*, for a novelist's moving depiction of the lives of India's poor in which lifetime bondage to a creditor appears as a rational response to an irrational world.

10. Nozick, *Anarchy*, 163. Nozick has three principles of justice: justice in acquisition, justice in transfer, and a principle of rectification.

11. Ibid., 30–35.

12. Ibid., 331. Nozick of course fails to consider that for slavery contracts to be valid, they must be underwritten by laws and enforced. Runaway slaves must be recaptured; defaulters on terms of agreement must be punished.

13. Indeed it is curious that given the centrality of the idea of "consenting parties" to the justification of market exchange, there has been so little attention paid to it in economics.

14. Nozick, "Coercion."

15. For objections to moralizing the concept of coercion, see Zimmerman, "Coercive Wage Offers"; G. A. Cohen, "The Structure of Proletarian Unfreedom." One worry is that Nozick's approach makes it impossible to ask whether a form of coercion, say by the state, might be justified. It also seems to ignore the ways that a form of coercion might benefit a person.

16. Of course the justification for the initial appropriation of natural resources is notoriously vexed. Locke thought that the justification rested on the fact that a person has a right to what he mixes his labor with (as long as it is not previously owned by someone else). Nozick notes the difficulties with this in his example of the person who "mixes his labor" with the ocean by throwing tomato juice into it.

17. See Nozick, *Anarchy*, 263–64.

18. Freeman, "Illiberal Libertarians."

19. I return later to the suggestion that libertarianism is not a stable theory.

20. Some instances of bonded labor do originate in force and are maintained by violence. See Bales, *Disposable People*.

21. See J. Buchanan, *The Limits of Liberty*, 59–60, for a discussion of slavery as the result of bargaining from an anarchistic equilibrium.

22. Randy Barnett may be unique among libertarians in advocating debt slavery for those who impose costs on others through wrongdoing. See *The Structure of Liberty*, 35. Thanks to Arthur Ripstein for the citation.

23. Yet even some left libertarians seem willing to countenance voluntary slavery. See Otsuka, *Libertarianism*, especially 122–25.

24. Thanks to Barbara Fried for suggesting that I separate out the different ways that an individual might have a right not to be in the circumstances that give rise to bonded labor.

25. In fact specific performance is an exceptional remedy for breach of contract in Anglo-American law. The normal remedy is money damages.

26. Not all de facto monopolistic markets violate Nozick's Lockean proviso. See below.

27. Nozick, *Anarchy*, 178–82.

28. Recall that Locke's founding principle was a positive duty to protect and preserve human life. It was this duty that was the basis of his restriction on individual property rights.

29. For a libertarian argument that stresses the negative efficiency consequences of government intervention in people's lives, see Friedman, *Capitalism*; Epstein, *Principles*.

30. Given its emphasis on protecting an agent's equal freedom to make her own choices and pursue her own projects, libertarian theory's silence on children is remarkable. Nozick, for example, merely notes in passing, "Children present yet more difficult problems. In some way it must be ensured that they are informed of the range of alternatives in the world. But the home community might view it as important that their youngsters not be exposed to the knowledge that one hundred miles away there is a community of great sexual freedom. And so on" (*Anarchy*, 330).

31. See also ibid., 38, arguing that children have a right not to be eaten by their parents(!).

32. Libertarians who base their doctrine on a principle of self-ownership have struggled with the question of why children are not owned by their begetters. See Steiner, "Self-Ownership." For criticism of Nozick's views, see Okin, *Justice*, chap. 4.

33. Rawls considered long-term stability crucial to the justification of his two principles of justice and devoted a large part of *A Theory of Justice* to this concern. See 434–41.

34. See E. Anderson, "Ethical Assumptions."

35. See Varian, *Microeconomic Analysis*, 94–97.

36. Bardhan, "Wages."

37. Bardhan, "Labor Tying."

38. Braverman and Stiglitz "Sharecropping."

39. Srinivasan, "On the Choice."

40. Genicot, "Bonded Labor," argues that the existence of "bonded labor hinders the development of welfare enhancing credit opportunities for laborers." Given poor peasants' lack of collateral, asymmetries of information, and ineffective enforcement institutions, credit contracts tend to be implicit self-enforcing agreements. The loss of future credit opportunities from lenders provides peasant borrowers with an incentive not to default on their loans. In the absence of such incentives enforcement would be extremely costly and creditors would have less reason to make such loans. By providing an alternative opportunity for obtaining credit besides formal credit institutions, bonded labor decreases the costs of reneging on the agreement. Bonded labor thereby renders the implicit promise to repay a loan from a formal credit institution unenforceable. Genicot argues that the existence of bonded labor can lead local credit institutions to deny loans to poor laborers; it might also prevent such institutions from forming or thriving. A ban on bonded labor, if this contributes to the creation of formal credit institutions, might make some poor laborers better off by enabling them access to credit on terms they would prefer.

41. See Parfit, *Reasons and Persons*.

42. As I discussed in chapter 2, this was a central concern of the classical political economists.

43. See Sen, *Inequality Reexamined*.

44. In many of these cases it might be argued that we have de facto monopoly pricing.

45. As the recent subprime loan crisis shows, even relatively educated Americans did not understand the terms of their loans.

46. Cited in Schaffner, "Attached Farm Labor." Prof. Mariana Mota Prado cautioned me that the language in this example may have other explanations, based on class and on culture.

47. Quoted in Bales, "The Social Psychology of Slavery," 2.

48. Hill, *Autonomy*.

49. Schaffner, "Attached Farm Labor," argues that employers attempt to manipulate the psychology of their employees to reduce the costs of enforcing the bondage relationship.

50. See Lane, *The Market Experience*, especially 235–59.

51. Thanks to Seana Shiffrin for suggesting that I emphasize my expansion of the vocabulary of endogeneity and underscore its relationship to skills as well as preferences.

52. Michael Blake raised this objection to my argument in discussion. But see Snyder, *A Well-Paid Slave*, for an argument that even high pay may not compensate for the right to exit. It is also worth pointing out that although Curt Flood was prohibited from playing for another baseball team, he was always free to leave the profession of baseball. (Military service is also exceptional in ways that perhaps justify its hierarchical and authoritative structure.)

53. For discussions of the role of work in sustaining personal welfare, self-respect, and social and civic status, see Estlund, *Working Together*; Schultz, "Life's Work."

54. Quoted in P. Brown, *Augustine*.

55. See Weiner, *Child and State*.

Chapter 9

1. Thanks to Caleb Perl and Jose Campos for research assistance. Thanks also to Joe Shapiro, whose undergraduate honors thesis at Stanford, "The Ethics and Efficacy of Banning Human Kidney Sales," prompted me to think harder about this topic. I was the co-advisor of his thesis with Ken Arrow. Thanks to Ben Hippen for comments on a longer version of this chapter. Thanks also to the audience at the Aristotelian Society, the editor of the Society's proceedings, David Harris, and to Annabelle Lever, Eric Maskin, and Josh Cohen for written comments.

2. This libertarian view confronts serious questions about the scope of control a person has over her body. For example, does a person have the right to sell all of her organs, even if it means her death? Does my right to use my body as I wish mean that I can walk naked into my office? More to the point, do rights to bodily autonomy and integrity entail rights to *sell* one's body or body parts? Cecile Fabre has recently argued that, under many circumstances, justice requires conferring on the sick a right to confiscate the superfluous body parts of healthy individuals. See, Fabre, "Whose Body." Her argument depends on a close analogy between body parts and external resources and perhaps an overly optimistic view about the state's ability to fairly enforce the organ distribution policy.

3. Among undeveloped nations only Iran presently has a legalized kidney market.

4. Goodwin, *Black Markets*, 119–22.

5. In *McFall v. Shimp*, 10 Pa. D&C.3d 90 (Ch. Ct. 1978) a man (McFall) who would surely die without a bone marrow transplant, sought an injunction to require his cousin (Shimp) to donate bone marrow, a procedure that would have posed little risk but considerable pain. The court refused to grant the injunction, and the man subsequently died. In *Curran v. Bosze*, 566 N.E.2d 1319 (Ill. 1990) the Illinois Supreme Court refused to grant a noncustodial parent's request that his own twin three-year-old children be compelled to undergo blood testing and possible bone marrow harvesting to save the life of their twelve-year-old half-brother. (The half-brother died while the case was still being decided.)

6. Or perhaps I should say *lists*, since in the United States there is a national list as well as lists at regional transplant centers.

7. Goodwin, *Black Markets*, 40. Goodwin also importantly notes that there are racial disparities in how long people have to wait for a kidney, as well as racial differences in rates of organ donation. African Americans, for example, wait longer on lists and also donate organs less frequently than whites.

8. This figure also includes those who die while waiting for a heart to become available for transplant.

9. See Living Legacy Registry, Donation Statistics, at http://livinglegacy.org.

10. Some object that opt-out systems do not really allow for individual consent because many people do not have adequate information about their society's default position on cadaver organs. According to critics, opt-out systems are really systems of organ conscription. Those who would not have wished to donate their organs after their death, if they had properly reflected on this while they were alive, are forcibly drafted

into donation: their actual consent is sidestepped. But *even if this were true*, that is, even if most people comply with such systems only out of ignorance, the critics' argument is insufficient to rebut those who favor such systems, since an analogous charge could be brought against opt-in systems. In opt-in systems there are likely to be people who have never thought about whether or not their organs should be available for others upon their death, yet would have ex ante preferred that they were. In opt-in donation systems, such people are simply presumed to have consented to nondonation and thus are forcibly drafted into nondonation; their consent to nondonation, in other words, is also sidestepped. Different attitudes about the respective degrees of coerciveness of opt-out and opt-in systems undoubtedly reflect different views about the extent to which an individual has strong ownership claims over her body parts, even after her death. The different default starting positions reflect, at least in part, different attitudes and preferences about social claims on cadaver organs. But these attitudes and preferences are themselves reciprocally influenced by framing effects and starting points. That is, *whichever* default position we choose for organ donation, opt in or opt out, may change the likelihood of certain choices over others. Initial allocations, expectations, and laws about a person's organs form a starting point that affects her individual preferences and judgments. Because every society must have some donation or nondonation starting point, every society faces the question of deciding how this starting point should be determined.

11. See the data collected by Spain's Organizacion Nacional de Transplantes, at http://ont.es. See also Newsletter *Transplant: International Figures on Organ Donation and Transplantation* vol. 10, no 1. Madrid, SpainFundacion Renal, 2005.

12. Coppen et al., "Opting-out Systems."

13. Those who receive their kidneys from live donors tend to fare better than those who receive their kidneys from cadavers. See Editorial, "Renal Transplantation from Living Donors," *British Medical Journal* 318 (1999): 409–10; Terasaki et al., "High Survival Rate."

14. See Healy, *Last Best Gifts.*

15. Cited in Seabright, *The Company*, 151–52.

16. Titmuss, *The Gift Relationship.*

17. Ibid., 314.

18. Arrow, "Gifts and Exchanges."

19. See Gneezy and Rustichini, "A Fine."

20. Frey and Oberholzer-Gee, "The Cost."

21. See E. Anderson, *Value.*

22. Strahilevitz, "How Changes."

23. Gneezy and Rustichini, "Pay Enough." Frey discusses the Dürrenmatt play in Frey, Oberholzer-Gee, and Eichenberger, "The Old Lady."

24. Thanks to Ben Hippen for the point that not all extrinsic rewards need have the same consequences for altruistic donation.

25. Ghods, Savaj, and Khosravani, "Adverse Effects."

26. Scheper-Hughes, "Keeping," 1645.

27. If we are concerned about desperation, banning kidney markets itself does nothing to rectify the desperate conditions that prompt such sales. If our concern with kidney markets is the desperation that is prompting the sale, it does no good to close off the sale but leave the circumstances that yielded the desperation in place. In fact given the desperation, sellers and buyers may still resort to a black market, with a host of attendant abuses even more exploitive, overreaching, or unfair than a legalized market would be.

28. Goyal et al., "Economic."

29. Indebtedness is a fact of life in many of the areas where kidney selling is widespread. The Goyal study found that 96 percent of sellers interviewed sold a kidney to pay off a debt; 74 percent were still in debt at the time of the survey, six years later. In fact this study of 305 kidney sellers in Chennai, India, found that after selling a kidney family income actually declined. Many sellers experienced pain and were unable to work. Participants were also paid little for their organs, and often substantially less than they were promised. So even when they were able to stave off the moneylenders for a few years, they were soon in debt again.

30. Goyal et al., "Economic," report that although people sell their kidneys to get out of debt, sellers are frequently in debt again within several years of the sale.

31. In the case of altruistic donation, our concerns about sellers' agency is presumably mitigated by the fact that the suppliers of kidneys are likely to come from many economic groups and not simply from the desperately poor, who also tend to be uneducated.

32. Recent studies have found that donating a kidney does not damage donors' health or reduce their life span, and they are less likely to develop kidney failure than the general population. See Ibrahim et al., "Long-Term Consequences." Of course, as I have stressed, the results of kidney donation in the developed world may not tell us very much about kidney donation in the undeveloped world. For one thing, donors in the United States, where this study was undertaken, are very carefully screened for health risks.

33. Joe Shapiro makes this observation as a framing background for his discussion of the morality of kidney markets. See "The Ethics."

34. C. Williams, "Note."

35. Titmuss, *The Gift Relationship*. Goodwin, *Black Markets*, draws attention to racial disparities in who gives and who gets an organ.

36. Ishiguro, *Never Let Me Go*. Recently, an article in the New York Times by Andrew Pollack raised concerns about the sale of plasma by poor Mexicans to centers run by pharmaceutical companies at the U.S. and Mexico border. See "Is Money Tainting the Plasma Supply?" December 6, 2010, Sunday Business section, p. 1.

37. Nancy Scheper-Hughes, quoted in Michael Finkel, "Complications," *New York Times Magazine*, May 27, 2001, 32. The term *transplant tourism* refers to wealthy individuals or their brokers from the developed world flying halfway around the world to less developed countries searching for organ sellers.

38. See Shapiro, "The Ethics," 120.

39. To what extent would the availability of kidneys through a market indemnify individuals against the effects of bad health choices? Thanks to Annabelle Lever for pressing this point.

40. L. Cohen, "Where It Hurts."

41. Ibid., 673.

42. Recall that in chapter 7 I made an analogous argument about child labor: the availability of child labor decreases the price of unskilled adult labor and thereby makes it harder for families to refrain from putting their children to work.

43. R. Dworkin, "Comment on Narveson," 39.

44. Walzer, *Spheres*, 102.

45. Roth, Sonmez, and Unver, "Pairwise Kidney Exchange."

46. The idea for this chart comes from Kanbur, "On Obnoxious Markets."

47. An earlier version of this chapter appeared as Satz, "The Moral Limits of Markets: The Case of Human Kidneys."

Conclusion

1. Ashley Conrad Walker suggested that my framework might apply to financial instruments and wrote a paper attempting to apply it. I am indebted to his discussion.

2. For a discussion of the state's interest in education, see Reich, *Bridging Liberalism*, 151–55. An important question is whether the existence of private schools threatens to create closed and exclusive groups who capture elite positions in society.

3. It is important to emphasize that the theory of noxious markets that I present here is not meant to be a substitute for a *full* theory of justice, even though justice-based considerations are clearly at work in my theory.

Bibliography

Adams, John. *Risk*. London: University College London Press, 1995.

Agarwal, Bina. *A Field of One's Own: Gender and Land Rights in South Asia*. Cambridge: Cambridge University Press, 1995.

Aigen, Betsy P. "Motivations of Surrogate Mothers: Parenthood, Altruism and Self Actualization." 1996. Available at www.surrogacy.com/psychres/article/motiv.html.

Akerlof, George. "The Market for 'Lemons': Quality Uncertainty and the Market Mechanism." *Quarterly Journal of Economics* 84, no. 3 (1970): 488–500.

Alexander, C. F. "All Things Bright and Beautiful." In *The Oxford English Dictionary of Quotations*. London: Oxford University Press, 1954.

Alexander, Priscilla. "Prostitution: A Difficult Issue for Feminists." In *Sex Work: Writings by Women in the Sex Industry*, ed. P. Alexander and F. Delacoste. Pittsburgh: Cleis Press, 1987.

Allen, Anita. "Surrogacy, Slavery and the Ownership of Life." *Harvard Journal of Law and Public Policy* 13, no. 1 (1990): 139–49.

Allen, D. "Young Male Prostitutes: A Psychosocial Study." *Archives of Sexual Behavior* 9, no. 5 (1980): 399–426.

Anderson, Elizabeth. "Against Desert: Markets, Equality and Pure Procedural Justice." Paper on file with author, 2006.

———. "Ethical Assumptions of Economic Theory: Some Lessons from the History of Credit and Bankruptcy." *Ethical Theory and Practice* 7 (2004): 347–60.

———. "Is Women's Labor a Commodity?" *Philosophy and Public Affairs* 19, no. 1 (1990): 71–92.

———. *Value in Ethics and Economics*. Cambridge, MA: Harvard University Press, 1993.

———. "What Is the Point of Equality?" *Ethics* 109, no. 2 (1999): 287–337.

Anderson, Scott. "Prostitution and Sexual Autonomy: Making Sense of the Prohibition of Prostitution." *Ethics* 112 (2002): 748–80.

Arrow, Kenneth. "Gifts and Exchanges." *Philosophy and Public Affairs* 1, no. 4 (1972): 343–62.

———. "Uncertainty and the Welfare Economics of Medical Care." *Journal of Health Politics, Policy and Law* 26, no. 5 (2001): 851–83.

Baldwin, James. "A Talk to Teachers." In *The Price of the Ticket: Collected Non-Fiction 1948–1985*. New York: St. Martin's Press, 1985. (Originally delivered October 16,

1963, as "The Negro Child—His Self-Image," published in *The Saturday Review*, December 21, 1963.)

Baldwin, Margaret. "Split at the Root: Prostitution and Feminist Discourses of Law Reform." *Yale Journal of Law and Feminism* 5 (1992): 47–120.

Bales, Kevin. *Disposable People: New Slavery in the Global Economy*. Berkeley: University of California Press, 1999.

———. "The Social Psychology of Slavery." *Scientific American*, April 24, 2002.

Bardhan, Pranab. "Labor Tying in a Poor Agrarian Economy: A Theoretical and Empirical Analysis." *Quarterly Journal of Economics* 98, no. 3 (1983): 501–14.

———. "A Note on Interlinked Rural Economic Arrangements." In *The Economic Theory of Agrarian Institutions*, ed. Pranab Bardhan. Oxford: Clarendon Press, 1991.

———. "Wages and Employment in a Poor Agrarian Economy: A Theoretical and Empirical Analysis." *Journal of Political Economy* 87, no. 3 (1979): 479–500.

Barnett, Randy. *The Structure of Liberty*. Oxford: Oxford University Press, 1998.

Bartels, Dianne, R. Priester, D. Vawter, A. Caplan. *Beyond Baby M*. New York: Springer Verlag, 1990.

Basu, Kaushik. "Child Labor: Cause, Consequence and Cure." *Journal of Economic Literature* 37, no. 3 (1999): 1083–1119.

———. "Economics and Law of Sexual Harassment in the Workplace." *Journal of Economic Perspectives* 17 (2003): 141–57.

Becker, Gary. *The Economic Approach to Human Behavior*. Chicago: University of Chicago Press, 1976.

Bennett, John G. "Ethics and Markets." *Philosophy and Public Affairs* 14, no. 2 (1985): 195–204.

Bhatty, K. "Educational Deprivation in India: A Survey of Field Investigations." *Economic and Political Weekly*, July 4 and 18, 1998, 1731–40.

Bianchi, Suzanne, et al. "Is Anyone Doing the Housework? Trends in the Gender Division of Household Labor." *Social Forces* 79, no. 1 (2000): 191–228.

Birdsall, Nancy. "The World Is Not Flat: Inequality and Injustice in Our Global Economy." WIDER Annual Lecture. 2005.

Blaug, Mark. *Economic Theory in Retrospect*. 3rd ed. Cambridge: Cambridge University Press, 1978.

Bloch, Marc. *Feudal Society*. Trans. L. A. Manyon. Chicago: University of Chicago Press, 1961.

Bohm-Bawerk, Eugen V. *Capital and Interest: A Critical History of Economical Theory*. Whitefish, MT: Kessinger Publishing, 2007. (Originally published in 1884.)

Bowen, William, and Derek Bok. *The Shape of the River: Long-Term Consequences of Considering Race in College and University Admissions*. Princeton, NJ: Princeton University Press, 1998.

Bowles, Samuel. "Endogenous Preferences: The Cultural Consequences of Markets and Other Economic Institutions." *Journal of Economic Literature* 36 (1998): 75–111.

———. "Mandeville's Mistake." Working paper, University of Massachusetts, 1989.

———. "What Markets Can and Cannot Do." *Challenge*, July–August 1991: 11–16.

Bowles, Samuel, and Herbert Gintis. "Contested Exchange: New Microfoundations for the Political Economy of Capitalism." *Politics and Society* 18, no. 2 (1990): 165–222.

Brandt, Richard. *A Theory of the Good and the Right.* New York: Prometheus Books, 1979.

Braverman, A., and J. Stiglitz. "Sharecropping and the Interlinking of Agrarian Markets." *American Economic Review* 72, no. 4 (1982): 695–715.

Brighouse, Harry. "Egalitarianism and Equal Availability of Political Influence." *Journal of Political Philosophy*, vol. 4, no. 2 (1996): 118–41.

——. "What Rights (If Any) Do Children Have?" In *The Moral and Political Status of Children*, ed. David Archard and Colin Macleod. Oxford: Oxford University Press, 2002.

Brown, D., A. Deardorff, and R. Stern. "Child Labor: Theory, Evidence and Policy." In *International Labor Standards—Issues, Theories and Policy Options*, ed. Kaushik Basu, H. Horn, L. Roman, and J. Shapiro. Oxford, UK: Basil Blackwell, 2003.

Brown, Peter. *Augustine of Hippo.* Berkeley: University of California Press, 2000.

Browne, J., and M. Stears. "Capabilities, Resources and Systematic Injustice." *Politics, Philosophy and Economics* 4, no. 3 (2005): 355–73.

Buchanan, Allen. *Ethics, Efficiency and the Market.* Totowa, NJ: Rowman & Allanheld, 1985.

Buchanan, James. *The Limits of Liberty: Between Anarchy and Leviathan.* Chicago: University of Chicago Press, 1975.

Burra, N. *Born to Work: Child Labor in India.* Oxford: Oxford University Press, 1995.

Calabresi, Guido, and Philip Bobbitt. *Tragic Choices: The Conflicts Society Confronts in the Allocation of Tragically Scarce Resources.* New York: Norton, 1978.

Calabresi, Guido, and Douglas Melamed. "Property Rules, Liability Rules and Inalienability: One View of the Cathedral." *Harvard Law Review* 85 (1972): 1089–128.

Campbell, Nancy. "The Construction of Pregnant Drug Using Women as Criminal Perpetrators," *Fordham Urban Law Journal* 33 (January 2006): 101–121.

Cohen, G. A. "The Pareto Argument for Inequality." *Social Philosophy and Policy* 12 (Winter 1995): 160–85.

——. *Rescuing Justice and Equality.* Cambridge, MA: Harvard University Press, 2008.

——. "The Structure of Proletarian Unfreedom." *Philosophy and Public Affairs* 12, no. 3 (1983): 3–33.

Cohen, Lawrence. "Where It Hurts: Indian Material for an Ethics of Organ Transplantation." *Daedalus* 128, no. 4 (1999): 135–65.

Coppen, Remco, et al. "Opting-out Systems: No Guarantee for Higher Donation Rates." *Transplant International* 18 (2005): 1275–79.

Corea, Gena. *The Mother Machine.* New York: Harper and Row, 1985.

Crow, Ben. *The Diversity of Markets: How the Grain Trade Shapes Wealth and Poverty in Rural South Asia.* London: Macmillan, 2001.

Cunningham, Scott, and Todd Kendall. "Prostitution 2.0: The Internet and the Call Girl." Paper presented at the first annual meeting of the Economics of Risky Behavior conference, Washington, DC, March 2009. Available at www.iza.org/conference_files/riskonomics2009/Cunningham_S4817.pdf.

Decker, John. *Prostitution: Regulation and Control*. Littleton, CO: Fred Rothman, 1979.

Drew, D., and J. Drake. *Boys for Sale: A Sociological Study of Boy Prostitution*. Deer Park, NY: Brown Book, 1969.

Dreze, J., and H. Gazar. "Uttar Pradesh: The Burden of Inertia." In *Indian Development: Selected Regional Perspectives*, ed. J. Dreze and A. Sen. Delhi: Oxford University Press 1996.

Dworkin, Gerald. "Paternalism." In *Morality and the Law*, ed. Richard Wasserstrom. Belmont, CA: Wadsworth, 1971.

Dworkin, Ronald. "Comment on Narveson: In Defense of Equality." *Social Philosophy and Policy* 1 (1983): 24–40.

———. *Sovereign Virtue*. Cambridge, MA: Harvard University Press, 2000.

———. "Sovereign Virtue Revisited." *Ethics* 113, no. 1 (2003): 106–43.

———. "What Is Equality, Part 2: Equality of Resources." *Philosophy and Public Affairs* 10, no. 4 (1981): 283–345.

Easterly, William. *The Elusive Quest for Growth*. Cambridge, MA: MIT Press, 2001.

Ehrenreich, Barbara, and Deidre English. *Witches, Midwives and Nurses: A History of Women Healers*. Old Westbury, NY: Feminist Press, 1973.

Elster, Jon. *Solomonic Judgments*. Cambridge: Cambridge University Press, 1989.

Epstein, Richard. *Principles for a Free Society: Reconciling Individual Liberty with the Common Good*. Reading, MA: Perseus Books, 1998.

Estlund, Cynthia. *Working Together*. Oxford: Oxford University Press, 2003.

Fabre, Cecile. *Whose Body Is It Anyway?* Oxford: Oxford University Press, 2006.

Fallon, P., and Z. Tzannatos. *Child Labor: Issues and Directions for the World Bank*. Washington, DC: World Bank Publications, 1998.

Field, Martha. *Surrogate Motherhood: The Legal and Human Issues*. Cambridge, MA: Harvard University Press, 1988.

Fogg-Davis, Hawley. "Racial Randomization: Imagining Nondiscrimination in Adoption." In *Adoption Matters*, ed. Sally Haslanger and Charlotte Witt. Ithaca, NY: Cornell University Press, 2005.

Foner, Eric. *Nothing but Freedom: Emancipation and Its Legacy*. Baton Rouge: Louisiana State University Press, 1983.

Frank, Robert. *Luxury Fever: Money and Happiness in an Era of Excess*. New York: Free Press, 1999.

Fraser, Nancy, and Axel Honneth, eds. *Redistribution or Recognition? A Political Philosophical Exchange*. London: Verso, 2003.

Freeman, Samuel. "Illiberal Libertarians: Why Libertarianism Is Not a Liberal View." *Philosophy and Public Affairs* 30, no. 2 (2001): 105–51.

———. "Rawls and Luck Egalitarianism." In *Justice and the Social Contract: Essays on Rawlsian Political Philosophy*. Oxford: Oxford University Press, 2007.

Frey, Bruno, and Felix Oberholzer-Gee. "The Cost of Price Incentives: An Empirical Analysis of Motivation Crowding Out." *American Economic Review* 87, no. 4 (1997): 746–55.

Frey, Bruno, Felix Oberholzer-Gee, and Reiner Eichenberger. "The Old Lady Visits Your Backyard: A Tale of Markets and Morals." *Journal of Political Economy* 104, no. 6 (1996): 1297–313.

Fried, Barbara. *The Progressive Assault on Laissez Faire: Robert Hale and the First Law and Economics Movement.* Cambridge, MA: Harvard University Press, 1998.

Friedman, Milton. *Capitalism and Freedom.* Chicago: University of Chicago Press, 1962.

Gandy, Patrick, and D. Deisher. "Young Male Prostitutes." *Journal of the American Medical Association* 212 (1970): 1661–66.

Gauthier, David. *Morals by Agreement.* New York: Oxford University Press, 1986.

Genicot, Garance. "Bonded Labor and Serfdom: A Paradox of Voluntary Choice." *Journal of Development Economics* 67, no. 1 (2002): 101–27.

Ghods, A. J., S. Savaj, and P. Khosravani. "Adverse Effects of a Controlled Living Unrelated Donor Renal Transplant Program on Living Related and Cadaveric Kidney Transplantation." *Transplantation Proceedings* 32, no. 3 (2000): 541.

Gneezy, Uri, and Aldo Rustichini. "A Fine Is a Price." *Journal of Legal Studies* 29, no. 1 (2000): 1–17.

———. "Pay Enough or Don't Pay at All." *Quarterly Journal of Economics* 115, no. 3 (2000): 791–810.

Goodwin, Michelle. *Black Markets: The Supply and Demand of Body Parts.* Cambridge: Cambridge University Press, 2006.

Gordon, Deborah. *Ants at Work: How an Insect Society Is Organized.* New York: Free Press, 1999.

Goyal, Madhav, et al. "Economic and Health Consequences of Selling a Kidney in India." *Journal of the American Medical Association* 288 (2002): 1589–93.

Greenwald, Harold. *The Elegant Prostitute: A Social and Psychoanalytic Study.* New York: Walker, 1970.

Grootaert, C., and R. Kanbur. "Child Labor: An Economic Perspective." *International Labour Review* 134, no. 2 (1995): 187–203.

Haddad, L., J. Hoddinott, and H. Alderman, eds. *Intrahousehold Resource Allocation in Developing Countries: Models, Methods and Policy.* Baltimore: Johns Hopkins University Press, 1977.

Harris, J. "The Survival Lottery." *Philosophy* 50 (1975): 81–87.

Haslanger, Sally. "Gender and Race: (What) Are They? (What) Do We Want Them to Be?" *Nous* 34, no. 1 (2000): 31–55.

Hausman, Daniel, and Michael McPherson. *Economic Analysis and Moral Philosophy.* Cambridge: Cambridge University Press, 1996.

Havel, Vaclav. *Summer Meditations: On Politics, Morality and Civility in a Time of Transition.* London: Faber and Faber, 1992.

Healy, Kieran. *Last Best Gifts: Altruism and the Market for Human Blood and Organs.* Chicago: University of Chicago Press, 2006.

Herzog, Don. "Externalities and Other Parasites." *University of Chicago Law Review* 67, no. 3 (2000): 895–923.

Hill, Thomas. *Autonomy and Self Respect.* Cambridge, England: Cambridge University Press, 1991.

Hirschman, Albert O. *Exit, Voice and Loyalty: Responses to Decline in Firms, Organizations and States.* Cambridge, MA: Harvard University Press, 1970.

———. *The Passions and the Interests: Political Arguments for Capitalism before Its Triumph.* Princeton, NJ: Princeton University Press, 1977.

———. *Rival Views of Market Society.* Cambridge, MA: Harvard University Press, 1992.

Hobbes, Thomas. *Leviathan.* Indianapolis: Hackett, 1994. (Originally published in 1651.)

Hobson, B. *Uneasy Virtue: The Politics of Prostitution and the American Reform Tradition.* Chicago: University of Chicago Press, 1990.

Hochschild, Arlie. *The Managed Heart: The Commercialization of Human Feeling.* New York: Basic Books, 1983.

Humphries, Jane. "Cliometrics, Child Labor and the Industrial Revolution." *Critical Review* 13, nos. 3–4 (1999): 269–83.

Ibrahim, Hassan N., Robert Foley, LiPing Tan, Tyson Rogers, Robert F. Bailey, Hongfei Guo, Cynthia R. Gross, and Arthur J. Matas. "Long-Term Consequences of Kidney Donation." *New England Journal of Medicine* 360 (January 29, 2009): 459–69.

International Labour Organization, "A Global Alliance against Forced Labour: Global Report under the Follow up of the ILO Declaration on Fundamental Principles and Rights at Work. Report of the Director-General." 2005.Available at: www.ilo.org/public/english/region/asro/manila/downloads/flexsum.pdf

Ishiguro, Kazuo. *Never Let Me Go.* New York: Knopf, 2005.

Jejeebhoy, S. J. "Family Size, Outcomes for Children and Gender Disparities: The Case of Rural Maharashtra." In *Fertility, Family Size, and Structure: Consequences for Families and Children,* ed. C. B. Lloyd. New York, Population Council, 1992.

Jevons, W. Stanley. *The Theory of Political Economy.* New York: Penguin, 1970. (Originally published in 1871.)

Kabeer, Naila. "Deprivation, Discrimination and Delivery: Competing Explanations for Child Labor and Educational Failure in South Asia." Working Paper 135, Institute of Development Studies, University of Sussex, 2001.

Kahneman, Daniel, J. Knetch, and R. Thaler. "Fairness and the Assumptions of Economics." In *Rational Choice: The Contrasts between Economics and Psychology,* ed. Robin M. Hograth and Melvin Reder. Chicago: University of Chicago Press, 1987.

Kahneman, Daniel, and Amos Tversky. "Prospect Theory: An Analysis of Decision under Risk." *Econometrica* 47 (1979): 263–91.

Kanbur, Ravi. "On Obnoxious Markets." In *Globalization, Culture and the Limits of the Market: Essays in Economics and Philosophy,* ed. Stephen Cullenberg and Prasanta Pattanaik. New Delhi: Oxford University Press, 2004.

Kane, E. *Birth Mother.* New York: Harcourt Brace Jovanovich, 1988.

Kant, Immanuel. *Groundwork of the Metaphysics of Morals.* Cambridge: Cambridge University Press, 1998. (Originally published in 1785.)

Kymlicka, Will. *Contemporary Political Philosophy: An Introduction.* Oxford: Oxford University Press, 2002.

Lane, Robert. *The Market Experience.* Cambridge: Cambridge University Press, 1991.

Lindblom, Charles. *The Market System: What It Is, How It Works, and What to Make of It*. New Haven, CT: Yale University Press, 2002.

Lindquist, John, et al. "Judicial Processing of Males and Females Charged with Prostitution." *Journal of Criminal Justice* 17 (1989): 277–91.

Loeb, Susanna. "Estimating the Effects of School Finance Reform: A Framework for a Federalist System." *Journal of Public Economics* 80 (2001): 225–47.

Loury, Glenn. *The Anatomy of Racial Inequality*. Cambridge, MA: Harvard University Press, 2002.

MacKinnon, Catherine. *Toward a Feminist Theory of the State*. Cambridge, MA: Harvard University Press, 1989.

MacLeod, Colin. *Liberalism, Justice, and Markets*. Oxford: Clarendon Press, 1998.

Marglin, Stephen. *The Dismal Science*. Cambridge, MA: Harvard University Press, 2008.

———. "What Do Bosses Do? The Origins and Functions of Hierarchy in Capitalist Production. Part I." *Review of Radical Political Economics* 6, no. 2 (1974): 60–112.

Marshall, T. H. "Citizenship and Social Class." In *Class, Citizenship and Social Development: Essays by T. H. Marshall*. Chicago: University of Chicago Press, 1977.

Marx, Karl. *Capital*. Vol. 1. New York: Vintage, 1977. (Originally published in 1867.)

———. "The Communist Manifesto." In *The Marx-Engels Reader*, ed. Robert Tucker. New York: Norton, 1978.

———. "Critique of the Gotha Program." In *The Marx-Engels Reader*, ed. Robert Tucker. New York: Norton, 1978.

———. "Economic and Philosophic Manuscripts of 1844." In *The Marx-Engels Reader*, ed. Robert Tucker. New York: Norton, 1978.

McMillan, John. *Reinventing the Bazaar: A Natural History of Markets*. New York: Norton, 2002.

Mill, John Stuart. *Utilitarianism*. New York: Macmillan, 1957. (Originally published in 1863.)

Mistry, Rohinton. *A Fine Balance*. New York: Vintage, 2001.

Mnookin, Robert H., and Lewis Kornhauser. "Bargaining in the Shadow of the Law: The Case of Divorce." *Yale Law Journal* 88, no. 5 (1979): 950–97.

Murphy, Liam, and Thomas Nagel. *The Myth of Ownership: Taxes and Justice*. Oxford: Oxford University Press, 2002.

Murthi, M., A. Guio, and J. Dreze. "Mortality, Fertility and Gender Bias in India: A District Level Analysis." *Population and Development Review* 21, no. 4 (1995): 745–82.

New Shorter Oxford English Dictionary. Oxford: Clarendon Press, 1993.

Nozick, Robert. *Anarchy, State and Utopia*. New York: Basic Books, 1974.

———. "Coercion." In *Philosophy, Science and Method: Essays in Honor of Ernest Nagel*, ed. Sidney Morgenbesser, Patrick Suppes, and Morton White. New York: St. Martin's Press, 1969.

Okin, Susan Moller. "A Critique of Pregnancy Contracts: Comments on Articles by Hill, Merrick, Shevory, and Woliver." *Politics and the Life Sciences* 8, no. 2 (1990): 205–10.

———. *Justice, Gender and the Family*. New York: Basic Books, 1989.

Okun, Arthur. *Equality and Efficiency: The Big Tradeoff.* Washington, DC: Brookings Institution Press, 1975.

Ostrom, Elinor. *Governing the Commons.* Cambridge: Cambridge University Press, 1990.

Otsuka, Michael. *Libertarianism without Inequality.* Oxford: Oxford University Press, 2003.

Overall, Christine. *Ethics and Human Reproduction: A Feminist Analysis.* Boston: Allen and Unwin, 1987.

Overvold, A. Z. *Surrogate Parenting.* New York: Pharos, 1988.

Parfit, Derek. *Reasons and Persons.* Oxford: Clarendon Press, 1984.

Parker, Philip. "Motivation of Surrogate Mothers: Initial Findings." *American Journal of Psychiatry* 140 (1983): 117–18.

Pateman, Carole. "Defending Prostitution: Charges against Ericsson." *Ethics* 93 (1983): 561–65.

———. *The Sexual Contract.* Stanford, CA: Stanford University Press, 1988.

Patterson, Orlando. *Slavery and Social Death.* Cambridge, MA: Harvard University Press, 1982.

Peterson, Richard. "A Re-evaluation of the Economic Consequences of Divorce." *American Sociological Review* 61, no. 3 (1996): 528–36.

Pettit, Philip. *Republicanism: A Theory of Freedom and Government.* Oxford: Oxford University Press, 1997.

Philips, Anne. *Which Equalities Matter?* Cambridge, UK: Polity Press, 1999.

Polanyi, Karl. *The Great Transformation: The Political and Economic Origins of Our Time.* Boston: Beacon Press, 2001.

Pollan, Michael. *The Omnivore's Dilemma: A Natural History of Four Meals.* New York: Penguin, 2006.

Posner, Richard. "An Economic Theory of Criminal Law." *Columbia Law Review* 85 (1985): 1193–231.

———. *Sex and Reason.* Cambridge, MA: Harvard University Press, 1992.

Potterat, John, et al. "Mortality in a Long Term Cohort of Prostitute Women." *American Journal of Epidemiology* 159, no. 8 (2004): 778–85.

Putterman, Louis. "On Some Recent Explanations of Why Capital Hires Labor." *Economic Inquiry* 22, no. 2 (1984): 171–87.

Radin, Margaret Jane. *Contested Commodities.* Cambridge, MA: Harvard University Press, 1996.

———. "Market-Inalienability." *Harvard Law Review,* volume 100, no. 8 (1987): 1849–1937.

———. "Residential Rent Control." *Philosophy and Public Affairs* 15, no. 4 (1986): 350–80.

Rawls, John. *A Theory of Justice.* Revised ed. Cambridge, MA: Harvard University Press, 1999.

Reich, Rob. *Bridging Liberalism and Multiculturalism in American Education.* Chicago: University of Chicago Press, 2002.

Ricardo, David. "An Essay on Profits: An Essay on the Influence of a Low Price of Corn on the Profits of Stock." John Murray: London, 1815. Available at http://socserv. mcmaster.ca/econ/ugcm/3ll3/ricardo/profits.txt.

———. *On the Principles of Political Economy and Taxation.* Ed. Piero Sraffa. Cambridge: Cambridge University Press, 1986. (Originally published in 1817.)

Rich, Adrienne. *Of Women Born: Motherhood as Experience and Institution.* New York: Norton, 1976.

Rix, S., ed. *The American Woman 1990–91.* New York: Norton, 1990.

Robbins, Lionel. *An Essay into the Nature and Significance of Economic Science.* New York: New York University Press, 1932.

Roemer, John. "Equality and Responsibility." *Boston Review* 20 (April–May 1995): 3–16.

Rosen, Ruth. *Prostitution in America: 1900–1918.* Baltimore: Johns Hopkins University Press, 1982.

Roth, Alvin, Tayfun Sonmez, and M. Utku Unver. "Pairwise Kidney Exchange." *Journal of Economic Theory* 125, no. 2 (2005): 151–88.

Rothschild, Emma. *Economic Sentiments: Adam Smith, Condorcet and the Enlightenment.* Cambridge, MA: Harvard University Press, 2001.

Rousseau, J. J. *Social Contract and Discourses.* London: J. M. Dent. (Originally published in 1762.)

Saletan, William. "Fetal Foreclosure." *Slate*, March 24, 2009. Available at www.slate. com.

Sandel, Michael J. *What Money Can't Buy: The Moral Limits of Markets.* Tanner Lectures on Human Values, vol. 21, ed. Grete B. Peterson. Salt Lake City: University of Utah Press, 2000.

Satz, Debra. "Child Labor: A Normative Perspective." *World Bank Economic Review* 17, no. 2 (2003): 297–309.

———. "Equality, Adequacy and Education for Citizenship." *Ethics* 117, no. 4 (2007): 623–48.

———. "The Limits of the Market: A Map of the Major Debates." In *International Encyclopedia of the Social and Behavioral Sciences*, ed. J. Smelser and Paul Baltes. Oxford: Pergamon, 2001.

———. "Markets in Women's Reproductive Labor." *Philosophy and Public Affairs* 21, no. 2 (1992): 107–31.

———. "Markets in Women's Sexual Labor." *Ethics* 106, no. 1 (1995): 63–85.

———. "The Moral Limits of Markets: The Case of Human Kidneys." *Proceedings of the Aristotelian Society* 108, part 3 (2008): 269–88.

———. "Noxious Markets: Why Some Things Should Not be for Sale." In *Globalization, Culture, and the Limits of the Market: Essays in Economics and Philosophy*, ed. Stephen Cullenberg and Prasanta Pattanaik. New Delhi: Oxford University Press, 2004.

———. "Remaking Families: A Review Essay." *Signs* 32, no. 2 (2007): 523–38.

———. "Voluntary Slavery and the Limits of the Market." *Law and Ethics of Human Rights* 3, no. 1 (2009): article 5.

Scanlon, T. M. "Preference and Urgency." *Journal of Philosophy* 72, no. 19 (1975): 655–69.

Schaffner, Julie. "Attached Farm Labor, Limited Horizons and Servility." *Journal of Development Economics* 47 (1995): 241–70.

Schapiro, Tamar. "What Is a Child?" *Ethics* 109, no. 4 (1999): 715–38.

Schelling, Thomas. *Choice and Consequence*. Cambridge, MA: Harvard University Press, 1984.

Scheper-Hughes, Nancy. "Keeping an Eye on the Global Traffic in Human Organs." *Lancet* 361 (2003): 1645–48.

Schultz, Vicky. "Life's Work." *Columbia Law Review* 100 (2000): 1881–1964.

Schwartzenbach, Sybil. "Contractarians and Feminists Debate Prostitution." *New York University Review of Law and Social Change* 18 (1990–91): 103–30.

Seabright, Paul. *The Company of Strangers: A Natural History of Economic Life*. Princeton, NJ: Princeton University Press, 2004.

Sen, Amartya. *Development as Freedom*. New York: Knopf, 2000.

———. *Inequality Reexamined*. Cambridge, MA: Harvard University Press, 1992.

———. *On Economic Inequality*. Oxford: Oxford University Press, 1997.

———. "Well-being, Agency, and Freedom: The Dewey Lectures 1984." *Journal of Philosophy* 82, no. 4 (1985): 169–221.

———. *On Ethics and Economics*. Oxford: Blackwell Publishing, 1987.

Sereny, Gita. *The Invisible Children: Child Prostitution in America, West Germany and Great Britain*. London: Andre Deutsch, 1984.

Shalev, Carmel. *Birthpower*. New Haven, CT: Yale University Press, 1989.

Shapiro, Joseph. "The Ethics and Efficacy of Banning Human Kidney Sales." Honors thesis, Ethics in Society Program, Stanford University, 2003.

Shaw, George Bernard. *Mrs. Warren's Profession*. New York: Cosimo Classics, 2006. (Originally published in 1906.)

Shrage, Laurie. *Moral Dilemmas of Feminism: Prostitution, Adultery and Abortion*. New York: Routledge, 1994.

———. "Should Feminists Oppose Prostitution?" *Ethics* 99 (1989): 347–61.

Shue, Henry. *Basic Rights: Subsistence, Affluence and U.S. Foreign Policy*. Princeton, NJ: Princeton University Press, 1996.

Silbert, Mimi. "Sexual Assault on Prostitutes. Phase II, Final Report, Grant 1 RO1 MH 32782." Washington, DC: National Institute of Mental Health, 1982.

Smith, Adam. *An Inquiry into the Nature and Causes of the Wealth of Nations*. Indianapolis: Liberty Classics, 1976. (Originally published in 1776.)

———. *The Theory of the Moral Sentiments*. Ed. D. D. Raphael and Al Macfie. Indianapolis: Liberty Classics, 1976. (Originally published in 1759.)

Snyder, Brad. *A Well-Paid Slave: Curt Flood's Fight for Free Agency in Professional Sports*. New York: Viking, 2006.

Srinivasan, T. N. "On the Choice among Creditors and Bonded Labor Contracts." In *The Economic Theory of Agrarian Institutions*, ed. P. K. Bardhan. Oxford: Oxford University Press, 1989.

Steiner, Hillel. "Self-Ownership, Begetting and Germ-Line Information." In *A Companion to Genethics*, ed. Justine Burley and John Harris. London: Blackwell, 2002.

Steinfeld, Robert J. *Coercion, Contract and Free Labor in the Nineteenth Century*. Cambridge: Cambridge University Press, 2001.

Stiglitz, Joseph. "The Causes and Consequences of the Dependence of Quality on Price." *Journal of Economic Literature* 25 (March 1987): 1–48.

Strahilevitz, Lior Jacob. "How Changes in Property Regimes Influence Social Norms: Commodifying California's Carpool Lanes." *Indiana Law Journal* 75 (2000): 1231–96.

Sunstein, Cass. "Neutrality in Constitutional Law (with Special Reference to Pornography, Abortion, and Surrogacy." *Columbia Law Review* 92, no. 1 (1992): 1–52.

Sunstein, Cass, and Richard Thaler. "Libertarian Paternalism Is Not an Oxymoron." *University of Chicago Law Review* 70, no. 4 (2003): 1159–1202.

Taylor, Michael. *Anarchy and Cooperation*. London: Wiley, 1976.

Terasaki, Paul I., et al. "High Survival Rate of Kidney Transplants from Spousal and Living Unrelated Donors." *New England Journal of Medicine* 333 (1995): 333–36.

Titmuss, Richard. *The Gift Relationship: From Human Blood to Social Policy*. New York: Pantheon, 1971.

Tobin, James. "On Limiting the Domain of Inequality." *Journal of Law and Economics* 13, no. 2 (1970): 263–77.

Treblicock, Michael. *The Limits of Freedom of Contract*. Cambridge, MA: Harvard University Press, 1997.

Tremain, Shelley. "Dworkin on Disablement and Resources." *Canadian Journal of Law and Jurisprudence* 9 (1996): 343–59.

Tribe, Lawrence. *Abortion: The Clash of Absolutes*. New York: Norton, 1990.

Varian, Hal. *Intermediate Microeconomics: A Modern Approach*. 5th ed. New York: Norton, 1999.

Veblen, Thorstein. *The Theory of the Leisure Class*. New York: Macmillan, 1899.

Walkowitz, Judith. *Prostitution and Victorian Society*. Cambridge: Cambridge University Press, 1980.

Walzer, Michael. *Spheres of Justice: A Defense of Pluralism and Equality*. New York: Basic Books, 1983.

Warnock, Mary. *A Question of Life: The Warnock Report on Human Fertilisation and Embryology*. Oxford: Basil Blackwell, 1985.

Weiner, Myron. *Child and State in India*. Princeton, NJ: Princeton University Press, 1992.

Weitzman, L. J. *The Divorce Revolution: The Unexpected Social and Economic Consequences for Women and Children in America*. New York: Free Press, 1985.

Wertheimer, Alan. *Coercion*. Princeton, NJ: Princeton University Press, 1987.

White, Stuart. *The Civic Minimum: On the Right and Obligations of Economic Citizenship*. Oxford: Oxford University Press, 2002.

Williams, Andrew. "Dworkin on Capability." *Ethics* 113, no. 1 (2002): 23–39.

Williams, Bernard. Book review of Thomas Schelling, *Choice and Consequence*. *Economics and Philosophy* 1 (1985): 142–46.

Williams, Christian. "Note. Combating the Problems of Human Rights Abuses and Inadequate Organ Supply through Presumed Donative Consent." *Case Western Reserve Journal of International Law* 26 (1994): 315.

Wolff, Jonathan. "Addressing Disadvantage and the Human Good." *Journal of Applied Philosophy* 19, no. 3 (2002): 207–18.

———. "Market Failure, Common Interests, and the Titanic Puzzle." In *Egalitarianism: New Essays on the Nature and Value of Equality*, ed. K. Lippert-Rasmussen and N. Holtung. Oxford: Oxford University Press, 2007.

Young, Iris. *Justice and the Politics of Difference*. Princeton: Princeton University Press, 1990.

Zelizer, Vivianna. *Pricing the Priceless Child: The Changing Social Value of Children*. New York: Basic Books, 1985.

Zimmerman, David. "Coercive Wage Offers." *Philosophy and Public Affairs* 10, no. 1 (1981): 121–45.

Index

Adams, John, 108
agency interests. *See* interests
Anderson, Elizabeth, 101
    on best understandings of a good's
      value, 81
    on contract pregnancy, 121, 124–25
    on degradation in prostitution, 142–43
Anderson, Scott, 149
Arrow-Debreu general equilibrium model, 33
asymmetry thesis, 115–19
Augustine, 188

Baby M case, 122, 129
baby selling, 123–24
Baldwin, James, 48
Bardhan, Pranab, 180
basic interests. *See* interests
Bennett, Jonathan, 216
Bentham, Jeremy 51
blood diamonds, 3, 33
bodily integrity. *See* kidney market
bonded labor, 171–88
    and slavery, 171–72
    as a psychological phenomenon, 184
Bowles, Sam, 211n2, 212n33
Brandt, Richard, 153
Braverman, A., 180
Buffett, Warren, 207

capabilities, 50, 182
    as endogenous to markets, 103, 186
child
    best versus basic interests of, 161–62
    defined, 156–57
child labor, 155–69
    and asymmetric vulnerability, 159
    and extremely harmful outcomes,
      159–62

    and girls, 168
    policy, 162–66
    versus forced labor, 159–60
    and weak agency, 157–59
choice sets, endogeneity of, 180–81
classical political economists, vision of,
    39, 61
coercion, 174–75
Cohen, Lawrence, 200
commercial surrogacy. *See* contract
    pregnancy
contract pregnancy
    and asymmetry thesis, 115–17
    contrasted with adoption and in vitro
      fertilization, 127
    contrasted with artificial insemination,
      128–29
    and control over women's bodies,
      128–30
    essentialist defense of, 117–21
    and gender equality, 127–34
    and interests of children, 125–27
    markets in, 115–34
    and mother's bonds with children,
      123–25
    and mother's bonds with fetus,
      121–122
    and race, 131
    and specific performance, 129
    versus wage labor, 132–34
Corn Laws, 53–54
cost of production theory, 51–52
cost-benefit analysis, 19
credit derivatives, 207–8
credit market, 47–48
crowding out, and intrinsic motivation,
    193–95

debt peonage. *See* bonded labor

debt slavery. *See* bonded labor
democracy, and equal provision of goods, 106–9
disability, Dworkin on, 71–72
distributional equality. *See* general egalitarianism
Dreze, Jean, 158
Durrenmatt, Friedrich, 194
Dworkin, Gerald, 87
Dworkin, Ronald, 8, 35, 66–75, 86–87, 92, 201
  and bad gambles, 74–76
  equality of resources, 66–76
  role of the auction, 67–68
  role of the hypothetical insurance market, 68–69

economics, 4, 31–33
  See also classical political economists; welfare economics
education, markets and, 48–49, 101–2, 106
efficiency, 18
  See also Kaldor Hicks efficiency; Paretianism
egalitarianism, 8, 76–79, 112
  See also general egalitarianism; specific egalitarianism
envy free, 67
equal concern and respect, 66, 72
equal status, 99, 100–101
  in a democratic society, 100–104, 208–9
  and kidney markets, 197–99
essentialist thesis, 117–18, 140–44
exit, 25, 107
externality, 31–32
  and moralisms, 139
extreme harms. *See* noxious markets
extreme vulnerability. *See* noxious markets

France, Anatole, 27
free information, 27–28
freedom
  and markets, 21–26
  negative, 23
  positive, 24
Frey, Bruno, 193
Fried, Barbara, 215n37, 215n38, 215n47, 215n48, 215n50, 231n24

Gazdar, H., 158
gender inequality, 73–74, 128–32, 144–50

general egalitarianism, 8, 76–79, 209
  definition of, 63

Hausman, Daniel, 109
Havel, Vaclav, 207
Hill, Thomas, 184
Hirschman, Albert
  exit versus voice, 107
  passion versus interest, 24
  on vision, 213n1
Hobbes, Thomas, 41
Hume, David, 26
Humphries, Jane, 157

in vitro fertilization, 127
indentured servitude. *See* bonded labor
inequality. *See* general egalitarianism
interacting as equals, 89, 95
interests
  agency interests, 95
  basic interests, 95
  best interests, 161
  welfare interests, 95, 160
International Labour Organization, 155, 159, 164, 168
invisible hand, 28, 208
Ishiguro, Kazuo, 198

Jevons, William Stanley, 51, 57
Johnson, Anna, 131
justice, 19

Kabeer, Naila, 169
Kaldor-Hicks efficiency, 19–20, 182
Kanbur, Ravi, 94, 99, 211n8, 211n10, 212n5, 219n6, 220n9, 220n15, 221n22, 221n41, 228n2
Kant, Immanuel, 80
kidney donation, 190
kidney market, 189–205
  alternative regulations, 202–5
  and black market, 202–3
  and bodily integrity, 199–202
  as a desperate exchange, 194
  and equal status, 197–99
  and pecuniary externalities, 200–201
Kornhauser, Lewis, 16

labor, 132–34
  Smithean view of, 44–46

See also bonded labor; child labor;
    contract pregnancy
labor markets, 34, 50
    Marxist view of, 54–57
liberal neutrality, 133
libertarianism
    and children, 178–79
    and justification of bonded labor,
        174–79
Locke, John, 22
Lockean proviso, 177–78
Loeb, Susanna, 107

Malthus, Robert, 7, 53
marginalism, 57–60
    and cost of production theory, 58–59
    and utility theory, 59
marginalization, 145
market
    abstract, 91
    and black market, 111
    complete, 32–33
    definition of, 15–16
    and efficiency, 17–21
    and freedom, 21–26
    and gendered division of labor,
        72–74
    heterogeneous, 7, 44–49, 210
    as a mechanism, 65
    moral view of, 65, 66–76
    regulating versus blocking, 104–5
    and trust, 28–29
    in votes, 34, 102–3
    See also noxious market
market failure, omnipresence of, 31
market system, 16, 91
Marshall, T. H., 6
    view of citizenship, 100–102
Marx, Karl, 39, 51, 58, 60, 61
    on capitalism's defining features, 55
    on immiseration of workers, 56
    labor markets, 54–57
    on liberating character of a market
        system, 23
McMillan, John, 212n27, 212n30
McPherson, Michael, 109
Menger, Carl, 57
military service, and markets, 34, 103
Mill, John Stuart, on autonomy, 40, 61, 173
Mnookin, Robert, 16

monopolies, 29–31
Montesquieu, Baron de, 40
moral hazard, 74
multiple equilibria, 181

National Organ Transplantation Act, 190
natural lottery, 71
noxious markets
    basic parameters, 9, 94–100
    effects on democracy, 10, 100–104
    and equal provision of goods, 108
    extreme harms for individuals and for
        society, 94–96
    extreme vulnerability, 97–98
    limits of my approach to, 110–12
    parameters, characterized, 9
    weak agency, 96–97
Nozick, Robert
    on coercion, 174–75
    consenting acts, 16
    on Lockean proviso, 177–78

Okin, Susan Moller, on consequences
    of contract pregnancy for children,
    125–26
opt out versus opt in organ donation, 78,
    191

Paretianism
    and bonded labor, 179–82
    moral limits of, 18–19
    and Smith, 49–51
Pareto improvement, 77, 180
Pareto Optimum, 18
Pareto, Vilfredo, 39, 49
Parfit, Derek, 181
Pateman, Carole, 119, 120, 140–41
paternalism, 78, 87, 157, 159
Patterson, Orlando, 143
pecuniary externalities. *See* kidney market
Pigou, A. C., 39
Polanyi, Karl, social embeddedness of
    markets, 39
preferences, 20, 61, 69–70
    versus urgency, 79
presumed consent, 190
principal-agent problem, 77
Programa de Educacion, Salud y
    Alimentacion, 166
property rights, 26–27, 176–79

prostitution, 135–53
  definition of, 137–38
  economic approach to, 138–40
  egalitarian approach to, 144–50
  essentialist approach to, 140–44
  legalization of, 150–53
  and negative image effect, 149
  and sexual autonomy, 149
  as theater of inequality, 147

Quesnay, Francois, 40

Radin, Margaret Jane, 142
  on flourishing, 81
Rawls, John, 71
Ricardo, David, 7, 39, 51, 53–54, 60
rights, 6, 100, 105
Robbins, Lionel, 33
Rodbertus, Karl, 43
Rousseau, J. J., 22, 97

Sandel, Michael, 81, 101
Sanders Amendment, 159
Scanlon, Thomas, preference and urgency, 79
Schelling, Thomas, 77, 78, 87–88, 106
  on Titanic cases, 84–85
Scheper-Hughes, Nancy, 198
Sen, Amartya, 40, 160, 212, 214, 215
  on capabilities, 50
  and intrinsic value of freedom, 22
  on welfare interests versus agency
    interests, 95
servility, 184–85, 188
  undermined by markets, 24–25, 42–43
Sex markets. *See* prostitution
slavery, 140, 143
Smith, Adam, 7, 26, 28, 39, 58, 60, 61, 93
  approach as opposed to Paretianism,
    48–51
  on effects of market on feudal
    dependency, 24–25
  on labor markets, 44–47, 50–51
  on price and value, 51–52
  view of markets, 41–51
social bases of self respect, 187
social democratic account, 209

specific egalitarianism, 79–84, 209–10
  definition of, 64
specific performance, 129, 187
Srinivasan, T. N., 180
St. James, Margo, 148
stability, and libertarianism, 179
status inequality, 110, 153
stereotyping, 130–31, 145
Stern, William. *See* Baby M case
Stiglitz, Joseph, 180
  on the invisible hand, 28
stigma, 146
Summers, Lawrence, 82
  memo on toxic waste markets, 83–84

theory of diminishing returns, 53–54
Titanic cases, 64–65, 84–89
  and noxious markets, 105–6
Titmuss, Richard, 80, 192–193
Tobin, James, 8, 34, 63–64, 209
Torrens, Robert, 53
toxic waste markets, 109–10.
  See also Summers, Lawrence
tragic choices, 91
Treblicock, Michael, 99, 219

Uniform Anatomical Gift Act, 190
Utility, 59–60

votes, markets in, 34, 102–3

Walras, Leon, 49, 51, 57, 58
Walzer, Michael, 35, 80–81, 101, 106, 167
Warnock Report on Human Fertilisation
  and Embryology, 120, 122, 124
weak agency, 96–97
  See also noxious markets
Weber, Max, 22
Weiner, Myron, 162
welfare economics, 179–82
  fundamental theorem of, 18
welfare interests. *See* interests
West, Sir Edward, 53
Whitehead, Mary Beth. *See* Baby M case
Wolff, Jonathan, 108, 216
work, 185–86
Worst Forms of Child Labor Convention, 159